COMPLETE FLAGS OF THE WORLD

DK

DK | Penguin Random House

SEVENTH EDITION
Senior Editor Simon Mumford
Managing Editor Francesca Baines
Managing Art Editor Philip Letsu
US Editor Jennette ElNaggar
Flag illustrations and 3-D flag maps Simon Mumford
Authenticity Reader Bianca Hezekiah
Production Editor George Nimmo
Production Controller Sian Cheung
Jacket Design Development Manager Sophia MTT

Art Director Karen Self
Associate Publishing Director Liz Wheeler
Publishing Director Jonathan Metcalf

This book has been produced in association with the Flag Institute, UK.
We would like to dedicate this book to the late Dr. William G. Crampton and Michael Faul, both of the Flag Institute, without whom it would not have been possible.

Vexillology artwork and consultant
Graham Bartram, Chief Vexillologist of the Flag Institute
www.flaginstitute.org

This American Edition, 2021
First American Edition, 1997 published as The Ultimate Pocket Flags of the World
Published in the United States by DK Publishing
1450 Broadway, Suite 801, New York, NY 10018

21 22 23 24 25 10 9 8 7 6 5 4 3 2 1
001–325623–Dec/2021

Published in Great Britain by Dorling Kindersley Limited

A catalog record for this book is available from the Library of Congress
ISBN 978-0-7440-4562-8

Printed and bound in the UAE

COMPLETE FLAGS OF THE WORLD

Contents

ASIA

AUSTRALASIA & OCEANIA

Flag Directory

Flag Directory (continued)

U

V

Y

Z

A Brief History of Flags

Flags are a part of everyday life. They are used by countries, provinces, cities, international bodies, organizations, and companies. Flags are a potent symbol of a country's nationhood, and their design is often closely interwoven with the history and struggles endured by its people to establish a national identity or to gain its independence. A country's flag is therefore often a huge source of pride and a focal point for the historical, social, and geographical elements that define a nation.

EARLY FLAGS

The earliest known flags were used in ancient China around 1000 BCE. The ancient civilizations of Greece, Rome, and the Middle East used them in a variety of ways, but it was the Romans who developed a sophisticated system of symbology for military use. Each unit of their army had its own standard, including the famous eagles of the legions. The Romans also introduced the *vexillum*, a square flag used by their cavalry, from which the term "vexillology"—the study of flags—originates. The *vexillum* did not resemble a modern flag because it was fixed to a horizontal pole. Flags attached to one side of an upright pole were introduced to the West by the Arabs in the 1st century, and flags with actual designs on them became widespread during the Crusades.

An early Roman *vexillum*, the first true flag

Flag bears the name of the legion

CHINESE PIRATE FLAG

For centuries, piracy was prevalent on the South China Seas, with most pirate ships hoisting flags to bring them good fortune. These flags were often beautifully drawn and tended to depict gods and goddesses who were thought to rule the waves.

A Chinese pirate flag from around 1850 depicting the goddess T'ien Hou

The shield is the focal point of the armorial bearings
The lion is the crest of the Churchill family

The heraldic family banner of British prime minister Sir Winston Churchill

HERALDRY

In Europe during the Middle Ages, heraldry—the art of producing and recording coats of arms—became a popular means of identifying kings and noblemen. Since then, heraldry has influenced flags greatly, laying down rules for their design and use, and creating new flag types. Owners of coats of arms often had heraldic flags made for them, which were used to symbolize their power and authority. Traditionally there are four types: the long *standard*, the rectangular *banner*, the *badge-flag*, and the *pennon*. A coat of arms consists of the following parts: a shield, which can contain symbols relevant to the history of the bearer's family; supporters (a human or animal figure) on either side of the shield; a helmet with a wreath; mantling (the strips of cloth hanging from the wreath); and a crest on top of the shield. There may also be a scroll displaying a motto.

FLAGS FOR IDENTIFICATION

Since the days of the first warships and the earliest trading vessels, flags have been used at sea. Today such ships—as well as passenger vessels and other boats used for recreation—still use flags. Many flag traditions started out at sea, including ships raising the national flag of the country at whose port they are arriving, which is known as flying a "courtesy flag." On leaving port, many ships hoist the blue flag with a white square in the center, called the Blue Peter.

SIGNALING WITH FLAGS

One of the oldest uses for flags is for signaling between ships at sea. In the wars between the Greeks and Persians (547–478 BCE), signals were made by both sides with flaglike objects called "vexilloids." The first system of flag signals to use letters and numbers dates from the 17th century, which evolved into semaphore signaling in the 19th century. Mariners relied on semapohores during this period because it was the fastest means of communication between vessels.

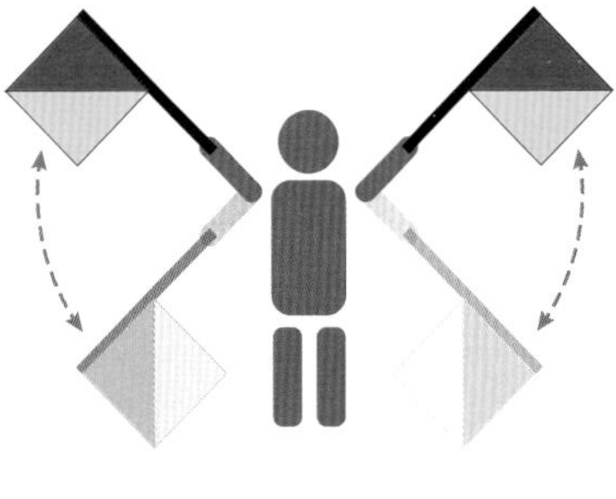

Semaphore flags can be used for signaling between ships at sea

A Brief History of Flags (continued)

FLAGS IN POLITICS

With the growth of independent nation states, flags have become more important in politics. Many newly independent states choose flags based on the political parties that secured their independence. Revolutionary movements usually have their own flags, and private and professional organizations are also increasingly adopting flags.

Flags in the political arena can become very potent symbols to harness and mobilize public support. In Europe, for example, the socialist movement has used red in its flags to represent its cause (the color has been associated with left-wing politics since the French Revolution). The anarchist movement, meanwhile, often uses the color black. One of the most common symbols to represent peace, togetherness, and inclusivity is a rainbow. The environmental organization Greenpeace, for example, has adopted this motif to symbolize its determination to protect the environment by peaceful means.

The symbol of a rainbow in flags promotes the idea of peace and togetherness

FLAGS IN SPORT

Flags are used for signaling and identification in many sports, including motorsports, golf, gymnastics, skiing, cross-country events, and team sports such as baseball and soccer. They are employed as signals, markers, and as decorations. In addition, both individual and national teams have their own flags bearing their colors and badge, which help them and their fans form a collective identity.

Motorsports fans wave flags in the stands to show support for their favorite teams

NASA astronaut John W. Young salutes the US flag during the Apollo 16 moon landing

Reciprocally, sports fans wave flags in the stands to show their support for their team, or individual players. Flags are also used to signal the beginning and ending of certain sporting events. Each Olympic Games, for example, has its own flag, as well as the Olympic Standard (the flag bearing the five colored rings), which are both raised and lowered to mark the opening and closing of the Games. In addition, when medals are presented to the victors at the Olympics, their national flags are raised to celebrate the achievement.

KEY FLAGS IN WORLD HISTORY

Throughout history, certain flags have provided the inspiration for the design of others. For example, the American Stars and Stripes of 1777 has inspired more flags than any other. A similar degree of influence has been exerted by the French *Tricolore* from 1794, giving rise to the Dutch flag and its major derivative, the Russian Tricolor, which in turn formed the basis of many flags of the countries in eastern Europe.

SECTIONS OF THIS BOOK

This book deals predominantly with national, international, and subnational flags, as well as national coats of arms, and is arranged continent by continent. Among national flags are the state ensign and state flag, for government use only on sea and land; the civil ensign and civil flag, for private and commercial use, and the naval ensign, flown by warships. Subnational flags may be of states (US), provinces (Canada), cantons (Switzerland), and overseas territories or other such areas. The book also includes a section on flags adopted by international organizations, a brief list of some of the more well known disputed territories, and finally offers an overview of the use of signal flags.

Parts of the Flag

The study of flags is known as "vexillology." Over the years, vexillologists have established a set of flag terminologies to describe the parts, patterns, and other elements that make up a modern-day flag. The diagram below illustrates the main parts of a flag. Many of these terms are used throughout the book in the detailed flag descriptions.

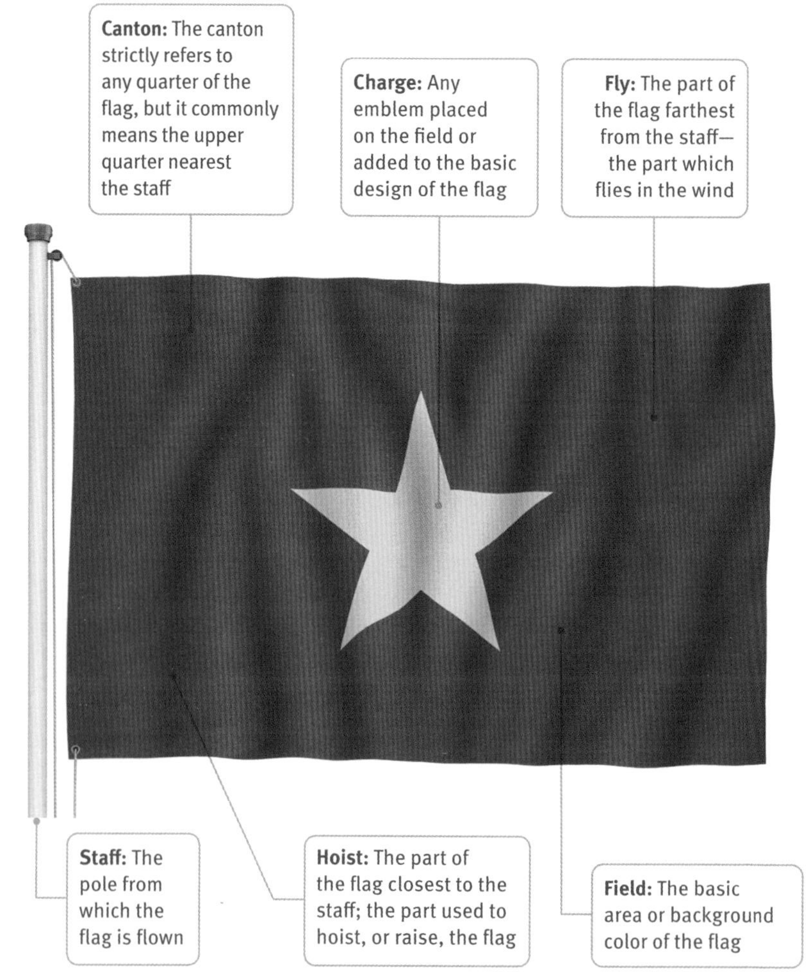
Canton: The canton strictly refers to any quarter of the flag, but it commonly means the upper quarter nearest the staff
Charge: Any emblem placed on the field or added to the basic design of the flag
Fly: The part of the flag farthest from the staff—the part which flies in the wind
Staff: The pole from which the flag is flown
Hoist: The part of the flag closest to the staff; the part used to hoist, or raise, the flag
Field: The basic area or background color of the flag

Ratio describes the relative proportions of height against width. For example, ratio: 1:2 represents a flag twice as wide as it is high.

Heraldic Terms

Heraldry is the art of producing and recording coats of arms. The practice of heraldry is nearly 900 years old and has had a great influence on flags, creating new kinds of flags and laying down the ground rules for their design and use. The diagram below describes the main elements that are usually included in a coat of arms.

Crest: The element that appears at the extreme top of the arms, above the shield

Wreath or Torse: The rope of colors placed above the helmet or shield

Mantling: The strips of cloth hanging or flying from the wreath

Chief: The top third of the shield

TO·LEAD·IS·TO·SERVE

Supporters: The figures, human or animal that hold the shield

Scroll: The strip—usually below the shield—that contains the motto

Shield: The basic unit on which the coat of arms is portrayed

Compartment: The base, often a mound, on which the shield stands

Flag Colors

RED: SYMBOLIC USES

Flag colors generally carry symbolic meaning. Red is one of the most commonly used colors and traditionally represents strength, bravery, revolution, hardiness, and bloodshed. Below are some examples.

Albania: strength and valor at war

China: the Communist revolution

Kyrgyzstan: the valor of *Manas* the *Noble*

Morocco: descent of royal *Alaouite* family

Tunisia: blood shed in 1574 Turkish conquest

Turkey: sacrifices made for independence

GREEN: SYMBOLIC USES

Green is traditionally a healing color, and is often used to represent nature, agriculture, and fertility, as well as other positive themes such as hope and love. It is also the color of Islam as it recalls the Prophet Muhammad's favorite color.

Brazil: the reigning house of Braganza

Mauritania: Islam; bright future and growth

Pakistan: Islam; hope, joy, and love

Saudi Arabia: the Muslim Wahabi sect

Turkmenistan: life, prosperity, and peace

Zambia: lush flora and rich natural resources

BLUE: SYMBOLIC USES

Blue is universally associated with water and sky. In flags, the color has historically symbolized justice, prosperity, and perseverance. Island nations, or those with an extensive coastline, often feature blue as a key part of their flag design.

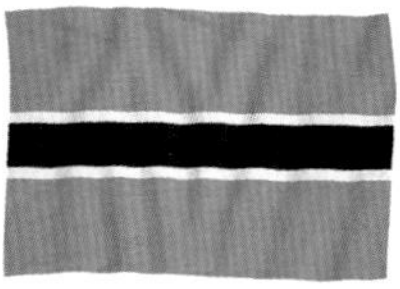

Botswana: water (a resource for agriculture)

El Salvador: *añil* (a source for indigo dye)

Kazakhstan: cultural and ethnic unity

Micronesia: Pacific Ocean; UN flag

Somalia: sky and Indian Ocean

St. Lucia: Caribbean Sea and Atlantic Ocean

YELLOW: SYMBOLIC USES

Yellow typically represents the sun, wealth, and plentitude. The color appears in many flags of African nations, often to denote that the land is bathed in sunshine. Agricultural prosperity and crops are also symbolized with yellow.

Bhutan: civil tradition and temporal authority

Brunei: royalty (Sultan of Brunei)

Columbia: sunshine; the abundance of gold

Ecuador: crops and fertile soil

Grenada: wisdom and wealth

Ukraine: vast grain fields

Flag Colors (continued)

BLACK: SYMBOLIC USES

Black usually carries a strong or serious message often linked to a period of struggle. In flags, the shade has been used to symbolize determination, ethnic heritage, and the fortitude required to defeat one's enemies.

Afghanistan: a troubled past pre-independence

Angola: the African continent it belongs to

Estonia: fertile soil; Estonia's dark history

Iraq: determination in the face of adversity

Libya: Senussi Dynasty of 1837; resistance

Papua New Guinea: native art and clothing

WHITE: SYMBOLIC USES

A plain white flag is the universal symbol for truce. Usually, white flags traditionally represent aspirational themes such as peace, purity, and innocence. However, in some countries it is the color of mourning.

Algeria: peace (after Algerian War 1954–62)

Cyprus: peace (between Turks and Greeks)

Finland: snow (covering the land in winter)

Israel: light, honesty, and innocence

Singapore: everlasting purity and virtue

South Korea: purity and peace

PAN-AFRICAN COLORS: SYMBOLIC USES

Pan-Africanism is the concept of solidarity between groups of African descent. Red, yellow, green, and black are colors commonly used to represent Pan-Africanism. These colors have important individual meanings.

Benin

Ethiopia

Ghana

Guinea-Bissau

Red: the blood uniting all people of black African ancestry

Yellow: a reference to the sun; the presence of precious resources, particularly gold

Green: the abundant flora and natural wealth of Africa

Black: a symbol of black people

PAN-ARABIC COLORS: SYMBOLIC USES

The Pan-Arabic colors are black, white, green, and red. They were first combined in the flag of the Arab Revolt in 1916. Each of the Pan-Arabic colors is meant to represent a specific Arab dynasty, or era. The eras are listed below.

Iran

Jordan

Kuwait

United Arab Emirates

Black: Abbasid Caliphate (750–1258 AD)

White: Ummayad Caliphate (661–750 AD)

Green: Fatimid Caliphate (909–1171 AD)

Red: rulers of the Maghreb and Al-Adalus (647–732 AD)

Types of Flags

There are broadly three types of flag useage indicated in this book, National, Civil, and State.

National flag: This is a term used to describe a nation's flag that can be used for both Civil and State purposes.

Civil flag: May be flown by anyone, regardless of any government links.

State flag: Used exclusively for offical government purposes and are often charged with coats of arms or other official symbols.

General flag designs

Tricolor

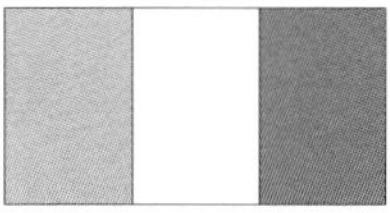

A flag of three stripes of three colors, either horizontal or vertical.

Tribar

A flag of three stripes of two colors, horizontal or vertical.

Bicolor

A flag of two stripes of different colors, either horizontal or vertical.

Cross

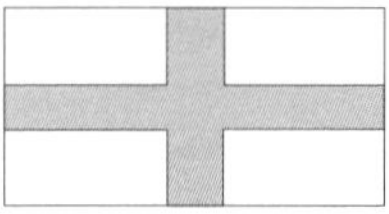

A cross is vertical, centrally placed, and extends across the whole flag.

Scandinavian cross

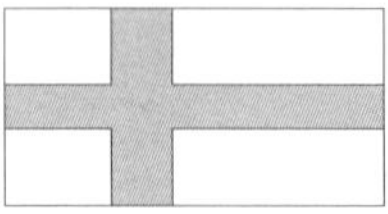

A cross with the upright set closer to the hoist than to the fly.

Bend

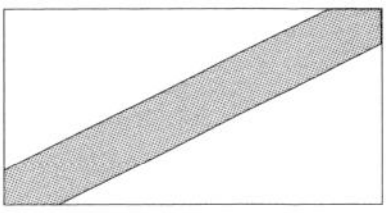

A flag divided by a diagonal strip.

Saltire

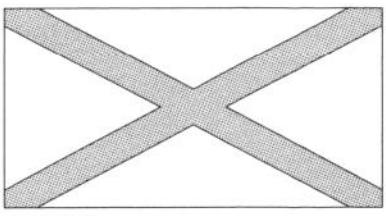

A diagonal cross stretching from corner to corner of the flag.

Triangle

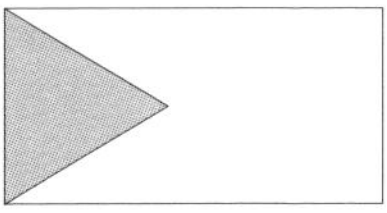

A flag divided by a triangle of a different color, usually at the hoist.

Serration

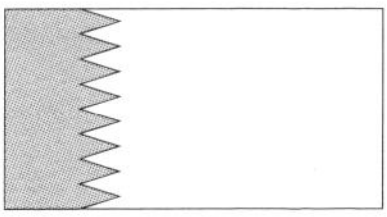

A narrow strip of color separating two broader stripes or larger areas.

Canton

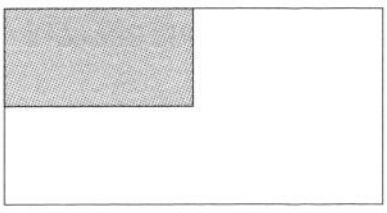

A flag charged with a design in the corner, usually at the hoist.

Quartered

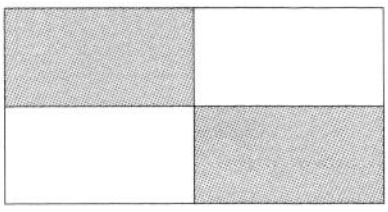

A flag divided into four equal sections of differing design.

Bordered

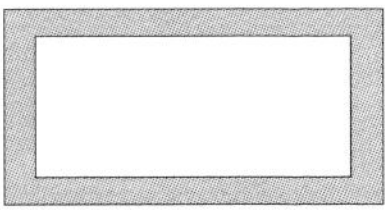

A flag where the central color is surrounded by a different color.

Flag Identification Guide

The flags in this guide have been grouped into the various design types found in vexillology (see pp.20–21). Within each category they have been arranged by color, starting with the color that is most common in the group.

It is interesting to note that many neighboring countries have flags with similar colors and design elements, though sometimes the opposite is true. The final group contains flags that share the traits of several design types.

TRICOLOR

Netherlands (p.170)

Luxembourg (p.187)

Croatia (p.215)

Russia (p.228)

Slovakia (p.213)

Slovenia (p.214)

Paraguay (p.95)

Serbia (p.218)

France (p.186)

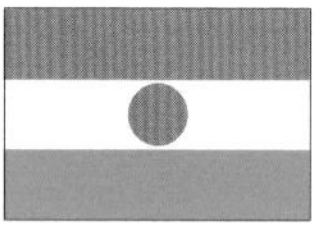

Niger (p.117)

India (p.264)

Ivory Coast (p.128)

Ireland (p.175)

Hungary (p.211)

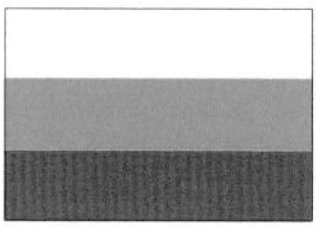

Bulgaria (p.222)

Iran (p.253)

Italy (p.196)

Mexico (p.57)

Yemen (p.246)

Egypt (p.104)

TRICOLOR (continued)

Syria (p.241)

Iraq (p.252)

Libya (p.103)

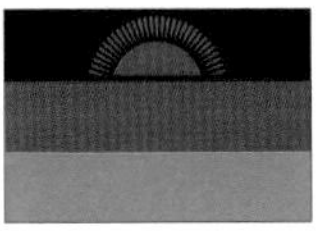

Malawi (p.142)

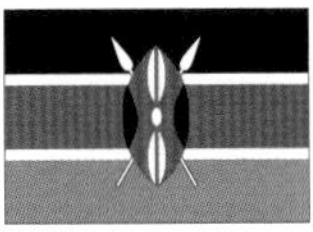

Kenya (p.112)

Afghanistan (p.260)

Germany (p.165)

Belgium (p.174)

Bolivia (p.94)

Ghana (p.130)

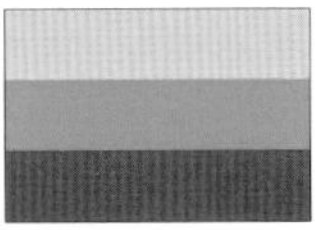

Lithuania (p.163)

Myanmar (Burma) (p.268)

Ethiopia (p.109)

Guinea (p.125)

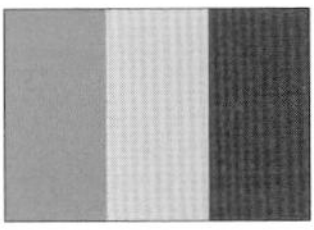

Mali (p.120)

Senegal (p.121)

Cameroon (p.134)

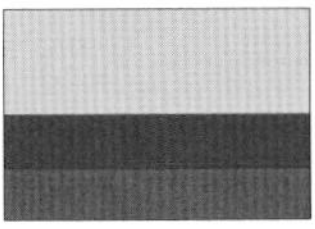

Colombia (p.80)

Ecuador (p.84)

Venezuela (p.81)

Chad (p.118)

Romania (p.224)

Andorra (p.189)

Moldova (p.225)

Flag Identification Guide (continued)

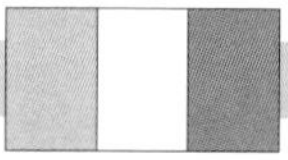

TRICOLOR (continued)

Sierra Leone (p.126)

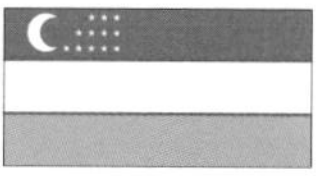

Uzbekistan (p.255)

Tajikistan (p.259)

Lesotho (p.147)

Estonia (p.161)

Gabon (p.137)

Rwanada (p.113)

St. Vincent & Grenadines (p.74)

Azerbaijan (p.236)

Armenia (p.237)

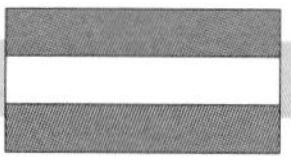

TRIBAR

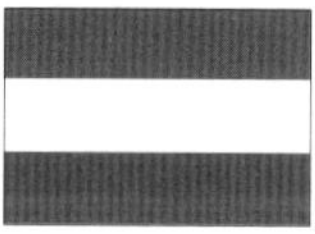

Austria (p.208)

Lebanon (p.240)

Canada (p.34)

Peru (p.85)

Latvia (p.162)

Nicaragua (p.62)

El Salvador (p.60)

Honduras (p.61)

Argentina (p.97)

Guatemala (p.58)

Nigeria (p.133)

Spain (p.191)

TRIBAR (continued)

Cambodia (p.271)

Laos (p.270)

Mongolia (p.257)

Barbados (p.75)

BICOLOR

Indonesia (p.278)

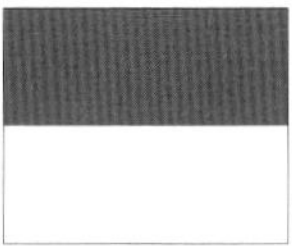
Monaco (p.188)

Singapore (p.280)

Poland (p.164)

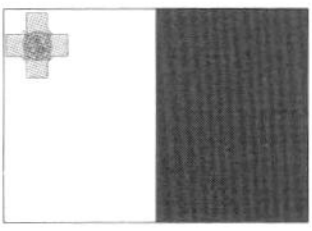
Malta (p.197)

Burkina Faso (p.129)

Belarus (p.226)

Portugal (p.190)

Algeria (p.101)

San Marino (p.199)

Haiti (p.68)

Liechtenstein (p.207)

Angola (p.139)

Vatican City (p.198)

Ukraine (p.227)

Pakistan (p.261)

Flag Identification Guide (continued)

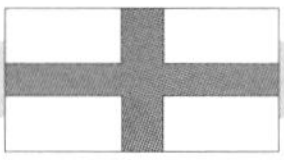

CROSS

Switzerland (p.200)

Georgia (p.239)

Dominican Republic (p.69)

Dominica (p.72)

SCANDINAVIAN CROSS

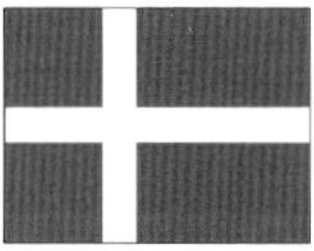

Denmark (p.158)

Norway (p.157)

Iceland (p.156)

Sweden (p.159)

Finland (p.160)

BEND

Congo (p.138)

St. Kitts & Nevis (p.70)

Tanzania (p.141)

Solomon Islands (p.296)

Namibia (p.145)

Congo, Dem. Rep. (p.116)

Trinidad & Tobago (p.77)

Brunei (p.281)

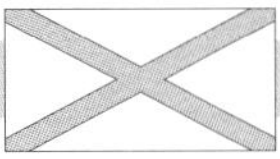

SALTIRE

Burundi (p.114)

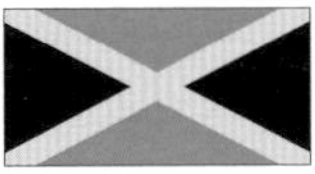

Jamaica (p.65)

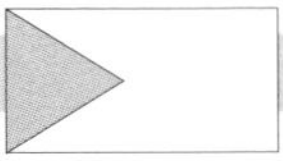

TRIANGLE

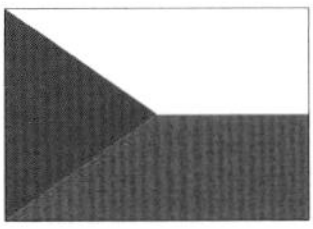

Czechia (Czech Republic) (p.212)

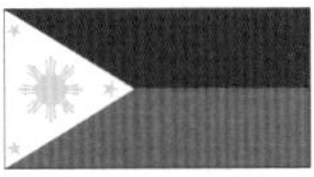

Philippines (p.282)

Cuba (p.66)

Djibouti (p.108)

Equatorial Guinea (p.135)

Sudan (p.105)

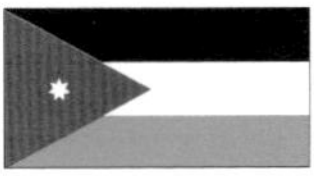

Jordan (p.244)

South Sudan (p.106)

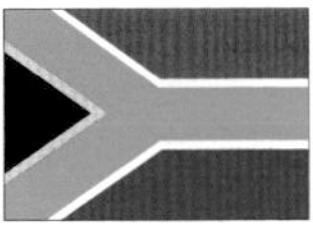

South Africa (p.149)

Vanuatu (p.293)

East Timor (p.279)

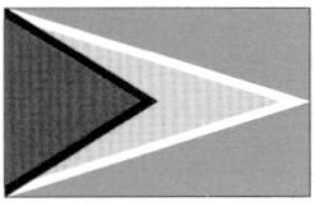

Guyana (p.82)

São Tomé & Príncipe (p.136)

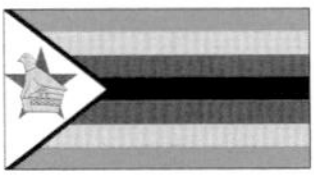

Zimbabwe (p.143)

Mozambique (p.144)

Comoros (p.151)

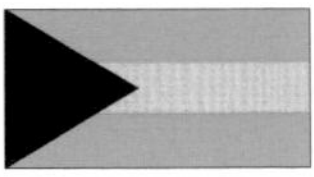

The Bahamas (p.67)

Eritrea (p.107)

Flag Identification Guide (continued)

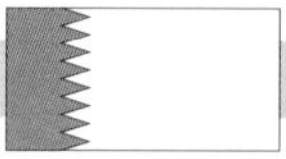

SERRATION

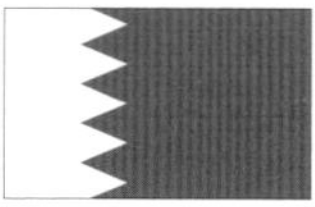

Bahrain (p.250)

Qatar (p.249)

CANTON

Chile (p.93)

Taiwan (p.283)

Samoa (p.303)

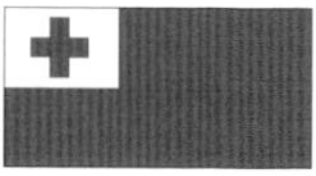

Tonga (p.304)

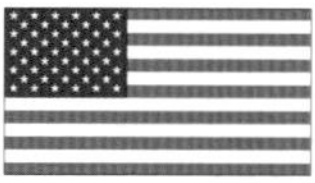

USA (p.39)

Liberia (p.127)

Malaysia (p.273)

Australia (p.290)

New Zealand (p.305)

Tuvalu (p.302)

Fiji (p.294)

Greece (p.223)

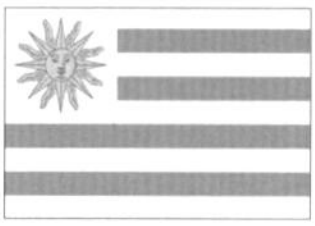

Uruguay (p.96)

Togo (p.131)

QUARTERED

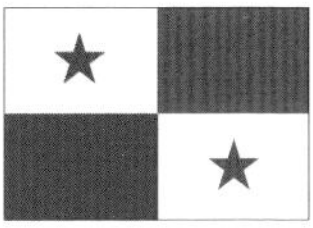
Panama (p.64)

BORDERED

Montenegro (p.217)

Maldives (p.265)

Grenada (p.76)

Sri Lanka (p.266)

PLAIN WITH EMBLEM

Vietnam (p.272)

China (p.284)

Kyrgyzstan (p.258)

Morocco (p.100)

Turkey (p.238)

Tunisia (p.102)

Albania (p.220)

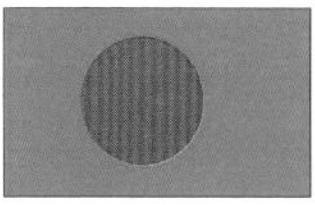
Bangladesh (p.267)

Brazil (p.86)

Mauritania (p.119)

Zambia (p.140)

Saudi Arabia (p.245)

Flag Identification Guide (continued)

PLAIN WITH EMBLEM (continued)

St. Lucia (p.73)

Palau (p.297)

Somalia (p.110)

Micronesia (p.298)

Kosovo (p.219)

Japan (p.287)

South Korea (p.286)

Cyprus (p.242)

OTHER TYPES

Israel (p.243)

Costa Rica (p.63)

Thailand (p.269)

North Korea (p.285)

Cape Verde (p.123)

Belize (p.59)

Botswana (p.146)

Kiribati (p.301)

United Kingdom (p.176)

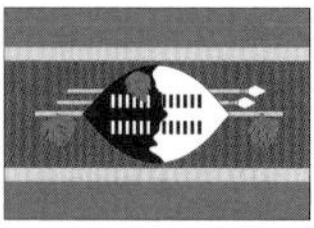
Eswatini (p.148)

Nauru (p.300)

Kazakhstan (p.256)

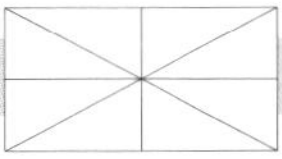

OTHER TYPES (continued)

Bosnia & Herzegovina (p.216)

Marshall Islands (p.299)

Mauritius (p.153)

The Gambia (p.122)

Central African Republic (p.115)

Seychelles (p.150)

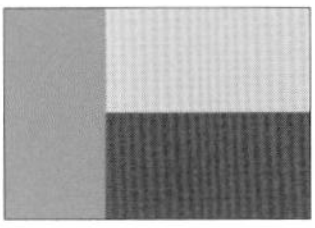

Benin (p.132)

Guinea Bissau (p.124)

UAE (p.248)

Kuwait (p.251)

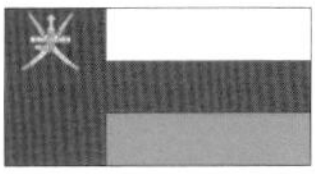

Oman (p.247)

Madagascar (p.152)

Suriname (p.83)

Turkmenistan (p.254)

Antigua & Barbuda (p.71)

Papua New Guinea (p.295)

Uganda (p.111)

North Macedonia (p.221)

Bhutan (p.263)

Nepal (p.262)

North & Central America

23
2
1
8
19
3
7
9
20
21
13
15
11
4
14
22
17
10
18
6

Canada

Adopted February 15, 1965 | **Ratio** 1:2 | **Usage** National and Civil

Red represents the sacrifice made by Canadians during the First World War

White represents the snowy north of Canada

A stylized maple leaf has been Canada's national emblem for more than 150 years

An earlier flag, the "Pearson's Pennant," did not meet with universal approval. Efforts to reach a new consensus resulted in a design by George Stanley featuring the traditional Canadian maple leaf emblem and the national colors of red and white. The "Maple Leaf Flag," was adopted by Parliament in 1965.

THE ROYAL STANDARD

This standard shows the Arms of Canada, with the personal emblem of Queen Elizabeth II. The quarters show the arms of England, Scotland, Ireland, and France, the historical origin for the majority of European settlers to Canada. The lowest stripe shows the red maple leaf, which is Canada's national emblem.

CANADIAN ROYAL STANDARD

The maple leaves represent Canada's national emblem

The quarters of the shield represent England, Scotland, Ireland, and France—the homelands of many Canadian people

Provincial and official flags

The date when each province joined the Confederation is shown next to the province name.

Alberta 1905

The shield dates from 1907 and was placed on a blue field to make a flag in 1967. The shield depicts a scene from the vast wheat lands of the west under St. George's Cross.

British Columbia 1871

This flag, adopted in 1960, is an armorial banner of the arms, granted in 1906. The sun placed over heraldic waters represents the province's position on the west coast.

Manitoba 1870

The flag is intended to recall and to preserve the old Canadian Red Ensign, with Manitoba's shield, depicting a buffalo on a rock, in the fly. It was adopted in 1966.

New Brunswick 1867

Another armorial banner, authorized in 1965. The galley ship represents shipbuilding, once an important industry, and the lion represents New Brunswick's ties with Britain.

Provincial and official flags (continued)

Newfoundland & Labrador 1949

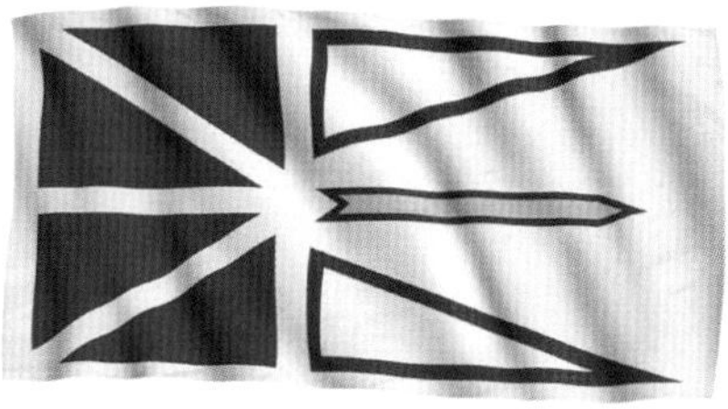

The colors of the flag represent all aspects of the province, such as snow, ice, and the sea. The design is intended to recall the Union Jack, the territory's previous flag.

Northwest Territories 1870

The flag was a competition winner in 1969. It contains the shield from the arms adopted in 1956. The lakes are represented by blue, and snow by white.

Nova Scotia 1867

This flag is theoretically the oldest flag of a British Dominion. "Nova Scotia" means "New Scotland." Its flag has a St. Andrew's Cross in reversed colors, with the Scottish Royal Arms.

Nunavut 1999

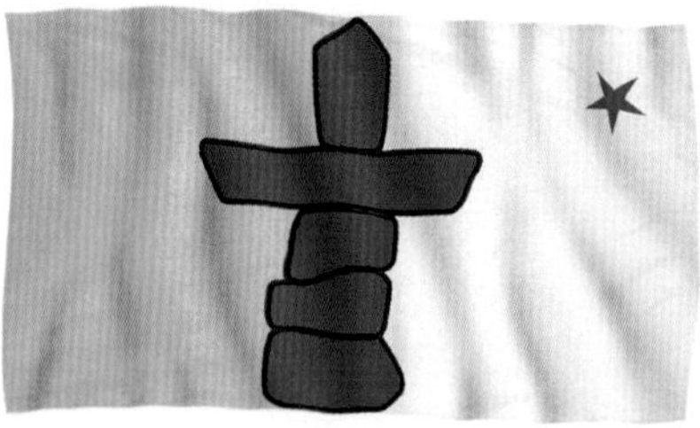

The figure on this flag symbolizes the stone monuments used to mark sacred places. The North Star represents the leadership of the community's elders.

Ontario 1867

The flag was adopted in 1965 and also attempts to recall and preserve the Canadian Red Ensign. The shield is from the arms of 1868 and was the first design to use a maple leaf.

Prince Edward Island 1873

The flag is a banner of the arms granted in 1905. It depicts an island, with a great British oak and its "descendants," under the protection of a British lion.

Quebec 1867

Adopted in 1948, this flag is a modern version of the *Fleurdelysé*, an old French-Canadian flag. The *fleur-de-lis* flower is symbolic of France.

Saskatchewan 1905

Adopted in 1969, the flag combines the provincial shield (representing forests and grain) with the floral emblem—the western red lily.

Provincial and official flags (continued)

Yukon 1898

Accepted in 1967, the flag uses the 1956 coat of arms. Forests, snows, and waters are symbolized by the colors.

Cape Breton Island 1994

This flag was designed by Kelly Gooding as part of a competition and was adopted in 1994 by Cape Breton Island in Nova Scotia. The bird is a bald eagle.

Labrador 1973

The spruce sprigs on this regional flag denote the three races of the larger Newfoundland & Labrador Province.

Governor-General of Canada 1981

This flag, dating from 1981, does not use the British Royal Crest; it has its own crest of a lion holding up a maple leaf.

United States of America

Adopted July 4, 1960 | **Ratio** 10:19 | **Usage** National and Civil

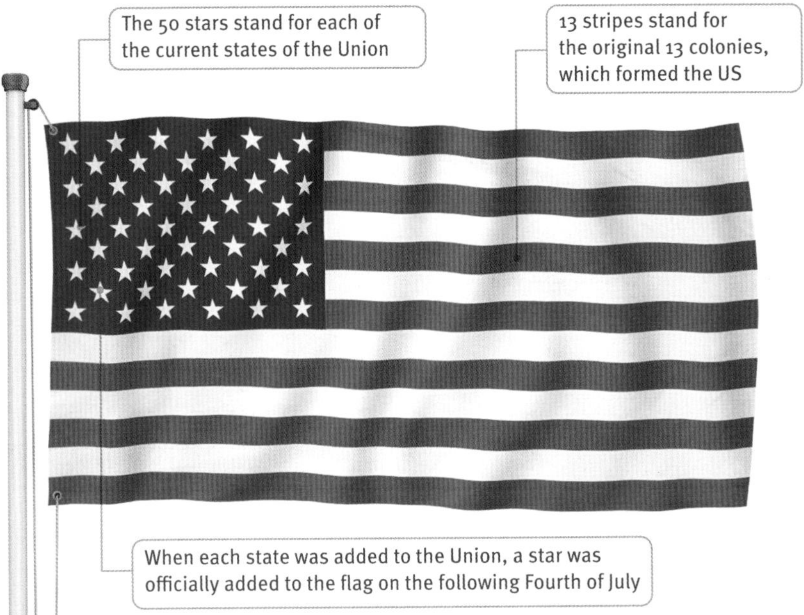
The 50 stars stand for each of the current states of the Union
13 stripes stand for the original 13 colonies, which formed the US
When each state was added to the Union, a star was officially added to the flag on the following Fourth of July

The first flag used by the Americans was an adaptation of the British Red Ensign, known as the "Grand Union Flag" (see p.40). From this developed the distinctive "Stars and Stripes," as it is known today, which still has the 13 stripes for each of the original colonies to join the Union, and a star for each state, which is now part of the US. The latest star was added on July 4, 1960, after Hawaii joined the US in 1959.

A TRULY NATIONAL FLAG

The flag of 1777 (see p.40), marked a break with old colonial ties. It became the first of a new kind of flag, one that celebrated national pride. Its basic design and color combination was soon copied by other new nations.

The Stars and Stripes is an all-purpose flag, but the US is rich in flags of many other kinds.

THE PRESIDENT'S STANDARD

The presidential standard, in use today, contains the President's version of the national arms, and a ring of 50 stars. The coat of arms depicts a spread eagle holding a shield in the style of the Stars and Stripes, 13 arrows, and 13 olive leaves, indicating the country is prepared for either war or peace. The motto "*E Pluribus Unum*" meaning "Out of many, one," reflects the federal nature of the United States of America.

US: Historical flags

The flags of the Revolutionary and the Civil War still have an influence on the American flags of today.

The Grand Union Flag

The first American flag was adapted from the British Red Ensign of the time. It was known as the "Grand Union Flag," i.e. of the union of 13 colonies. These were represented by the 13 stripes of red and white. The flag was introduced in December 1775 for use on land and at sea.

The first Stars and Stripes

On June 14, 1777, the Union Jack was removed from the flag in favor of a blue canton with 13 stars, representing a new constellation, which now also represented the United States of America. This was the first use of stars in this way, and set a precedent for many later flags.

The Flag of 1795

When two new states joined the Union in 1795, two new stars and two new stripes were added to the flag, making 15 stripes and 15 stars. This set a precedent for adding new stripes and stars when each new state joined the Union. The flag soon became known as the "Star-Spangled Banner."

The Flag of 1818

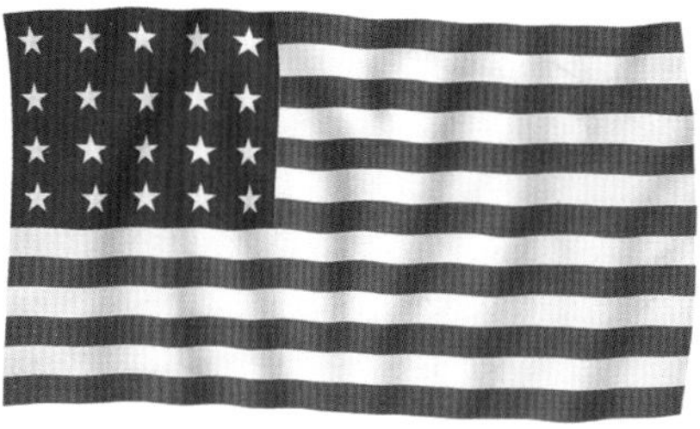

Five new states were formed after 1795, but a new flag was not designed until 1817, when Congress decreed that in order to preserve the appearance of the flag, in future only new stars would be added and it would revert to 13 stripes. The new stars were added on July 4, 1818, and this system has been followed ever since.

The Stars and Bars

When the southern states seceded from the Union in 1861, it marked the start of the Civil War. These states formed the Confederacy (or Confederate States) and created their own flag on March 4, 1861. Known as the "Stars and Bars," it originally had 7 stars, but these increased to 13 in the course of 1861, as more states joined the Confederacy.

The Confederate Battle Flag or "Second Naval Jack"

The Confederate Battle Flag with its distinctive saltire on a red field (Southern Cross) was introduced in September 1863 and was used by the Confederate Army during the Civil War. Modern use of this flag carries the legacy of Confederate ideals and is usually a potent symbol for racism and white supremacy, even internationally.*

*The views represented by this flag do not reflect the opinions of the publisher or our contributors.

US: State flags

The date when each state joined the Union is shown beside the state name.

Alabama 1819

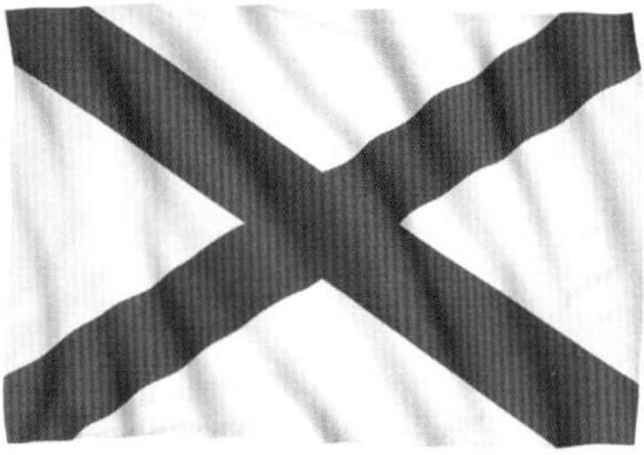

This flag, which was adopted in 1895, shows a red saltire on a white field. It is intended to recall the Southern Cross or Confederate Battle Flag.

Alaska 1959

The flag was designed by a schoolboy in 1926, when Alaska was still a territory. It depicts the Big Dipper and the northern Pole star. Gold also represents Alaska's mineral reserves.

Arizona 1912

The red and yellow rays recall the period of Spanish rule, and the copper star represents mineral riches. The flag was designed locally and adopted in 1927.

Arkansas 1836

The flag recalls the Southern Cross. The lower stars represent former colonial powers and the upper star stands for the Confederacy. The flag was adopted in 1913.

California 1850

The flag is based on that of the California Republic declared at Sonora in 1846; it did not become the state flag until 1911. It depicts a grizzly bear and a star representing freedom.

Colorado 1876

The C-shaped emblem contains the colors of Spain, which once laid claim to this area. The gold ball also represents the state's mineral riches. The flag was adopted in 1911.

Connecticut 1788

The arms date back to the seal of 1784, and the blue field to the Civil War period, when the flag was a Union color. This design was adopted in 1897.

Delaware 1787

The arms date back to 1777 and the flag, adopted in 1913, includes the date Delaware joined the Union. The colors recall the uniforms worn during the Revolutionary War.

US: State flags (continued)

Florida 1845

This is another flag which recalls the Southern Cross used by the Confederacy during the Civil War. The original flag, adopted in 1868, had only the seal; the red saltire was added in 1900.

Georgia 1788

The revised state flag for Georgia was introduced in 2003, following objections to the inclusion of the Confederate flag on the previous two designs. The three bars evoke pre-1956 versions of the flag.

Hawaii 1959

The state flag, originally representing the independent kingdom, was adopted in 1845. The Union Jack recalls a flag given to the King by an army officer in 1793. The stripes stand for the main islands.

Idaho 1890

The flag, originally a military color, bears the state seal in the center; beneath it is a scroll with the state's name. The flag in this form was adopted in 1927, with new specifications in 1957.

Illinois 1818

Created in 1915, the central emblem of the Illinois flag, depicts elements from the state seal, including a bald eagle and a shield of the Stars and Stripes. The name was added beneath this in 1970.

Indiana 1816

The flag was the winning entry in a design competition held in 1916 and was officially adopted in 1917. The stars in the outside circle are for the original states and bottom arc is for the subsequent ones.

Iowa 1846

The red, white, and blue colors stand for French Louisiana, of which Iowa was once a part. In the center is the seal of 1847. The flag was adopted in this form in 1921.

Kansas 1861

The flag of Kansas follows a very common seal and name pattern. The original flag of 1925 had the seal, recalling settlement and agriculture, and a sunflower—the state flower. The name was added in 1963.

US: State flags (continued)

Kentucky 1792

This is another flag derived from the militia colors. The flag was adopted in 1918 and regularized in 1962. Like many state flags, it contains the seal, the state name, and a wreath of goldenrod—the state flower.

Louisiana 1812

The pelican, representing self-sacrifice and the state's role as protector, has long been the badge of Louisiana, but the flag was only adopted in 1912 and slightly modified in 2006. In 2010 the pelican was completely redrawn to look more natural.

Maine 1820

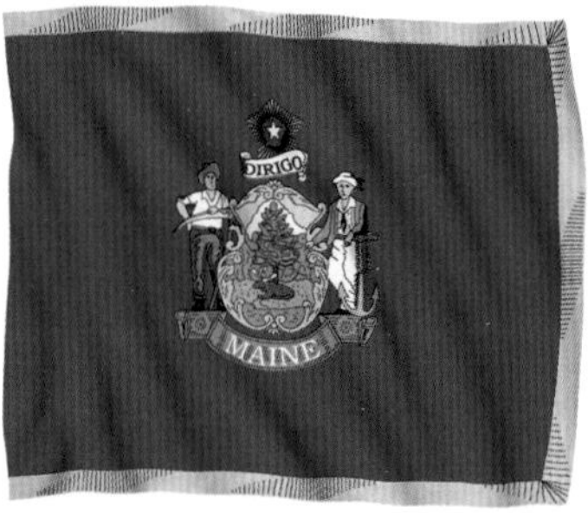

The flag dates from 1909 when the arms, adopted in 1820, were placed on a blue field. The star and motto recall Maine's northerly location. It was the northernmost state of the Union, until Michigan joined in 1837.

Maryland 1788

This is the only flag which is a true heraldic banner, reproducing the arms of the Baltimore family, once the "proprietors" of the state. Each side of the family is represented by two quarters. It was adopted in 1904.

Massachusetts 1788

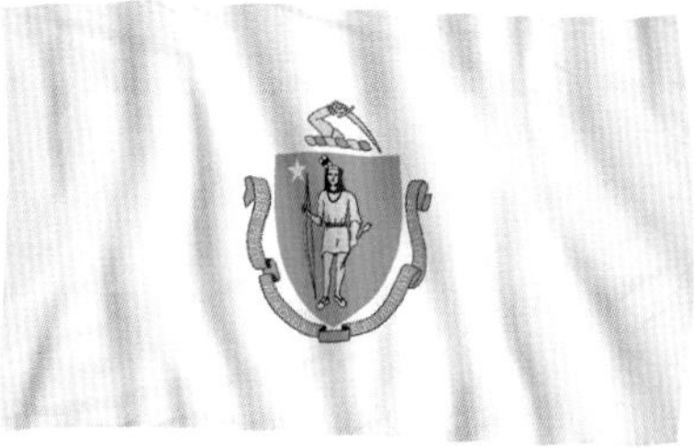

The flag was originally adopted in 1908 and revised in 1971, replacing a pine tree with the coat of arms adopted in 1780. The arms depict a Native American holding a downward facing bow, denoting peace, and a star that signifies statehood.

Michigan 1837

The arms was adopted in 1832, and placed on a blue field to make the state flag in 1911. The mottoes translate to "I will defend," and "If you seek a pleasant peninsula, look about you."

Minnesota 1858

The motto on this flag, "The North Star," was retained from when the state was the northernmost in the Union. The flag was originally adopted in 1893 and revised in 1957.

Mississippi 1817

The previous flag of Mississippi, which dated from 1894, contained elements associated with the Confederacy. This was replaced in 2021, following a flag design competition and referendum where the new flag, featuring a magnolia blossom, was chosen.

US: State flags (continued)

Missouri 1821

The colors of the flag recall when the region was under French control. The 24 stars stand for Missouri being the 24th state to join the Union. Within the seal itself are another 24 stars. The flag was adopted in 1913.

Montana 1889

The flag is derived from the former state militia colors, while the motto, "Gold and Silver," is in Spanish, recalling Spain's claim to the area. The flag was adopted in 1905 and had the name added in 1981.

Nebraska 1867

The flag of Nebraska was adopted in 1925 and uses the seal that was adopted in 1867. This depicts an allegorical landscape, symbolic of the state's agricultural and industrial development.

Nevada 1864

The flag emerged from a design competition and was adopted in 1929. It was revised in 1991, and the state name was placed underneath the boughs of the sagebrush and the star, which represents the state.

New Hampshire 1788

The design was adopted in 1909, making use of the seal, which dates back to 1775. It depicts a ship, the *Raleigh*, being built on the docks of the town of Portsmouth during the Revolutionary War.

New Jersey 1787

The buff field recalls the uniforms worn during the Revolutionary War. The flag with the arms was adopted in 1896 and made widely available in 1938.

New Mexico 1912

This flag was adopted in 1925 and uses the sun symbol of the indigenous *Zia Pueblo* people, while the colors represent the Spanish colonial era.

New York 1788

The flag dates originally from flags used in the Revolutionary War, but in this form only from 1901. Prior to that the flag had a buff field. The two figures symbolize liberty and justice. The coat of arms dates from 1777.

US: State flags (continued)

North Carolina 1789

The original flag was adopted in 1861 at the outbreak of the Civil War and used colors derived from the Stars and Bars. The present design dates from 1885. It contains the initials of the state in the blue stripe.

North Dakota 1889

The flag was originally used by the state militia—the North Dakota Infantry—and was adopted in 1911, almost without alteration, explaining its squarish shape. A version of the national arms is in the center.

Ohio 1803

The pennant-shaped flag of Ohio is derived from a cavalry guidon of the Civil War period. The 17 stars recall that Ohio was the 17th state to join the Union, and the circle or "O" refers to the state's initial.

Oklahoma 1907

The basic design emerged from a design competition and was adopted in 1925. The flag includes many indigenous symbols, including Osage emblems for peace and a blue field alluding to the flag of the Choctaw people. The name was added in 1941.

Oregon 1859

This is now the only state flag with a different design on its reverse. The obverse shows the seal within 33 stars, the state's name, and its date of admission. It was adopted in 1925.

Pennsylvania 1787

The coat of arms of the state was adopted in 1777 and regularized in 1875. It was placed on a blue field to make the flag in 1907. The shield is supported by two horses.

Rhode Island 1790

The anchor, symbolic of hope, has long been the emblem of Rhode Island. The flag, based on a Revolutionary War flag, was adopted in 1877 and modified in 1897.

South Carolina 1788

The flag was adopted in 1861 at the very start of the Civil War but contains emblems used during the Revolutionary War and also used in the state arms. The central palmetto is the state tree.

US: State flags (continued)

South Dakota 1889

The flag of South Dakota was adopted in 1963 on the basis of previous models and had the former motto "The Sunshine State" around the seal. This was changed to "The Mount Rushmore State" in 1992.

Tennessee 1796

The three stars represent the three geographical divisions of the state, while its general appearance recalls the Confederate Flag or Southern Cross. The flag was adopted in 1905.

Texas 1845

The flag copies the colors of the Stars and Stripes, but with only one star, which dates back to the one found on the plain blue flag of the Republic of Texas. It was adopted in 1839 and retained after Texas joined the Union.

Utah 1896

The beehive in the flag recalls the emblem of the provisional Mormon state of Deseret, and the date commemorates their settlement of the region. In 2011, a new version of the flag corrected the previously misplaced date of 1847 by adding it to the shield, a mistake that had persisted for 89 years.

Vermont 1791

The arms, including the Lone Pine emblem, date back to when Vermont was independent from 1777–1791. The present flag, based on the former militia flag, was adopted in 1923. The state name appears on a scroll.

Virginia 1788

The state arms was adopted in 1776. The seal, showing Liberty Triumphing over Tyranny, was placed on the flag in 1861 at the start of the Civil War. The design has been used ever since.

Washington 1889

Washington is known as "The Evergreen State," and this is reflected by its flag. It is the only state with a green flag. The seal dates from 1889 and was placed on the flag in 1923.

West Virginia 1863

The coat of arms dates from 1863 when West Virginia seceded from Virginia. The current version of the flag was adopted in 1929 and has the arms within a wreath of rhododendron, the state flower.

US: State and overseas territory flags

The date when each state or territory joined the US is shown besides the name.

Wisconsin 1848

The flag is derived from the militia colours of the Union in 1863. It depicts the state seal, supported by a miner and a sailor. The shield also recalls mining and sailing. The name and the date were added in 1980.

Wyoming 1890

The flag emerged from a design competition and was adopted in 1917. The flag has been revised several times; at one time the buffalo containing the arms faced the fly. The colors are based on those of the national flag.

District of Columbia 1791

The flag of the Federal District of Columbia (also known as Washington, DC) is based on a banner of the arms of the Washington family, which originated in England and dates back to 1592. It was adopted in 1938 by a Congress Commission.

Overseas territory flags

American Samoa 1900

A self-governing US dependency, American Samoa's flag uses its colors to represent the connection to the United States. A bald eagle carrying Samoan emblems symbolizes the political relationship between the two nations.

Guam 1917

The flag was designed locally and adopted in 1917. In the center of the flag, in the US colors, is the seal of the territory, which depicts an idealized landscape. The flag can be flown only with the US flag.

US: Military flags

Northern Mariana Islands 1972

The original flag was adopted in 1972 but has undergone several modifications, including the addition of the flower-wreath. It also depicts a gray latte stone, representing the islands' Chamorro culture.

Puerto Rico 1952

Based on the flag of Cuba, this design was approved in 1895 by members of of the Puerto Rican Revolutionary Committee in New York City. The flag was subsequently banned from use until Puerto Rico became a "Commonwealth" under US sovereignty in 1952.

Virgin Islands (US) 1921

The flag dates from 1921 and uses part of the US seal, with the initials of the islands. The three arrows in one claw stand for the main islands; in the other claw is an olive branch.

Military flags

US Army 1956

The flag bears a blue replica of the War Office Seal on a white field. It was officially adopted by President Eisenhower. The date 1775 underneath the banner refers to the year the army was formed.

US Air Force 1951

The flag includes the coat of arms of the US Air Force, the Air Force Seal, and 13 stars representing the 13 original colonies. The version of the flag that is used for parades has a gold border.

US: Military flags (continued)

US Navy 1959

The flag bears the seal of the US Navy on a dark blue field and has a yellow banner underneath inscribed with "United States Navy". The flag is flown in the Navy's offices, during parades, and on other ceremonial occasions.

US Marines 1939

The gold and scarlet colors of the flag are also the official colors of the Marines Corps. The flag bears the Corps' emblem in the center and is also known as the "Battle Color". The flag is used to represent the Corps' units and formations.

US Coast Guard 1964

The flag bears the Great Seal of the USA on a white field. It is used in parades and ceremonies. The Coast Guard motto "*Semper Paratus*", which appears at the bottom of the flag, means "Always Ready".

US Space Force 2019

The flag includes the Delta Wing Emblem of the US Space Force. The largest star is Polaris and the smaller stars represent the space assets protected by the Space Force. The Roman numerals represent 2019, the year the Space Force was founded.

Mexico

Adopted November 2, 1821 | **Ratio** 4:7 | **Usage** National and Civil

The basic design is derived from the French *Tricolore*
Red, white, and green are the colors of the national liberation army in Mexico
The coat of arms incorporates the badge of Mexico City

When Mexico gained independence from Spain in 1821 a new flag was devised based on the French *Tricolore*. The colors were derived from those used in the flag of the Liberation Army.

A darker shade of green and the coat of arms on the center stripe distinguishes the flag from that of Italy.

THE AZTEC INHERITANCE

The central emblem is the Aztec pictogram for Tenochtitlán (now Mexico City), the center of their empire. It recalls the legend that inspired the Aztecs to settle on what was originally a lake island.

The form of the coat of arms was most recently revised in 1968.

ARMS OF MEXICO

The lake, with an island, represents Tenochtitlán
Ribbon in the national colors
Aztec legend held that they should found their city on the spot where they saw an eagle on a cactus, eating a snake

Guatemala

Adopted August 17, 1871 | **Ratio** 5:8 | **Usage** National and State

Blue and white are the colors of the original flag of the United Provinces of Central America
The coat of arms was adopted in 1968

In Guatemala, the flag of the United Provinces of Central America, horizontal stripes of blue-white-blue, was used until 1851, when a pro-Spanish government added the red and yellow of Spain to the flag. On August 17, 1871, the original colors were restored as vertical stripes, and with Guatemala's own coat of arms.

THE QUETZAL BIRD

The new coat of arms shows the quetzal, Guatemala's national bird, standing on a scroll giving the date of the Declaration of Independence. The present form of the arms was adopted in 1968. When used at sea for civil purposes, the flag does not contain the arms.

ARMS OF GUATEMALA

The date of the Declaration of Independence
Rifles and swords represent defense of freedom
LIBERTAD 15 DE SEPTIEMBRE DE 1821
The quetzal bird with its distinctive tail feathers is a symbol of liberty

Belize

Adopted September 21, 1981 | **Ratio** 2:3 | **Usage** National and State

Red stripes were added to denote the color of the opposition party
The 50 leaves recall 1950, the year the PUP came to power
SUB UMBRA FLOREO
The country's coat of arms was granted in 1907
Blue is the party color of the PUP

The flag is made up of a number of elements, the first of which was the coat of arms granted in 1907, which recalls the importance of the logging industry.

From 1968 onward, an unofficial national flag was in use. It was blue with a modified version of the arms—minus the Union Jack—on a white disk in the center. The colors were those of the People's United Party (pup). Around the arms was a wreath of 50 leaves, recalling 1950, when the PUP came to prominence.

On independence in 1981, this flag was retained, and the final elements of two red stripes were added to stand for the opposition party.

ARMS OF BELIZE

The figures, tools, and the mahogany tree represent the logging industry
Wreath of 50 leaves
SUB UMBRA FLOREO
National motto—"Sub Umbra Floreo," meaning "I Flourish in the Shade"

El Salvador

Adopted May 17, 1912 | **Ratio** 3:5 | **Usage** National and State

The flag is modeled on the flag of the United Provinces of Central America
The title of the state while it was part of the United Provinces of Central America surrounds the emblem
The emblem is surrounded by five flags, recalling the original five United Provinces of Central America

The flag of Central America was used as the national flag until 1865, when a flag based on the Stars and Stripes was adopted, with blue and white stripes and a red canton containing nine stars.

In 1912, the original design was readopted, with the arms of El Salvador positioned in the center.

TRIANGLES AND VOLCANOES

The coat of arms is similar to those of the United Provinces of Central America. The emblem is based on the Masonic triangle for equality and depicts the five original provinces with five volcanoes. Around the triangle are five national flags and a wreath, tied in the national colors.

ARMS OF EL SALVADOR

A triangle representing equality
The motto of Central America—"Dios, Union, Libertad," meaning "God, Union, Liberty"
The Cap of Liberty
Five volcanoes representing the original United Provinces

Honduras

Adopted March 7, 1866 | **Ratio** 1:2 | **Usage** National and Civil

The colors and pattern are the same as the flag of the United Provinces of Central America
Five stars recall the five original members of the United Provinces of Central America

In 1823, Honduras joined the United Provinces of Central America and adopted their flag. In 1866, it was amended: five blue stars were placed in the center to represent the five original Central American provinces. The state flag has the arms of Honduras in the center in place of the stars.

The arms was created in 1838 and revised in 1935. The central feature is a pyramid in Maya style rising from the sea. Around this is a blue band with the name of the state and the date of the Declaration of Independence. Beneath it is a landscape strewn with allegorical items representing mineral and timber industries.

ARMS OF HONDURAS

The cornucopias are symbolic of prosperity and agricultural wealth
A Maya pyramid
The landscape depicts mines, mining tools, forests, and logging tools

Nicaragua

Adopted September 4, 1908 | **Ratio** 3:5 | **Usage** National and Civil

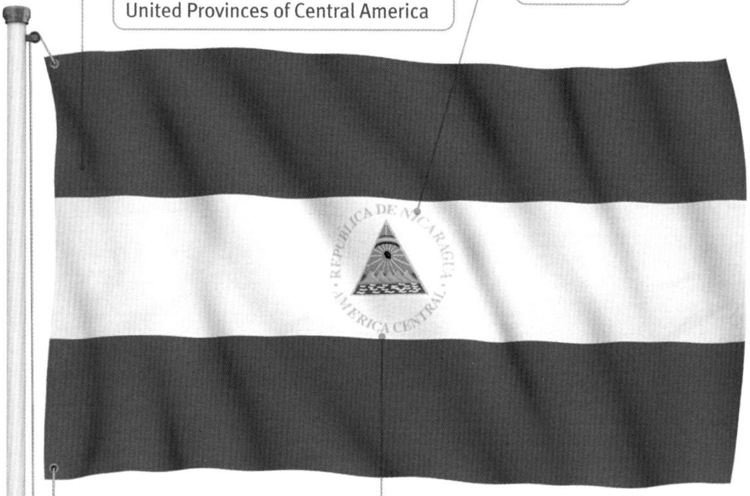
Apart from the text around the arms, the flag is identical to that of the United Provinces of Central America
Arms of Nicaragua
REPUBLICA DE NICARAGUA
AMERICA CENTRAL
"America Central" recalls the United Provinces of Central America

The flag and the arms of Nicaragua in use today are the most similar to those used by the United Provinces of Central America. The triangle, volcanoes, rising sun, Cap of Liberty, and rainbow all appeared on the original emblem. The coat of arms used today contains the name of the state, *Republica de Nicaragua*, whereas in 1823, the title was *Provincias Unidas del Centro de America*.

In 1908 the decision to revert to the emblems that are used by the United Provinces of Central America was made to reflect Nicaragua's aspirations for the rebirth of the political entity formed by the five nations.

ARMS OF NICARAGUA

The rays of the sun and the rainbow are symbolic of the bright future
REPUBLICA DE NICARAGUA
AMERICA CENTRAL
The Cap of Liberty represents national freedom
The five volcanoes represent the original five member states

Costa Rica

Adopted November 27, 1848 | **Ratio** 3:5 | **Usage** National and State

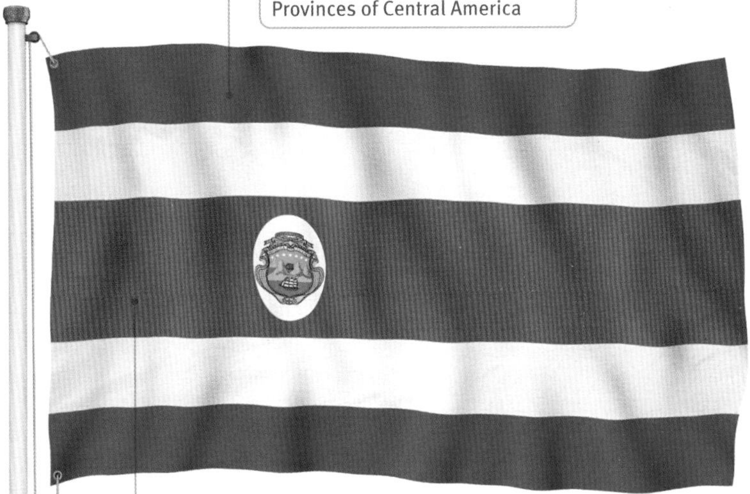
Blue and white were the colors of the original flag of the United Provinces of Central America
Red, white, and blue recall the colors of the French *Tricolore*

The Central American flag remained in use in Costa Rica until 1848 when, inspired by the French Revolution, it was decided to incorporate the French colors into the national flag. This was done by adding a central red stripe. The coat of arms was also revised and placed in the center of the flag. In 1906, it was placed in a white disk on the red stripe, and later on an oval, set toward the hoist.

The coat of arms depicts the isthmus between the Pacific Ocean and the Caribbean Sea. The stars stand for the seven provinces and the Central American union is recalled by *"America Central"* on the upper scroll.

ARMS OF COSTA RICA

Seven stars for the seven provinces
The Caribbean Sea
The Pacific Ocean
AMERICA CENTRAL
REPUBLICA DE COSTA RICA
"America Central" recalls the former United Provinces of Central America
Three volcanoes on the isthmus

Panama

Adopted November 3, 1903 | **Ratio** 2:3 | **Usage** National and Civil

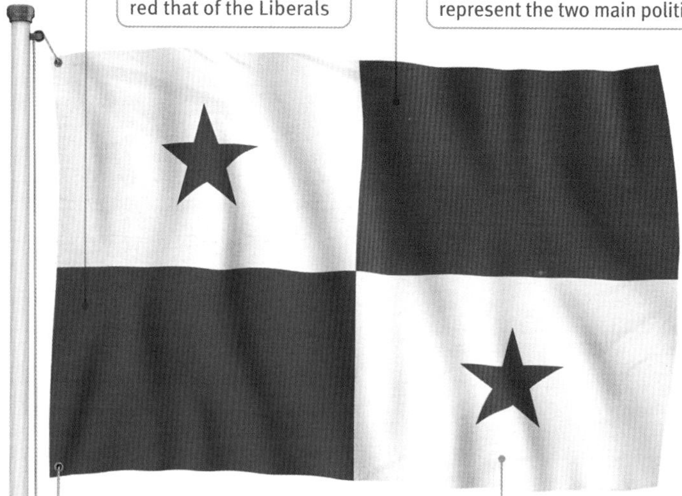
Blue was the color of the Conservatives and red that of the Liberals
Although inspired by the Stars and Stripes, the stars and quarters are said to represent the two main political parties
White symbolizes peace in the country

The first flag, proposed back in 1903, consisted of seven horizontal stripes of red and yellow, with a blue canton containing two golden suns, joined by a narrow line to depict the oceans to be united by the Panama Canal.

However, this was not accepted by the Panamanian leader, Manuel Amador Guerrero, whose family designed a new flag. Although clearly modeled on the US flag, the stars and quarters are said to stand for the rival political parties, and the white for the peace in which they operate.

The coat of arms reflects Panama's transition from civil war to peace in 1903, and the increased prosperity this promised the people.

ARMS OF PANAMA

PRO MUNDI BENEFICIO
The shield depicts tools, weapons, a cornucopia, and a winged wheel, which together symbolize a move from war, to peace and prosperity
The national motto—"*Pro Mundi Beneficio,*" meaning "For the Benefit of the World"
The northern and southern hemispheres joined by the Panama Canal

Jamaica

Adopted August 6, 1962 | **Ratio** 1:2 | **Usage** National and Civil

Black, green, and gold are also Pan-African colors
"Hardships there are but the land is green and the sun shineth" is the local motto complementing the flag
Black reflects hardships
Green represents the land
Gold symbolizes the sun shining

The present design emerged after a public competition held in 1961. It was originally designed with horizontal stripes, but this was too similar to the then Tanganyikan flag, and as a result, the saltire was substituted.

The coat of arms, based on those granted to Jamaica on February 3, 1663, is among the oldest granted to a British colony. It was used on the former British flags of Jamaica.

THE QUEEN'S STANDARD
The flag for HM Queen Elizabeth II, was introduced after independence. It contains a banner of the arms, with the Queen's Cypher in the center. The field depicts the red Cross of St. George charged with pineapples.

BANNER OF THE QUEEN OF JAMAICA

The Royal Cypher is enclosed within a chaplet of roses
St. George's Cross
The four pineapples and cross are taken from the Arms of Jamaica

Cuba

Adopted June 25, 1848 | **Ratio** 1:2 | **Usage** National and Civil

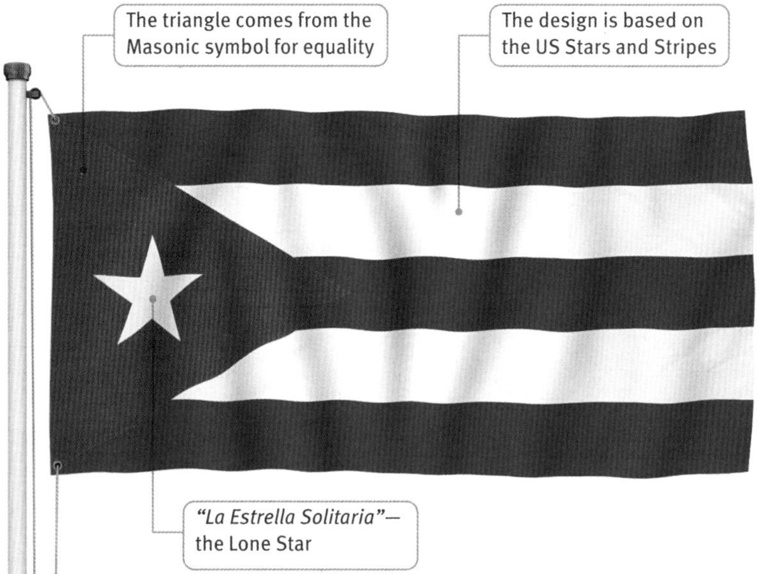
The triangle comes from the Masonic symbol for equality
The design is based on the US Stars and Stripes
"La Estrella Solitaria"—the Lone Star

The flag was designed in 1848 for the liberation movement, which sought to detach Cuba from Spain and make it into a state of the US. The "Lone Star" represented another star that would be added to "the splendid North American constellation."

The triangle is derived from the Masonic symbol for equality, while the five stripes stand for the five provinces of the time. The flag was briefly hoisted in 1850 at Cardenas but was not officially adopted until 1902, when independence was granted by the US.

Another flag from the 19th century is that of Carlos Manuel de Céspedes, used by the independence movement of 1868–1878. It is now used as the Jack of the Cuban navy.

FLAG OF CÉSPEDES

The flag is like that of Chile with the blue and red reversed

This flag was also modeled on the Stars and Stripes, using the same colors: blue, red, and white, and a star in the canton

The Bahamas

Adopted July 10, 1973 | **Ratio** 1:2 | **Usage** National

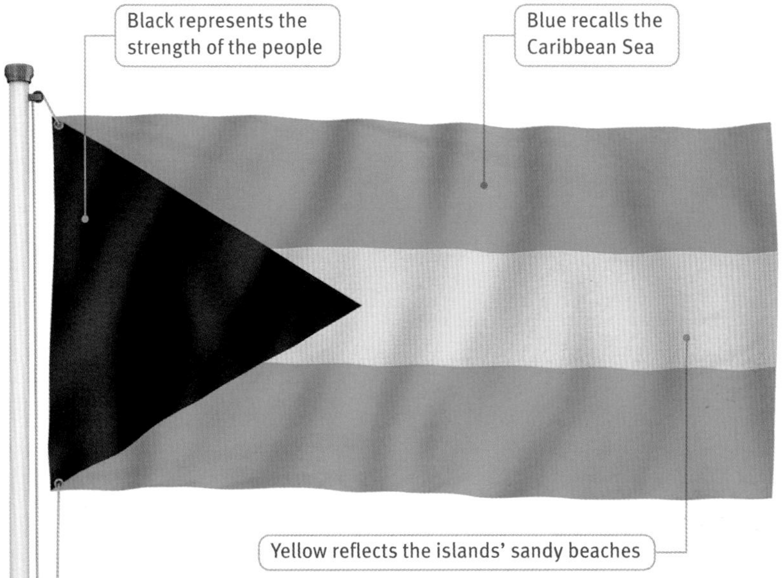
Black represents the strength of the people
Blue recalls the Caribbean Sea
Yellow reflects the islands' sandy beaches

The colors of the flag are intended to represent the aquamarine waters surrounding the islands and their golden sandy beaches. The black triangle at the hoist denotes direction and strength of purpose. The flag is based on designs by the Bahamian people, many of which also included the idea of sunrise, which has been incorporated into the coat of arms.

The Bahamas Civil Ensign (flown by merchant ships) is a familiar sight on the world's oceans, since many ships are registered in The Bahamas. The flag is based on the British Red Ensign—red with a Bahamian national flag in the canton—but is distinguished by the white cross, like the Cross of St. George, across the red field.

THE BAHAMAS CIVIL ENSIGN

The national flag is placed in the canton

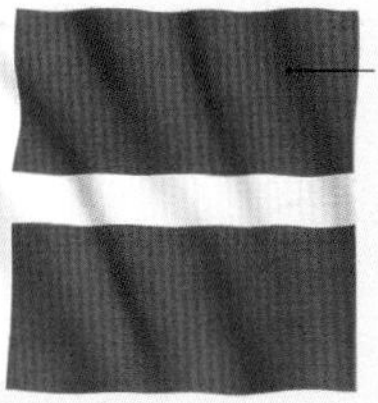
The civil ensign is distinguished from government and naval ensigns by its red field

Haiti

Adopted February 17, 1986 | **Ratio** 3:5 | **Usage** National and State

Blue and red are taken from the French *Tricolore*

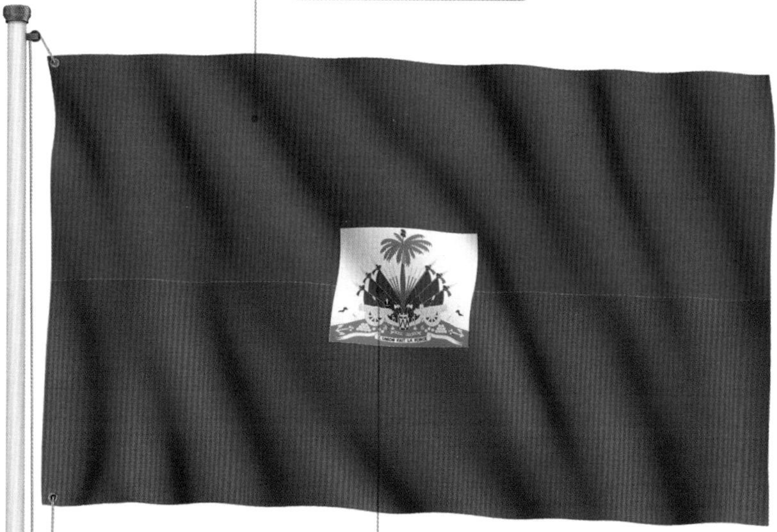

The coat of arms contains a depiction of the flag itself

The blue and red of the flag were retained after a French *Tricolore* was torn up by the rebel Jean-Jacques Dessalines in 1803. The two parts were stitched together horizontally to make a new flag.

However, a rival flag of vertical black and red panels was also used at various times, most recently in the period from 1964–1986, during the regime of the Duvalier family. Since 1843, the flag for official and state use has had the arms on a white panel in the center. The coat of arms depicts a trophy of weapons ready to defend freedom, and a royal palm topped with a Cap of Liberty for the country's independence.

ARMS OF HAITI

The Cap of Liberty

The national motto—"*L'Union Fait La Force,*" meaning "Union is Strength"

The royal palm symbolizes independence

Weapons reflect the people's willingness to defend their liberty

Dominican Republic

Adopted November 6, 1844 | **Ratio** 2:3 | **Usage** National and State

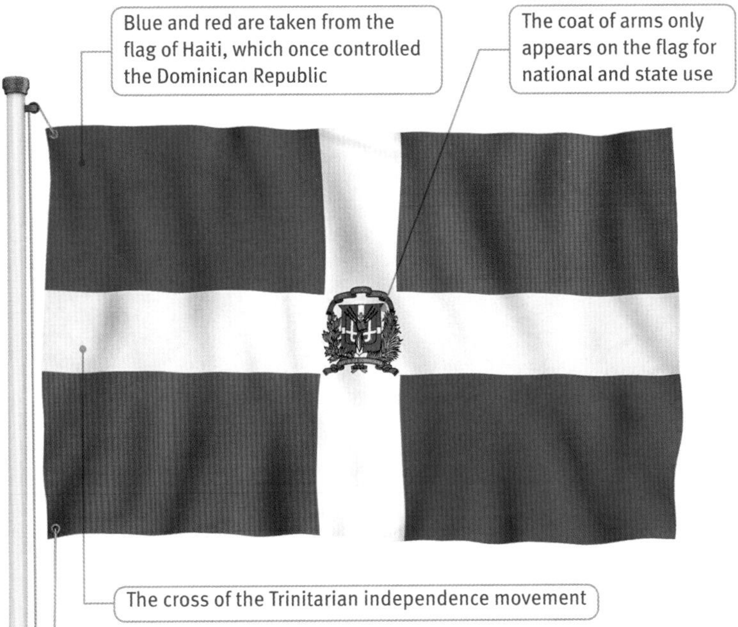
Blue and red are taken from the flag of Haiti, which once controlled the Dominican Republic
The coat of arms only appears on the flag for national and state use
The cross of the Trinitarian independence movement

The concept for the flag came from the leader of the Trinitarians, Juan Pablo Duarte. He altered the layout of the blue and red of the Haitian flag, placing a large white cross over it to symbolize faith.

A DISTINCTIVE NATIONAL FLAG

To create distinct flags for state and civil use, the coat of arms, adopted in 1844, was placed on the state flag. The civil flag, on both land and sea, does not carry the arms.

The arms depicts a Bible placed on a trophy of national flags and a shield of the same design. The Trinitarian motto is above this and the name of the state below.

ARMS OF DOMINICAN REPUBLIC

DIOS
PATRIA
LIBERTAD
REPUBLICA DOMINICANA
The password of the Trinitarian movement—*"Dios, Patria, Libertad"* ("God, Country, Freedom")
Gospel of St. John, a Trinitarian emblem
The lower scroll contains the state title

St. Kitts & Nevis

Adopted September 19, 1983 | **Ratio** 2:3 | **Usage** National and Civil

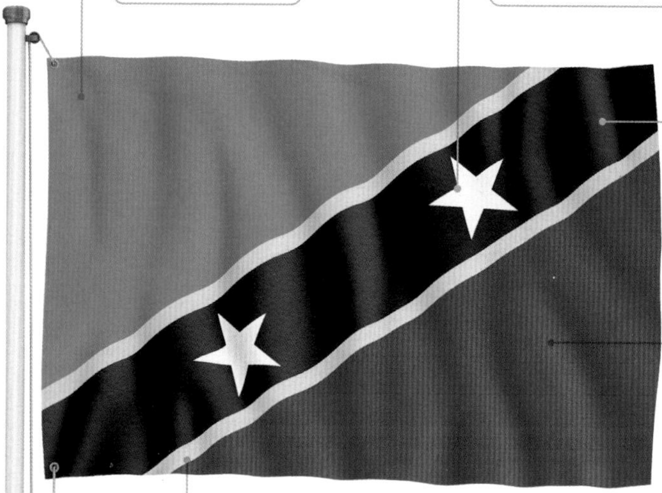

Green is symbolic of the fertile land
Two stars stand for hope and liberty
Black recalls St. Kitts' African heritage
Red recalls the struggle for freedom
Yellow reflects the country's sunny climate

The flag was the winning entry in a local competition that attracted 258 entries, and was the work of a student, Edrice Lewis. It was she who gave what is now the official interpretation of the flag—that its colors stand for the fertile land, year-round sunshine, the struggle for freedom, and the African heritage. The two stars stand for hope and liberty, not for the islands of St. Kitts and Nevis.

THE FLAG OF NEVIS

The island of Nevis has a flag of its own, which is bright yellow, with a stylized image of Nevis Peak. The national flag is in the canton. St. Kitts also has an ensign for the Coast Guard.

THE FLAG OF NEVIS

National flag in canton
Yellow for year-long sunshine
A graphic representation of Nevis Peak, a cone-shaped mountain in the center of the island

Antigua & Barbuda

Adopted February 27, 1967 | **Ratio** 2:3 | **Usage** National and Civil

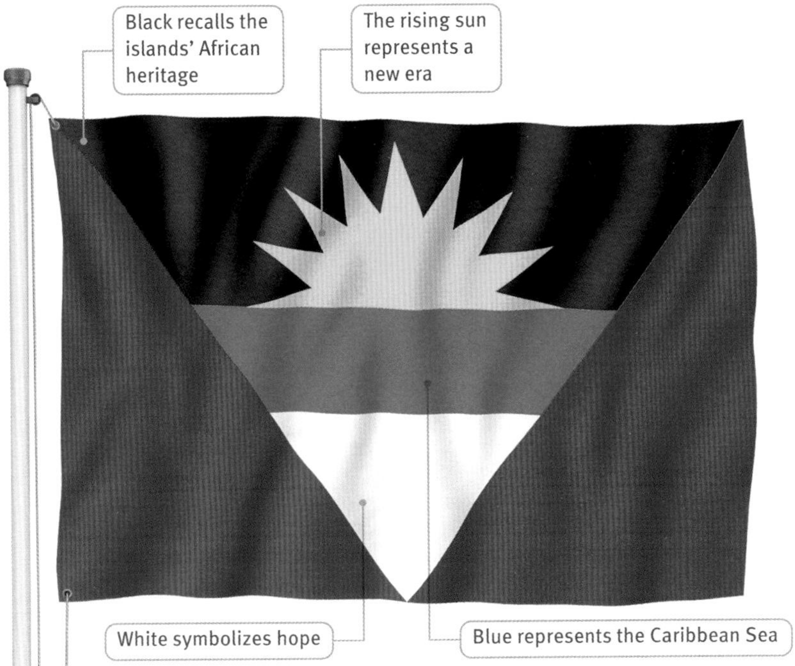
Black recalls the islands' African heritage
The rising sun represents a new era
White symbolizes hope
Blue represents the Caribbean Sea

The flag dates from the inception of self-government in 1967 and was the winning design in a competition that more than 600 local people entered.

THE SYMBOLISM OF THE FLAG

The designer, Reginald Samuel, interpreted it as representing the sun rising against the background of the peoples' African heritage in a new era. The overall V-shape stands for victory. It is on a red background, which symbolizes the dynamism of the population. Blue is for the sea, and white is for hope.

THE NEW NATIONAL FLAG

The flag was retained unchanged when Antigua became independent. The neighboring island of Barbuda does not have a separate flag, although, strangely, there is one for Redonda, an uninhabited island "micronation."

THE NATIONAL ARMS

The coat of arms was granted in 1977 and depicts a shield with a sugar mill, once the primary industry, on a background of white and blue waves. Above this is a sun on a black background. The shield stands on a sea island. The crest is a pineapple from the arms of the former colony of the Leeward Islands, of which Antigua was once a part. Beneath is a scroll with the national motto: "Each endeavoring, all achieving."

Dominica

Adopted November 3, 1978 | **Ratio** 1:2 | **Usage** National and Civil

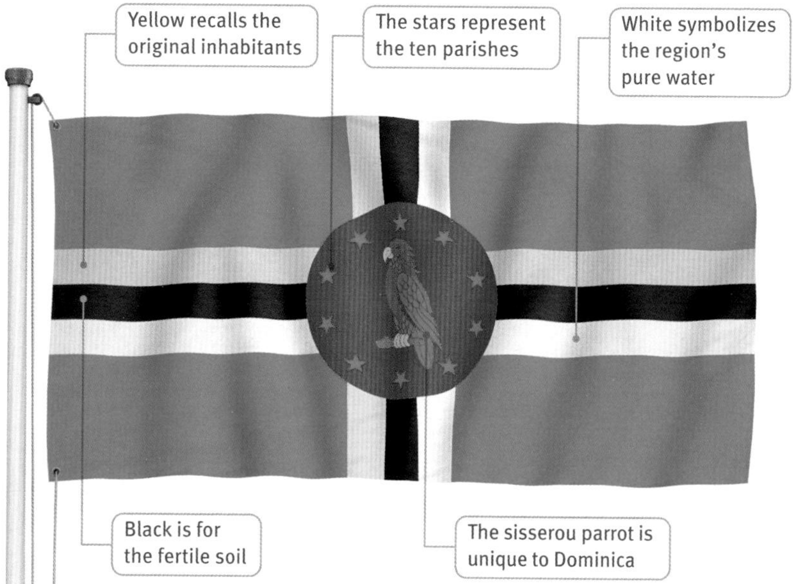

Yellow recalls the original inhabitants
The stars represent the ten parishes
White symbolizes the region's pure water
Black is for the fertile soil
The sisserou parrot is unique to Dominica

The flag adopted in 1978 features the national bird, the sisserou parrot, which also appears on the coat of arms granted on July 21, 1961. This parrot can be found only in Dominica. It is an endangered species; only a few pairs remain.

The green field represents the lush vegetation of the island. The cross represents the Christian faith and its Holy Trinity; its three colors recall the indigenous peoples, the fertile soil, and the pure water. The ten stars stand for the ten parishes and the red disk for social justice.

The flag of the president has a dark green field with the coat of arms in the center, crowned with a British lion. It depicts palm trees, a local frog species, and the sea.

THE PRESIDENT'S FLAG

The national motto is in Creole—"*Aprés Bondie C'est La Ter*," meaning "After the good Lord (we love) the soil"
APRES
BONDIE C'EST
LA TER
Two sisserou parrots support the coat of arms

St. Lucia

Adopted March 1, 1967 | **Ratio** 1:2 | **Usage** National and Civil

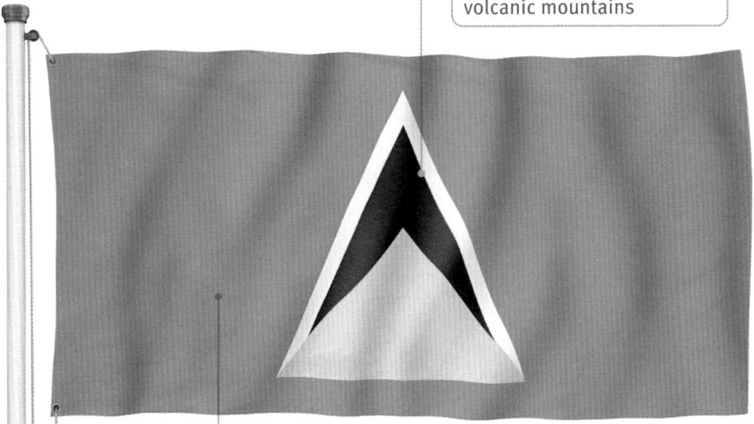
This symbol represents twin peaks of the Pitons—famous volcanic mountains
The blue field represents the sea

The flag was adopted when St. Lucia became a British Associated State in 1967. It was designed by a local artist, Dunstan St. Omer. The blue field represents the sea, from which arise the twin peaks of the Pitons said to be "rising sheer out of the sea and looking skyward—a symbol of hope." The yellow triangle stands for sunshine, and the black arrowhead on white, for the harmonious relationship between black and white people on the island. After independence was achieved in 1979, the height of the yellow triangle was increased.

A new form of the arms was also adopted, symbolizing the national motto: "The Land, the People, the Light."

THE GOVERNOR-GENERAL'S STANDARD

SAINT LUCIA
The state's title is placed on the scroll
The British Royal Crest of a crowned lion standing on a St. Edward's Crown

St. Vincent & the Grenadines

Adopted October 12, 1985 | **Ratio** 2:3 | **Usage** National and Civil

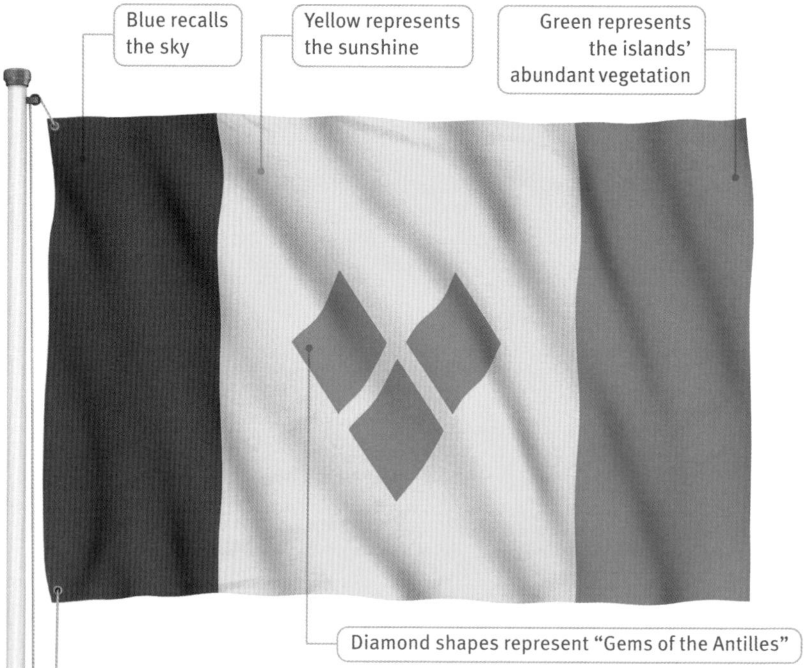
Blue recalls the sky
Yellow represents the sunshine
Green represents the islands' abundant vegetation
Diamond shapes represent "Gems of the Antilles"

The basic design and colors of the flag date from the flag hoisted on the day of independence in 1979. It had the arms of the islands placed on a stylized breadfruit leaf in the center. Its blue, yellow, and green stripes were derived from the common colors of the flags assigned to the Associated States by the College of Arms. The breadfruit recalled the British introduction of the breadfruit tree into the Caribbean from the South Seas in the late 18th Century.

Although this first flag was designed by a local islander, the design did not meet the approval of all the people of St. Vincent and the Grenadines, and, in 1985, moves were made to secure a new design.

A NEW NATIONAL FLAG

After a local competition failed to produce a satisfactory design, the problem was submitted to a Swiss graphic artist who suggested what is now the current design. In this, the "V" formed by the diamonds stands for St. Vincent, and the diamonds represent its local sobriquet the "Gems of the Antilles."

ARMS OF ST. VINCENT

The coat of arms was first introduced in 1912. It depicts two women, one standing holding an olive branch, the other kneeling to represent peace and justice, which is also the national motto—"*Pax, Justitia.*" This appears on a scroll at the base.

Barbados

Adopted November 30, 1966 | **Ratio** 2:3 | **Usage** National and Civil

Blue represents the sea
The trident broken from its shaft represents a break with the past
Gold reflects the golden sands of Barbados

The current flag was adopted at independence in 1966. It was the winning design in a national competition, which was won by Grantley Prescod, a local art teacher.

THE SYMBOLISM OF THE FLAG

Prescod interpreted the stripes as representing the blue seas and the golden sands that surround the island. The trident is adapted from the previous flag badge that depicted Britannia holding a trident (symbolic of her rule over the seas). Here the trident is without a shaft, indicating a break with its colonial past. It is also the emblem of the sea god, Neptune, and reflects the importance of the sea to Barbados.

ARMS OF BARBADOS

The coat of arms was granted by HM Queen Elizabeth II in 1966, on a visit to the island. The shield depicts a bearded fig tree, after which the island takes its name, between two "Pride of Barbados" flowers. The crest is an arm holding two sugarcanes in the form of a St. Andrew's Cross. This commemorates independence, which was achieved on St. Andrew's Day, November 30, in 1966.

Barbados also has a Governor's standard. It is the same as that of the Governor of St. Lucia, which features the Royal Crest of England with a British lion (see p.73), except that it bears the title "Barbados" on the scroll beneath the Royal Crest.

Grenada

Adopted February 7, 1974 | **Ratio** 3:5 | **Usage** National and Civil

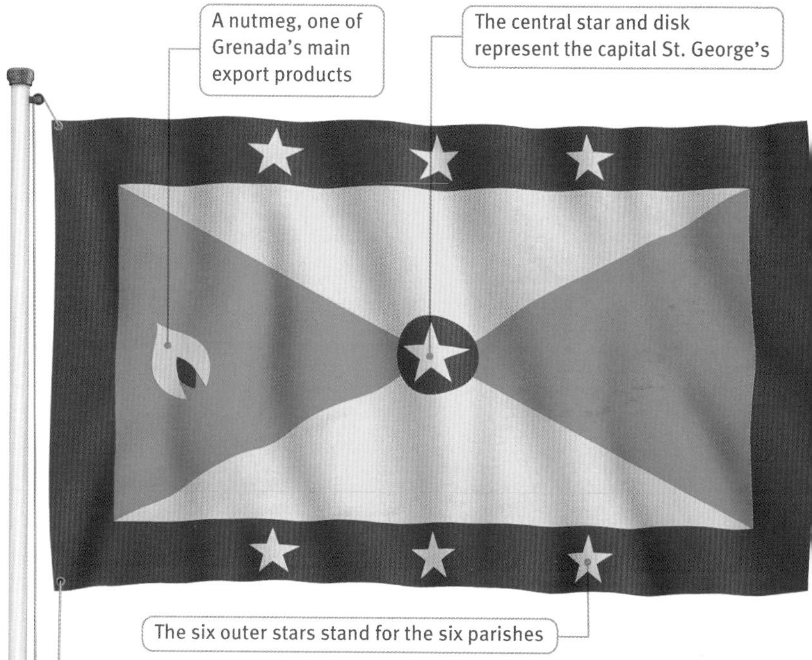
A nutmeg, one of Grenada's main export products
The central star and disk represent the capital St. George's
The six outer stars stand for the six parishes

The flag used prior to independence in 1967 also featured a nutmeg, since Grenada is a major world supplier of this commodity, and is known as the "Spice Island."

Other features of the flag derive from the coat of arms granted on December 6, 1973, including the red, yellow, and green colors.

SYMBOLISM OF THE FLAG

The yellow star on a red disk stands for the Borough of St. George's, Grenada's capital, and the other six stars for the remaining six parishes.

In the official interpretation the red stands for courage and vitality, the yellow for wisdom and warmth, and the green for vegetation and agriculture. When the flag is used at sea, its proportions are altered from 3:5 to a longer form (1:2).

THE NATIONAL ARMS

The coat of arms depicts the Santa Maria, Columbus's ship, a lion representing national liberty, and a lily emblem symbolizing the Virgin Mary. The shield is supported by two characteristic local creatures, an armadillo and a ramier pigeon. Beneath the shield is a representation of the Grand Etang lake, and, on a scroll at the base, what must be one of the world's longest national mottos: "Ever conscious of God we aspire, build and advance as one people."

Trinidad & Tobago

Adopted August 31, 1962 | **Ratio** 3:5 | **Usage** National and Civil

White represents the sea
Black symbolizes the strength of the people
Red stands for the people

Adopted at independence in 1962, the flag was chosen from designs sent in by the public. The same colors are used in the arms.

A flag for HM Queen Elizabeth II was adopted after independence, but it became obsolete following the formation of the republic.

The President has a flag of blue with the coat of arms in the center. It depicts the three ships of Columbus who landed here in 1498. Above the ships are two golden hummingbirds. The supporters of the coat of arms are also local birds and the whole shield stands on a scene depicting waves breaking against the rocky coasts of the islands.

Trinidad also has flags for the Prime Minister and other ministers.

THE PRESIDENT'S FLAG

The scarlet ibis is one of many local birds
The top of the shield depicts two hummingbirds
The *cocrico*—a local bird
In 1498, Columbus discovered Trinidad and his ships appear on the shield

12
7
5
6
9
2
8
1
4

South America

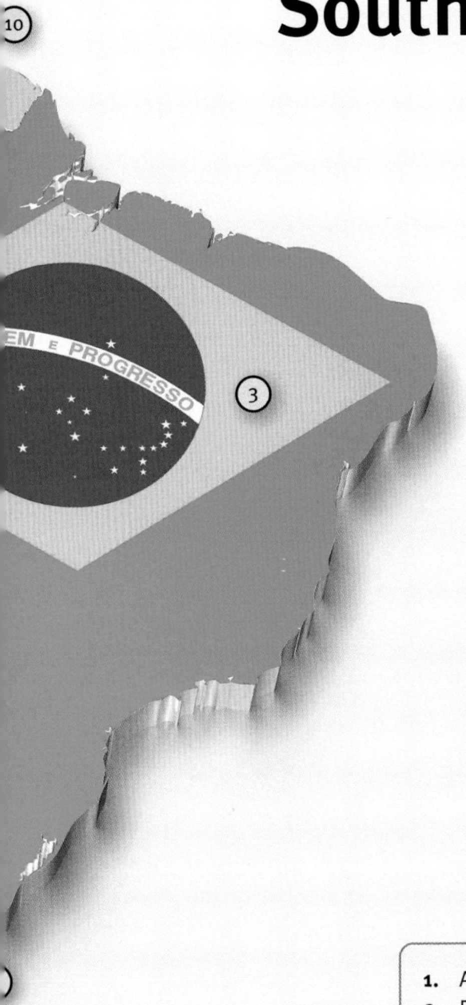

Colombia

Adopted December 17, 1819 | **Ratio** 2:3 | **Usage** National

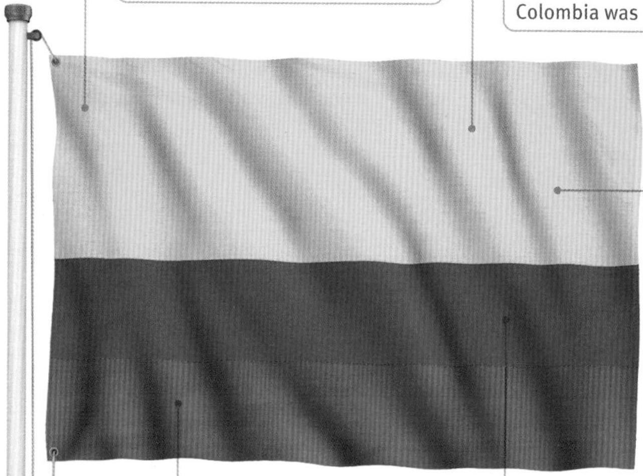
The colors are those of Francisco de Miranda, the liberation leader
The original yellow band was doubled in width when Greater Colombia was formed
Yellow recalls the federation of Greater Colombia
Red represents courage
Blue represents independence from Spain

The flag of Greater Colombia, adopted in 1819, was retained by Colombia after independence in 1830. For a while, the stripes were arranged vertically, but the original version was restored in 1861.

There are two variant flags. The civil ensign has a red-bordered, blue oval bearing a white star in the center, used to distinguish it from the flag of Ecuador. The state flag and naval ensign have the arms in the center.

THE NATIONAL ARMS

The coat of arms dates from 1834. It includes a pomegranate, the symbol of Granada in Spain, after which the area was once named.

ARMS OF COLOMBIA

LIBERTAD
Y ORDEN
National motto—*Libertad y Orden*, meaning "Liberty and Order"
The Cap of Liberty
A map of the Isthmus of Panama
The crest is a condor, frequently used in South American heraldry
A pomegranate recalls New Granada, Colombia's former name when a Spanish colony

Venezuela

Adopted March 12, 2006 | **Ratio** 2:3 | **Usage** National and Civil

The flag is an evolved form of the one flown by liberation leader Francisco de Miranda
Stars represent the eight provinces that supported independence
Red symbolizes courage
Blue represents Venezuela's independence from Spain

The Venezuelan flag was the invention of Francisco de Miranda, who initiated the freedom of New Granada in 1806. At that time it had no stars; they were added in 1836 to symbolize the provinces that had supported the Declaration of Independence in 1811. The original plain tricolor was altered in 1819, making the yellow double width, for use as the flag of Greater Colombia.

After independence in 1836, the flag reverted to stripes of equal width and the stars were added. The coat of arms dates from the 19th century but has altered frequently, especially the inscription. The present form dates from 2006.

ARMS OF VENEZUELA

The wheatsheaf represents fertility
A galloping horse symbolizes liberty
The name of the state, *Republica Bolivariana de Venezuela*
Two horns of plenty symbolize abundance
The flag and weapons represent independence and the early native people
The arms appear in the canton of the state flag and naval ensign

Guyana

Adopted May 26, 1966 | **Ratio** 3:5 | **Usage** National and Civil

Red recalls the people's dynamism and zeal for reform
The "Golden Arrow" represents a bright future
Green recalls the vast forests and fields
The white and black fimbriations were added by the College of Arms
Yellow is symbolic of mineral wealth

The flag is known as the "Golden Arrow" because of the arrowhead that flies across the green field. The College of Arms altered the original design's red field in 1966 and also added the black and white fimbriations. The green and yellow represent natural resources and the red "zeal and dynamism [of the inhabitants] in building the nation."

GUYANA'S ARMS

Guyana's arms includes a headdress symbolizing its indigenous population and is supported by two jaguars holding items representing its mining industry. The national motto, "One people, One Nation, One Destiny," appears on the scroll below the shield.

STANDARD OF GUYANA

An indigenous head-dress symbolizes the people of the country
A shield decorated with the national flower (*Victoria Regia* Lily)
A *Victoria Regia* water lily, growing from stylized heraldic water
Wavy lines represent the waters of Guyana; below is the Canje Pheasant
ONE PEOPLE
ONE NATION
ONE DESTINY

Suriname

Adopted November 25, 1975 | **Ratio** 2:3 | **Usage** National and Civil

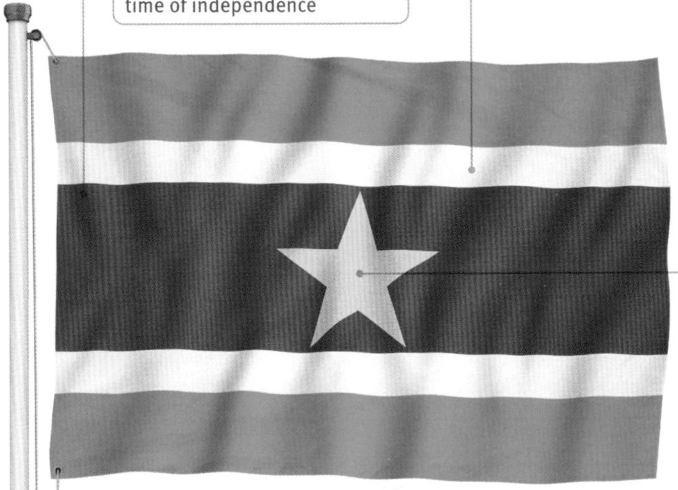
Green and red were the colors of the political parties at the time of independence
The white fimbriations represent justice and freedom
The star is an emblem of unity and hope

The flag was chosen in 1975 by a parliamentary commission, based on designs sent in by the public. The goal was to choose a flag that harmonized the colors of the main political groups (green and red) into a design suggestive of unity and progress. The star is thus the emblem of unity and hope for the future, and the white fimbriations, separating the red and green, stand for justice and freedom.

THE PRESIDENT'S STANDARD

This has a white panel in place of the star and contains the state arms. The coat of arms dates back to the 17th century and the time of Dutch rule but was revised in 1959 and again in 1975.

THE PRESIDENT'S STANDARD

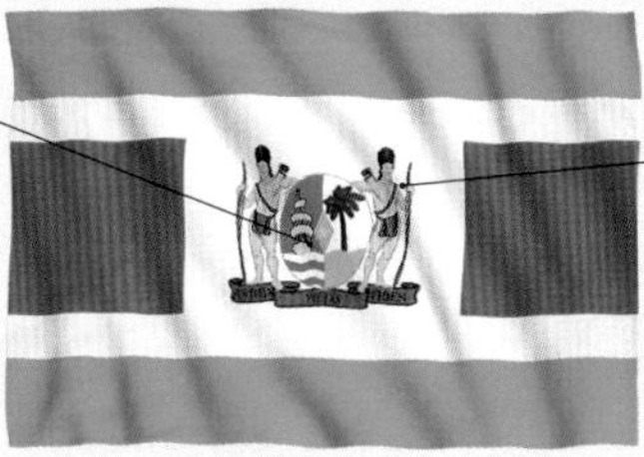
On the shield, a ship reflects commerce, a diamond, mining, and a tree, agriculture
The supporters are two Arawak figures, representing the indigenous people

Ecuador

Adopted September 26, 1860 | **Ratio** 1:2 | **Usage** National

Yellow, blue, and red are the colors of Venezuelan revolutionary Francisco de Miranda
Yellow symbolizes the crops and fertile soil
Blue recalls independence from Spain
Red symbolizes courage

The 1819 flag of Greater Colombia was restored in Ecuador in 1860, and since then the flags of Ecuador and Colombia have been very similar. The national arms were added to the center of the basic civil flag in 1900, creating a distinct flag for national and state purposes. The civil flag on land and at sea does not contain the arms, making it almost identical to the flag of Colombia, except for its proportions. When used abroad, the flag always contains the arms.

ARMS OF ECUADOR

The coat of arms dates from 1845 and depicts Mount Chimborazo and the mouth of the Guyas River.

ARMS OF ECUADOR

Four signs of the zodiac represent the months from March to May
An allegorical scene depicts Mount Chimborazo, South America's highest peak
An Andean condor symbolizes bravery and liberty
A ship at the mouth of the Guyas River representing commerce
The ax and fasces are symbols of republicanism

Peru

Adopted February 25, 1825 | **Ratio** 2:3 | **Usage** National

Red and white are the colors chosen by San Martín, *El Liberador* ("the Liberator")
The colors also recall those of the Incas, who ruled much of Peru until European colonization

The colors chosen by San Martín for the Peruvian Legion were red and white, said to be the colors of the Inca Empire, and the rising sun, also dating back to the Incas. The flag assumed its present form, dropping the sun in 1825, at the behest of Simón Bolívar, another famous liberator. As is usual in former Spanish colonies, the official flag, used by the government and the armed forces, has the coat of arms in the center.

The coat of arms dates from 1825 and depicts a cornucopia, a *cinchona* tree, and a *vicuña*, surrounded by state flags. The flags do not appear on the arms placed on the official flag.

ARMS OF PERU

A *vicuña*, the national animal of Peru
On the National Coat of arms, the wreaths are replaced by national flags
Cinchona, the source of quinine
A cornucopia symbolizing prosperity

Brazil

Adopted November 15, 1889 | **Ratio** 7:10 | **Usage** National and Civil

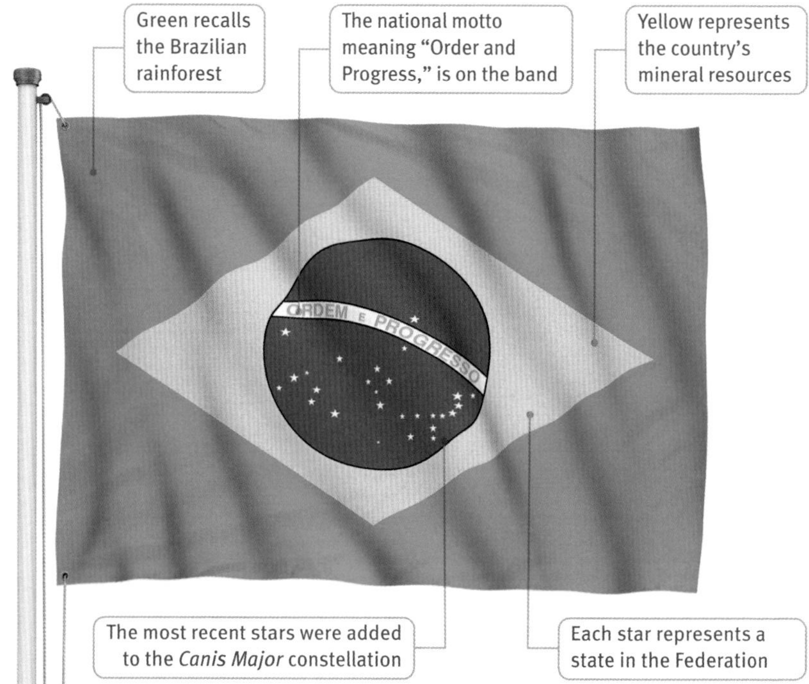
Green recalls the Brazilian rainforest
The national motto meaning "Order and Progress," is on the band
Yellow represents the country's mineral resources
ORDEM E PROGRESSO
The most recent stars were added to the *Canis Major* constellation
Each star represents a state in the Federation

The green field and yellow lozenge were part of the flag adopted in 1822 when independence was first achieved and the empire was declared. In 1889, the imperial arms were replaced by a view of the night sky as it appeared over Rio de Janeiro when the republic was formed. Each of the stars in the constellation represents a state of the Federation, including the Federal District. These have been altered from time to time, most recently in 1992 when the number of stars increased to 27.

THE CONSTELLATIONS

The constellations on Brazil's flag are represented in a realistic manner, with stars of varying sizes, although the size of star does not reflect the importance of the state. In 1992, new stars were added to the constellation of *Canis Major* in the lower left section of the sky. The country's national motto, "*Ordem e Progresso*," meaning "Order and Progress," appears on a band across the center of the night sky.

THE NATIONAL CAPITAL

In Brasília, the capital city since 1960, stands one of the world's tallest flagpoles, on which flies an enormous national flag.

Brazil also has flags for the president, the Ministry of Marine, and a naval Jack.

Brazil: State flags

Many of the flags recall historical events or the formation of the federal republic. The date of accession is next to the state name.

The Federal District 1960

The flag of the Federal District dates from 1969. The green rectangle contains four arrows representing the balance of centralization and devolution in Brazil.

Acre 1962

Adopted by the republic declared in 1899, when Acre was still part of Bolivia, the flag was retained by the state and the star was added to recall its joining the Federation.

Alagoas 1889

Based on the flag of 1894, this new version was instituted in 1963. In the center is the arms, also originally dating back to 1894. It recalls various aspects of the state's industry.

Amapá 1989

The flag was adopted in 1984 for the territory and retained for the state. It uses all the national colors, together with an outline of the fortress of Macapá, the state capital.

State flags (continued)

Amazonas 1889

The flag dates from the local uprising of 1897. The stars stand for the 25 municipalities, with the large one for Manaus, the state capital. The flag was regularized in 1982.

Bahia 1889

The flag dates back to the uprisings of 1789 and 1798, which are recalled by the white triangle. The flag in this form was first adopted in 1889, when Bahia joined the Federation.

Ceará 1889

The flag was instituted in 1922 and is very similar to the national flag. The arms depicts an allegorical landscape surrounded by stars. It dates from 1897 and was revised in 1967.

Espírito Santo 1889

The flag was created in 1947. The Portuguese motto meaning—"Work and Trust"—is from a Jesuit writer, and the pink and blue represent the local evening sky.

Goiás 1889

The flag is based on those promoted for the republic in 1889. This version has five stars for the Southern Cross similar to those in the national arms.

Maranhão 1889

The flag, adopted in 1889, features a star, which represents the state on the national flag, while the stripes stand for its ethnic mix.

Mato Grosso 1889

The flag is based on the national flag, but with local interpretations of the color arrangement and one star for the state. It was adopted in 1890.

Mato Grosso do Sul 1977

The design emerged from a competition held in 1978 after the new state was formed. The flag was instituted in 1979.

State flags (continued)

Minas Gerais 1889

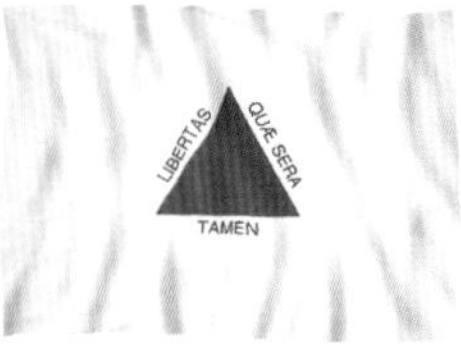

The flag contains a Masonic triangle of the *Inconfidência Mineira* (miners' revolt) of 1789, standing for equality.

Pará 1889

Adopted in 1898, the central white stripe of the flag symbolizes the Equator, Amazon River and the zodiac, the red represents sacrifices made and the star echoes the one for Pará on the national flag.

Paraíba 1889

The flag recalls Vargas' revolution in 1930. *Nego* ("I deny it") refers to the assassination of the state president.

Paraná 1889

The flag contains an emblem like the national flag, bearing the Southern Cross and name of the state.

Pernambuco 1889

This is the flag of the Pernambuco revolution of 1817, which later became the flag of the state when the events of 1817 were celebrated.

Piauí 1889

Based on the colors of the national flag, in this instance green represents hope and yellow, mineral wealth. The single star represents the state of Piauí. It was adopted in 1922.

Rio de Janeiro 1975

The state was reconstituted in 1975 to include the state of Guanabara. The new state took over the emblems of the former solo state of Rio de Janeiro.

Rio Grande do Norte 1889

Although it uses arms granted in 1909, the flag only dates from 1957, thus making it one of the newest flags of the original states.

Rio Grande do Sul 1889

The flag dates from the revolution of 1836, which created the Republic of Rio Grande do Sul. It was readopted in 1889; the arms were added in 1891.

Rondônia 1981

Rondônia's flag uses the four national colors and a single star symbol. It was adopted in 1981 after a design competition.

State flags (continued)

Roraima 1989

The flag, adopted when the territory became a federal state, uses the national colors and star, with a red line representing the Equator.

Santa Catarina 1889

The red and white flag precedes the republic. It was most recently regularized in 1953 when the arms were placed in the center.

São Paulo 1889

Originally intended to be the new national flag, this design was created in 1888 but only became officially adopted in 1946. The 13 stripes represent the days and nights spent fighting for the good of São Paulo during the republican revolution.

Sergipe 1889

The flag was created in the late 19th century and adopted in 1920. The stars represent the five major river estuaries in the state, and the green and yellow stripes echo the colors of the national flag.

Tocantins 1989

After achieving statehood, a flag and arms were adopted, using the national colors of blue and white.

Chile

Adopted October 18, 1817 | **Ratio** 2:3 | **Usage** National and Civil

Blue represents the clear Andean skies
White symbolizes the snow of the Andes
The flag is modeled on the US's Stars and Stripes
Red is for the blood shed for freedom

Adopted in 1817 after San Martín's victory at Chacabuco, the national flag of Chile was preceded by at least two other versions during the early years of separatism. The current flag was based on the Stars and Stripes.

The white star was reserved for use exclusively on the official flag until 1864, when the starred flag was made official for all purposes.

THE PRESIDENT'S STANDARD

The flag of the president is the same as the national flag, with the national arms in the center. The coat of arms dates from 1834. It is supported by a huemul deer and a condor. The crest is formed from the feathers of the rhea bird. The motto—"*Por La Razon o La Fuerza*"—means "By reason or by force."

THE PRESIDENT'S STANDARD

POR LA RAZON O LA FUERZA
A crest of feathers from the *rhea* bird
A *huemul* deer, of the high Andes
The condor is a common symbol on South American arms

Bolivia

Adopted November 30, 1851 | **Ratio** 15:22 | **Usage** National and Civil

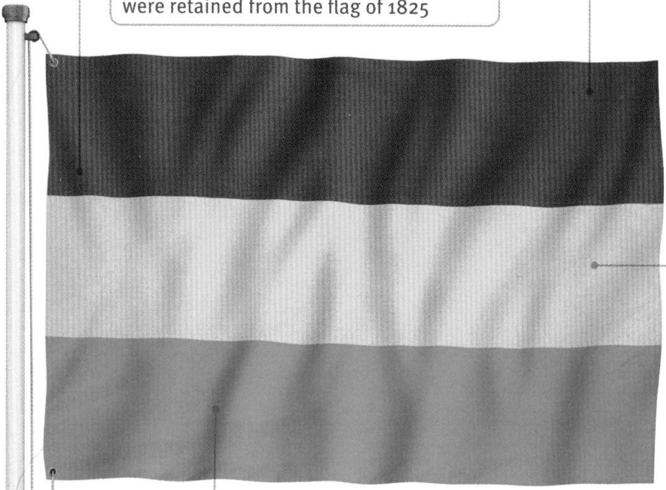
The order of the stripes was changed to red, yellow, green in 1851; red and green were retained from the flag of 1825
Red recalls valor
Yellow reflects Bolivia's mineral reserves
Green symbolizes fertility

The flag of 1825 had three stripes of green-red-green, with five gold stars within laurel wreaths. These stood for the original five departments.

A NEW TRICOLOR

In 1826, the flag was altered to three equal stripes of yellow, green, and red with the arms in the center. It was last altered in 1851, when the order of the stripes was changed to red, yellow, green.

The official flag still has the arms in the center. It was regulated in 1888 and features a stylized scene containing Mount Potosí, an alpaca, a wheatsheaf, and a breadfruit tree.

ARMS OF BOLIVIA

The weapons and flags represent the people's willingness to defend the state
The allegorical scene on the shield represents Bolivia's agricultural and industrial wealth
BOLIVIA
As on many South American arms, the crest is a condor
The nine stars represent Bolivia's nine departments

Paraguay

Adopted November 25, 1842 | **Ratio** 3:5 | **Usage** National and Civil

The red, white, and blue colors were influenced by the French *Tricolore*, which had become a symbol of liberation
REPUBLICA DEL PARAGUAY
On the reverse, the flag is charged with the Treasury Seal
The Star of May is used as a symbol of freedom on many South American flags

The colors of the flag and the Star of May emblem date from the Declaration of Independence. A number of variant designs existed prior to the current design, which was regularized in 1842. The current flag has a separate emblem on each side, dating from the time of José de Francia, in power from 1814–1840. During his regime one side of the flag carried the arms of Spain and the other the arms of Asunción.

The current emblems, used since 1842, have been redrawn several times, most recently in 2013. The national arms appear on the front (obverse) and the Treasury Seal on the back (reverse).

STATE ARMS ON THE OBVERSE

REPUBLICA DEL PARAGUAY
The Star of May recalls the date of independence
Name of the state

TREASURY SEAL ON THE REVERSE

PAZ Y JUSTICIA
The Cap of Liberty guarded by a lion
The motto, "*Paz y Justicia*" ("Peace and Justice")

Uruguay

Adopted July 11, 1830 | **Ratio** 2:3 | **Usage** National and Civil

The Sun of May has been a national emblem since the 19th century
White and blue are also the national colors of Argentina, from which this flag derives
The nine stripes represent the nine departments

The colors, blue and white, and the Sun of May on the current flag come from the Argentinian flag.

THE FLAG OF ARTIGAS

The colors were brought to Uruguay by José Artigas, who led the movement for separation. His flag was blue-and-white striped, with a red diagonal. Variations of this flag remained in use after Uruguay was annexed to Brazil in 1821.

When full independence was assumed, the present form of the flag was instituted. The nine stripes represent the nine departments. The Sun of May has been used as the national emblem since 1815 and now appears as the crest on the coat of arms.

FLAG OF ARTIGAS

This flag was used as a Jack for naval vessels until the late 1990s. The colors derive from those of Argentina's flag

Red represents the "*Banda Oriental*" (the "East Bank") of Uruguay

Argentina

Adopted February 27, 1812 | **Ratio** 9:14 | **Usage** National and Civil

Sky blue and white were formed into a flag by Manuel Belgrano, the leader of the revolution
Light blue and white are from the cockades used by revolutionaries in 1812
The sun was added in 1818 to create a flag for state use

At his encampment at Rosario in 1812, the revolutionary commander, Manuel Belgrano needed a flag. He devised one, using the sky blue and white colors of the cockades worn by supporters of independence. This flag was used in battle and although initially rejected by the provisional government, it later became the national flag.

THE SUN FLAG

In 1818, the sun emblem was added to the national flag, forming the state flag flown on government buildings and military bases. It is also the Argentine naval ensign. The sun is based on coins issued in Buenos Aires in 1813. The tradition of the "Sun of May," breaking through white clouds in a blue sky has no historical basis.

ARMS OF ARGENTINA

The Cap of Liberty
Sky blue and white are the national colors
The sun symbolizes the dawn of a new era and a new nation
A wreath of laurels

Africa

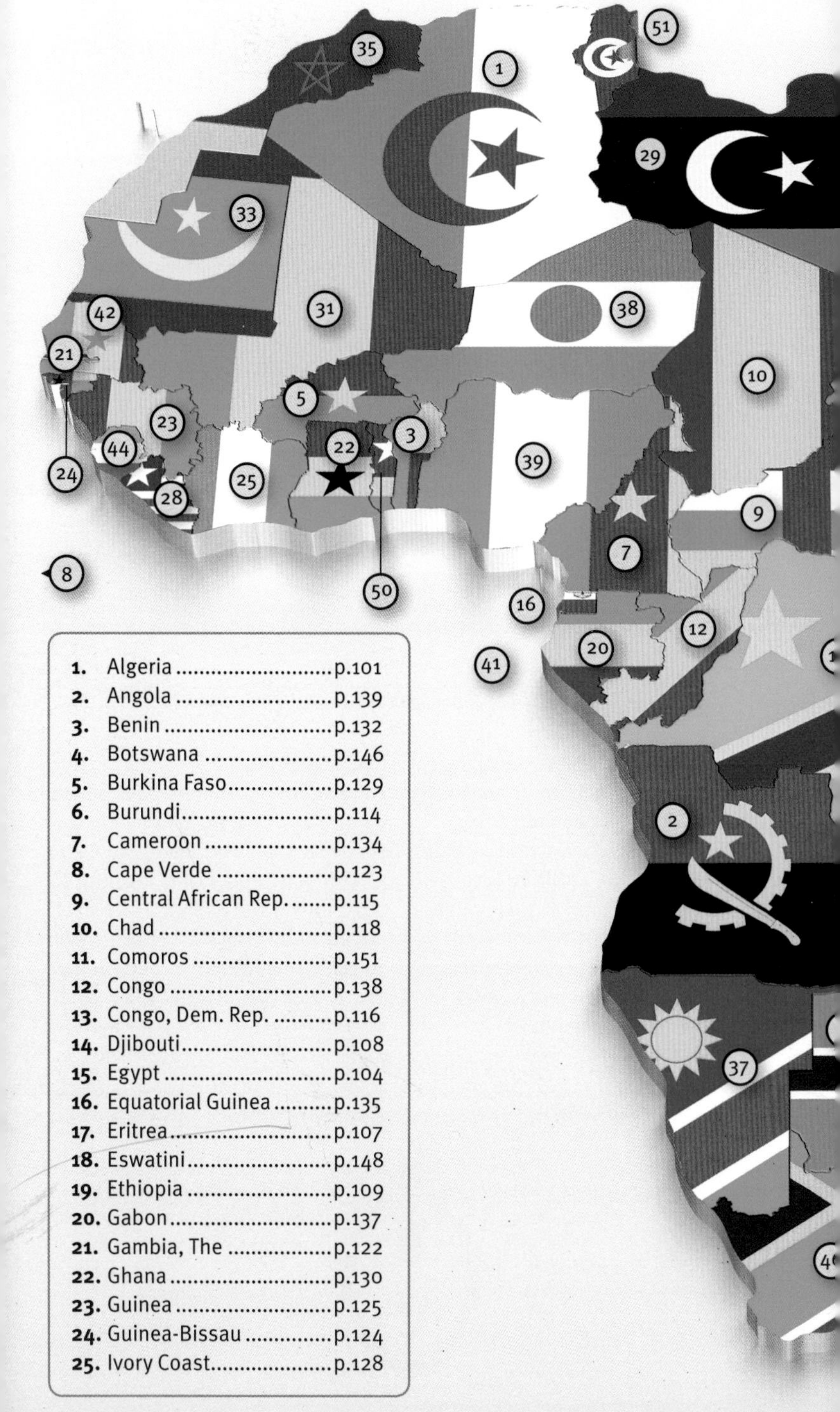
51
35
1
29
33
31
38
42
21
10
5
3
23
22
44
39
24
25
28
9
7
8
50
16
12
20
41
2
37

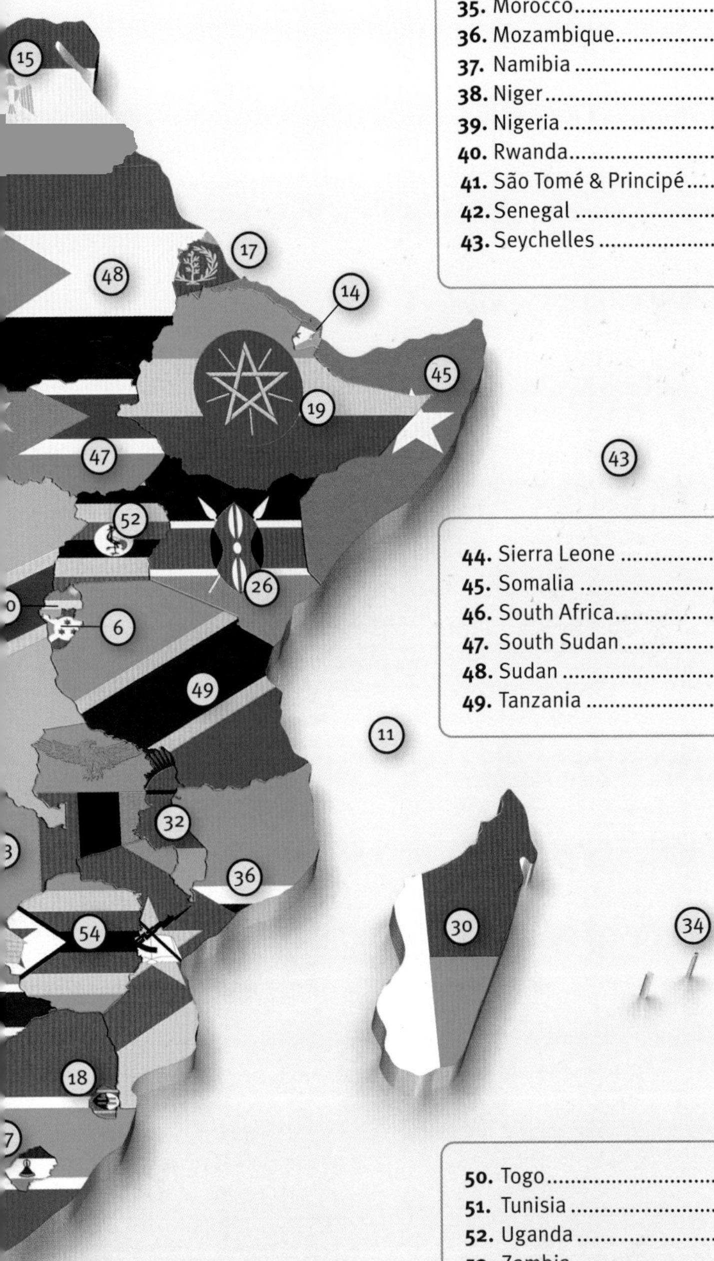
15
17
48
14
45
19
43
47
52
26
6
49
11
32
36
54
30
34
18

Morocco

Adopted November 17, 1915 | **Ratio** 2:3 | **Usage** National and Civil

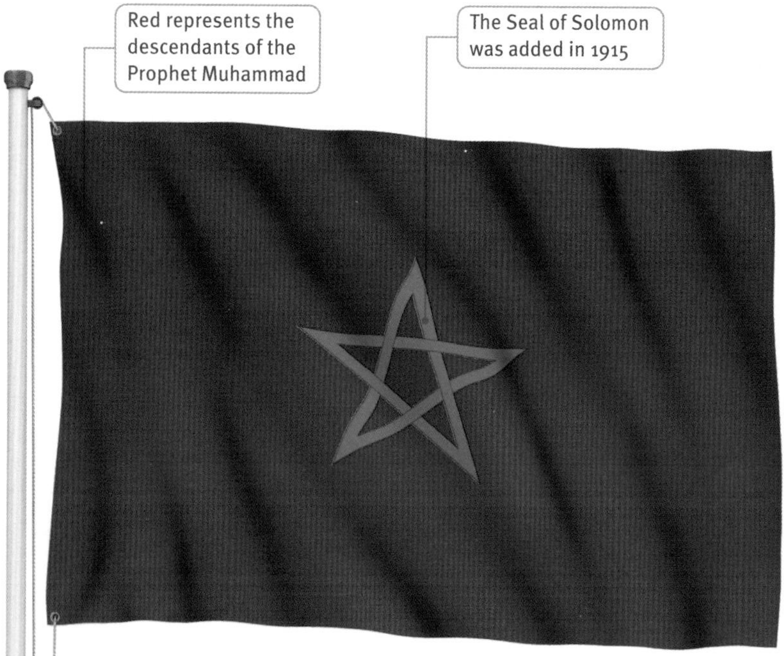
Red represents the descendants of the Prophet Muhammad
The Seal of Solomon was added in 1915

Red has considerable historic significance in Morocco, proclaiming the descent of the royal family from the Prophet Muhammad via Fatima, the wife of Ali, the fourth Caliph. Red is also the color that was used by the Sherifs of Mecca and the Imams of Yemen.

THE SEAL OF SOLOMON

Starting in the 17th century, when Morocco was ruled by the Hassani Dynasty, the flags of the country were plain red. In 1915, during the reign of Mulay Yusuf, the green "Seal of Solomon" was added to the national flag. The Seal is an interlaced pentangle, used as a talisman for centuries.

THE COLONIAL ERA

While Morocco was under French and Spanish control, the red flag with the Seal in the center remained in use but only inland; its use at sea was prohibited. When independence was restored in 1956, it once again became the national flag.

THE NATIONAL ARMS

After independence in 1958, Morocco adopted a national coat of arms. This depicts the sun rising over the Atlas Mountains. The arms also includes the Seal of Solomon from the national flag. On the scroll is an inscription from the Qur'an (Koran), which reads "If you assist God, he will assist you."

Algeria

Adopted July 3, 1962 | **Ratio** 2:3 | **Usage** National and Civil

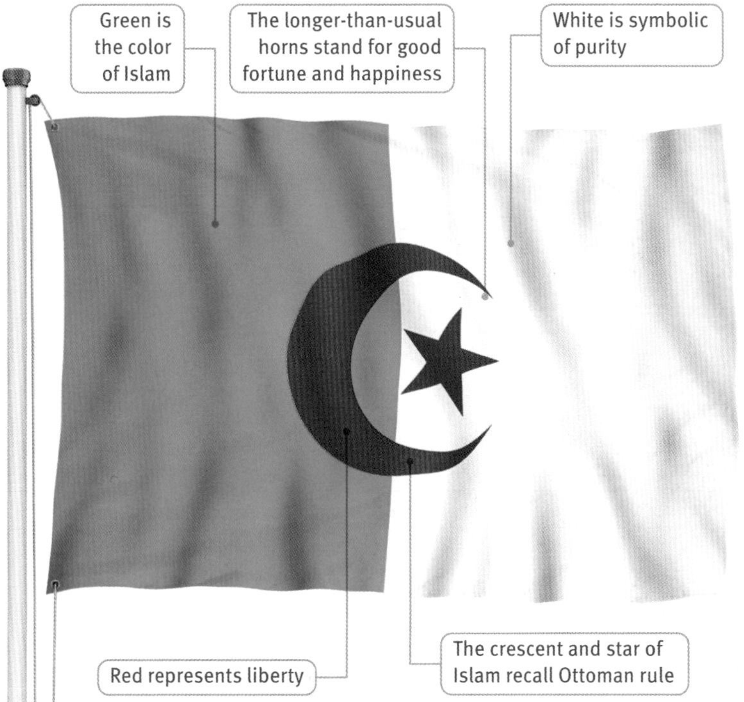
Green is the color of Islam
The longer-than-usual horns stand for good fortune and happiness
White is symbolic of purity
Red represents liberty
The crescent and star of Islam recall Ottoman rule

The flag of Algeria was adopted by the National Liberation Front (*Front de Libération National*) in 1954, based on an older design, created in 1928, by the nationalist leader Messali Hadj. From 1958–1962 it was the flag of the Provisional Government in exile, but it was retained when independence was achieved in 1962 and has remained unchanged ever since.

SYMBOLISM IN THE FLAG

The green in the hoist is the traditional color of Islam and the white represents purity. The horns of the crescent are longer than usual and represent increase or good fortune and happiness, while the whole emblem recalls the period of Ottoman rule during the 16th century and its color, red, is symbolic of liberty.

THE NAVAL ENSIGN

The naval ensign has two crossed anchors in the canton. This device is used on the naval ensigns of several Arab countries, following the example of Egypt.

THE EMBLEM OF ALGERIA

The state coat of arms is based on the well-known local emblem of the "Hand of Fatima." It also contains the crescent and star of Islam, alongside symbols reflecting both agriculture and industry.

Tunisia

Adopted 1835 | **Ratio** 2:3 | **Usage** National and Civil

Red taken from the flag of Turkey
The crescent and star of Islam

The flag is based on that of the Turkish Empire and was adopted by the "Bey," the hereditary ruler of Tunisia, in 1835, primarily as a military flag. During the French administration (1881–1957) it became a sea flag, with the French *Tricolore* in the canton; this was removed when independence was achieved in 1956.

ARMS OF TUNISIA

The coat of arms of Tunisia has been altered since the abolition of the monarchy, most recently in 1963, and unusually has the motto on a scroll actually on the shield. The motto reads—in Arabic—"Order, Liberty, Justice." The ship, lion, and balance were retained from the previous arms.

ARMS OF TUNISIA

The ship, lion, and balance symbolize the national motto
The ship also recalls early settlers
The national motto—"Order, Liberty, Justice"

Libya

Adopted August 3, 2011 | **Ratio** 1:2 | **Usage** National and Civil

Red recalls the blood shed for freedom
Green is the national color of Libya and also reflects the people's devotion to Islam
The crescent and star of Islam

The flag was designed by Omar Faiek Shennib after the formation of Libya in 1951. Following the revolution of 1969, the flag became three stripes of red, white, and black. In 1971, Libya joined the Federation of Arab Republics with Egypt and Syria and adopted a flag with a hawk emblem in the center and the country's name beneath it. When Libya quit the Federation, Colonel Gaddafi chose a plain green flag—the only national flag without a design, insignia, or any other detail. The country reverted to its original flag during the Arab Spring uprising in 2011, when Gaddafi was ousted after 42 years. The new national seal bears a crescent moon and star and the name of the new government.

NATIONAL FLAG OF LIBYA 1977–2011

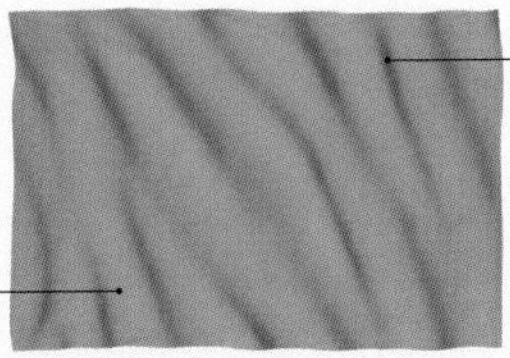
Green symbolizes Gadaffi's political philosophy (after his *The Green Book*)
The absence of design made this the only national flag to be a single plain color

Egypt

Adopted October 4, 1984 | **Ratio** 2:3 | **Usage** National and Civil

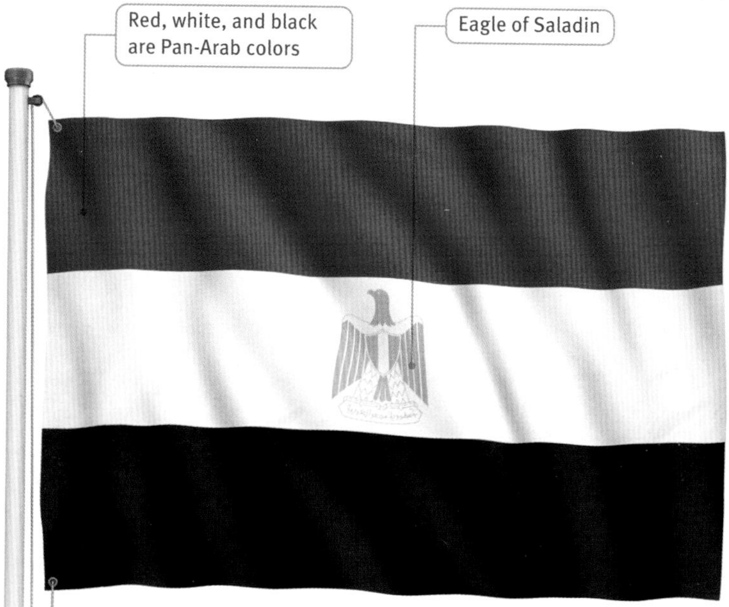
Red, white, and black are Pan-Arab colors
Eagle of Saladin

Egypt has a long and complicated history reflected in the various flag designs that have been used since the 1952 revolution.

THE UNITED ARAB REPUBLIC

When the United Arab Republic (UAR) was formed in 1958, they adapted the flag of the Liberation Rally (see below), which led the independence revolt of 1952–1953. In 1972, when the Federation was formed, the stars were replaced with the Hawk of the Quraish, in gold, above the state name.

In 1984, Egypt reverted to the gold eagle used by the Liberation Rally. These colors and the eagle emblem have been widely copied in other Arab countries.

FLAG OF THE LIBERATION RALLY 1952–1958

The gold eagle is said to be the Eagle of Saladin
The crescent and stars were retained from the old national flag

Sudan

Adopted May 20, 1970 | **Ratio** 1:2 | **Usage** National and Civil

Red represents socialism
White represents purity and optimism
Green is the color of Islam and prosperity
Black is for the pre-Islamic past

The flag used at independence was a horizontal tricolor of blue, yellow, and green, but following the formation of the Democratic Republic in 1968, a new flag was chosen in a competition.

A PAN-ARAB FLAG

The green triangle at the hoist represents Islam and prosperity. White represents purity and optimism, red is for socialism, and black for the country's pre-Islamic past.

In 1969, a new arms was adopted, with a secretary bird bearing a shield from the time of the Mahdi, (who briefly ruled Sudan in the 19th century). Two scrolls are placed above and below the bird.

ARMS OF SUDAN

The national motto—
"Al-nasr lina"
("Victory is ours")
The title of the state—
"Al-Jamhuriya as-Sudaniya"
("Republic of Sudan")
A secretary bird bears the shield

South Sudan

Adopted July 9, 2005 | **Ratio** 1:2 | **Usage** National and Civil

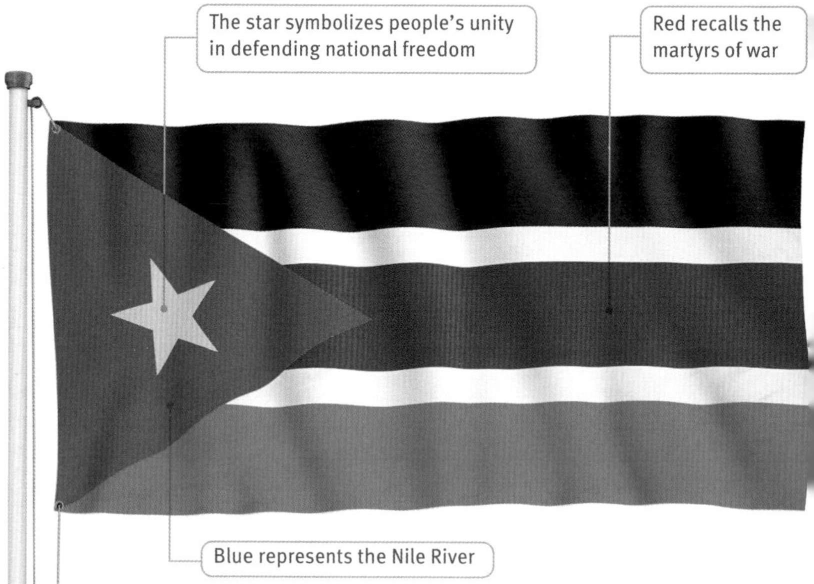
The star symbolizes people's unity in defending national freedom
Red recalls the martyrs of war
Blue represents the Nile River

During their struggle with the rest of Sudan in the 1990s, the South Sudanese created a banner of independence that was used by the Sudan People's Liberation Movement. This eventually became the new national flag following a peace agreement that ended the civil war. The flag was officially hoisted when the country declared itself a sovereign state on July 9, 2005 (although full independence was achieved in 2011).

The flag is made up of six different colors: black, red, green, white, blue, and yellow. The black represents the country's population; the red recalls the blood that was shed during the war; the green symbolizes the country's natural resources; and the white represents the peace it has achieved after the struggle. The hoist side includes a yellow star upon a blue chevron. The blue recalls the Nile River, a source of life, while the star symbolizes the determination of its people in their endeavor to build a brighter future.

Before full independence, South Sudan had adoped a national emblem, which depicted a traditional African shield bearing the country's flag, crossed by lances, and supported by a shoebill and rhinoceros. However, this was replaced by a new national coat of arms, approved by the government in 2011. The new coat of arms consists of an African Kingfisher Eagle holding a scroll that bears the name of the state in English in its talons. The bird of prey embodies strength, resilience, and vision, while the shield and crossed spears represent the people's willingness to protect their new state and defend their liberty.

Eritrea

Adopted May 24, 1993 | **Ratio** 1:2 | **Usage** National and Civil

An olive branch is encircled by a wreath representing Eritrean autonomy
Green, blue, and red are the colors of the Eritrean People's Liberation Front

The flag of the Eritrean People's Liberation Front (EPLF), which campaigned for independence, is green and blue with a red triangle bearing a gold star. The flag adopted at independence in 1993 retained the colors and pattern but replaced the star with an emblem representing Eritrean autonomy. This is an olive branch surrounded by a wreath of olive leaves. Originally this emblem was green on a blue flag, but it is now yellow.

THE PRESIDENT'S FLAG

The president's flag contains the national arms, which depicts a camel in a desert, with the name of the state underneath in English, Tigrinya, and Arabic.

THE PRESIDENT'S FLAG

The arms of Eritrea
The arms is surrounded by a wreath of leaves
The colors of the national flag are used

Djibouti

Adopted June 27, 1977 | **Ratio** 21:38 | **Usage** National and Civil

White, green, and light blue are the colors of the LPAI
Light blue represents the Issa people
The star represents the unity of the state
Green represents the Afar people, with their land and links to Islam

The national flag adopted in 1977 was an adaptation of the flag of the *Ligue Populaire Africaine pour l'Indépendance* (LPAI), which led Djibouti to independence. The LPAI flag had a red triangle with a white star. For the national flag, adopted at independence, the star was placed in an upright rather than a slanted position, and the proportions of the flag were lengthened. The colors stand for the Issas and the Afars, the two peoples of Djibouti at independence, and the red star for the unity of the diverse state.

The coat of arms is centered around a shield and spear, bordered by two hunting knives.

ARMS OF DJIBOUTI

A shield and weapons—two hunting knives and a spear
The red star is a traditional symbol of unity
Two hands represent the two peoples of Djibouti

Ethiopia

Adopted October 31, 1996 | **Ratio** 1:2 | **Usage** National and Civil

The colors date back to the 19th century
Green recalls the land and hope for the future
Yellow is the color of peace and love
The emblem represents diversity and unity
Red is symbolic of strength

The three traditional colors—green, yellow, and red—date back to the Emperor Menelik (1889–1913) and were first used in a flag in 1895.

The current flag and emblem were adopted after the defeat of the Marxist Mengistu regime, in power from 1974–1991. The emblem is intended to represent both the diversity and unity of the country.

ETHIOPIA AND THE RASTAFARI

In the 1930s the Ethiopian colors became popular with black activists in Jamaica who looked to Ethiopia for political and spiritual guidance. Since then, these colors (along with black from the flag of Marcus Garvey) have become linked with the Rastafarian movement and have spread to other African countries.

EMBLEM OF ETHIOPIA

Blue represents peace
The star represents diversity and unity
The sun's rays symbolize prosperity

Somalia

Adopted October 12, 1954 | **Ratio** 2:3 | **Usage** National and Civil

The five-pointed star represents the branches of the Somali race—in Ethiopia, Kenya, Djibouti, and the former British and Italian colonies
The blue is the same as that used by the United Nations

The flag was adopted by the Italian Trusteeship Territory in 1954 and was based on the blue and white flag of the United Nations, which was supervising the territory at the time. It was retained when Somalia became independent in 1960. The five-pointed star is said to stand for the five branches of the Somali ethnic group including those living in Ethiopia, Djibouti, and Kenya.

ARMS OF SOMALIA

The coat of arms was adopted in 1956. The leopards supporting the shield and the white star were also found on the arms used during the Italian administration.

ARMS OF SOMALIA

The shield is based on the national flag
Below the shield are two palm branches and two spears
The supporters are leopards; a leopard also featured on the shield of the colonial arms

Uganda

Adopted October 9, 1962 | **Ratio** 2:3 | **Usage** National and Civil

The colors of the flag represent the Ugandan people, sunlight, and brotherhood

The great crested crane is the national badge of Uganda

Black, yellow, and red are the party colors of the UPC

The dominant party at the time of independence in 1962 was the Uganda People's Congress (UPC), and the new national flag was an adaptation of its tricolor with the addition of the crane badge in the center. This dates back to before independence when the colonial badge of Uganda was the great crested crane. It also appears as one of the supporters on Uganda's coat of arms. The arms depicts a shield, in an allegorical landscape with tea and cotton plants.

THE PRESIDENT'S STANDARD

The flag for the president was adopted in 1963 and consists of the arms on a red field with the national colors along the lower edge.

THE PRESIDENT'S STANDARD

A kob (a type of antelope) is one of the supporters

Coffee and cotton are Uganda's most important crops

A great crested crane also supports the shield

Blue and white represent the waters of the Nile and of Lake Victoria

Kenya

Adopted December 12, 1963 | **Ratio** 2:3 | **Usage** National and Civil

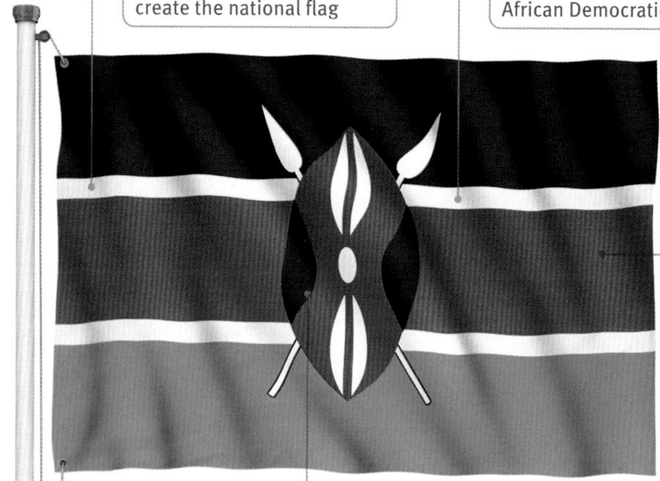

The white fimbriations were added to the KANU flag to create the national flag

White was added to represent the Kenya African Democratic Union

Red, black, and green are KANU party colors

The African shield is also used in the national arms

The flag adopted at independence in 1963 was based on that of the Kenya Africa National Union (KANU), the dominant political party. For the national flag, white fimbriations were added, and the shield and spears replaced the party symbol. A coat of arms, adopted in 1963, makes use of the same shield and spears, but with a white rooster in the center, grasping an ax.

Kenya was the first African country to use a shield in its coat of arms, a practice that has since been followed in many other new states. It was also the first to give the motto in a local language, in this case Swahili.

ARMS OF KENYA

The shield stands on a representation of Kirinyaga (Mount Kenya)

The rooster with an ax is the KANU party symbol

Harambee meaning "Pull Together" in Swahili

Rwanda

Adopted December 31, 2001 | **Ratio** 2:3 | **Usage** National and Civil

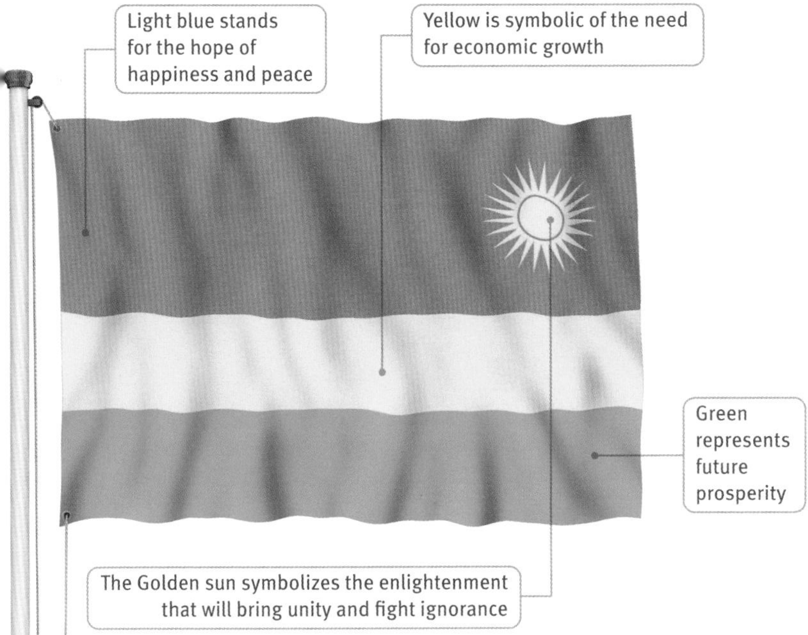
Light blue stands for the hope of happiness and peace
Yellow is symbolic of the need for economic growth
Green represents future prosperity
The Golden sun symbolizes the enlightenment that will bring unity and fight ignorance

In 2001 Rwanda adopted a new national flag, national arms, and a national anthem, in response to the government's desire to concentrate on future possibilities rather than the troubled past. It was decided that the old national symbols reinforced the ideas of ethnic separatism and violence that eventually led to the genocide of 1994. For the new flag, red and black, which have often been associated with blood and mourning, respectively, were removed, in favor of the more optimistic blue, yellow, and green. The new national symbols of Rwanda signify national unity, respect for work, patriotism, and confidence in the future.

ARMS OF RWANDA

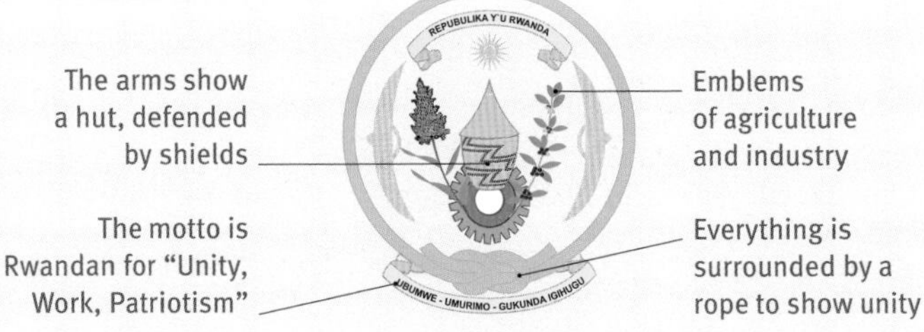
REPUBULIKA Y'U RWANDA
UBUMWE - UMURIMO - GUKUNDA IGIHUGU
The arms show a hut, defended by shields
The motto is Rwandan for "Unity, Work, Patriotism"
Emblems of agriculture and industry
Everything is surrounded by a rope to show unity

Burundi

Adopted March 28, 1967 | **Ratio** 3:5 | **Usage** National and Civil

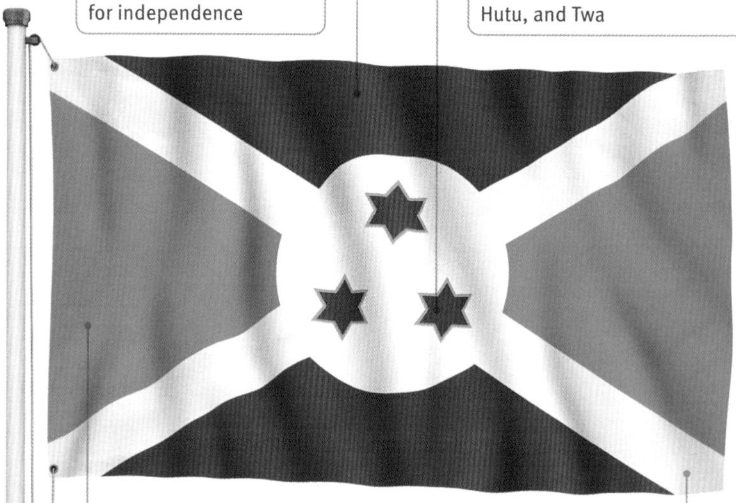
Red is symbolic of blood shed in the struggle for independence
The three stars represent the three ethnic groups, the Tutsi, Hutu, and Twa
Green represents hope
White signifies peace

The flag adopted at independence in 1962 had a drum—symbolic of the monarchy—and a sorghum plant in the central disk. When the kingdom was abolished, the drum was removed, and a year later in 1967 the sorghum plant was replaced by the three stars, said to symbolize the main ethnic groups.

THE NATIONAL ARMS

The coat of arms has also been altered. The royal drum that was above the shield was removed; a more republican motto was adopted and the four spears were reduced to three, again to represent the ethnic groups. The golden lion's face also featured on the royal badge.

ARMS OF BURUNDI

The lion's face has remained unchanged since the original 1962 arms
UNITE - TRAVAIL - PROGRES
Three spears represent Burundi's ethnic groups
The motto is "*Unité-Travail-Progrès*," meaning "Unity, Work, Progress"

Central African Republic

Adopted December 1, 1958 | **Ratio** 3:5 | **Usage** National and Civil

The star represents hope of a union under France
Red, white, and blue are taken from the French *Tricolore*
Red, yellow, and green are Pan-African colors
The vertical stripe represents unity and the blood of humanity

The flag is unique in that it combines the Pan-African colors with those of France, the former colonial power. This was done in the hope that neighboring states would join a federation under French protection, but this never materialized; the star represents the hope of achieving this goal. The state became an empire under the Emperor Bokassa from 1976–1979, but the national symbols were not changed.

The coat of arms is intended to symbolize both the Central African Republic and its important position in the center of Africa. The upper scroll bears the motto of the former ruling party; it means "A Man is a Man."

ARMS OF THE CENTRAL AFRICAN REPUBLIC

Zo Kwe Zo
UNITÉ
DIGNITÉ
TRAVAIL
An elephant and a baobab tree
The national motto – *Unité, Dignité, Travail*, meaning "Unity, Dignity, Work"
The central feature is a gold star on a map of Africa, symbolizing the position of the Central African Republic
The hand was the party emblem of the ruling party in 1963, when the arms was adopted

Dem. Rep. of the Congo

Adopted February 18, 2006 | **Ratio** 3:4 | **Usage** National and Civil

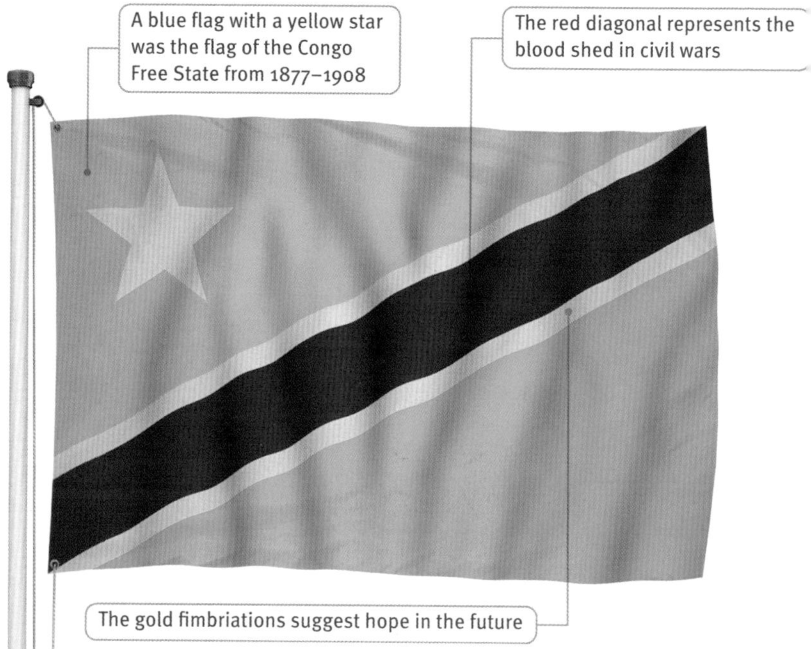
A blue flag with a yellow star was the flag of the Congo Free State from 1877–1908
The red diagonal represents the blood shed in civil wars
The gold fimbriations suggest hope in the future

The flag of the Democratic Republic of the Congo is similar to the Congo Free State flag used between 1963–1971, which was blue with a central gold star. At independence in 1960, six stars were added down the hoist for the then six provinces. In 1964, the design changed to one like the present flag with its distinctive diagonal stripe.

In 1971, the name of the country changed to Zaïre, and the flag was based on that of the ruling party. In 1997, the 1960 flag (and country name) were restored, until replaced by the present design in 2006.

FLAG OF CONGO 1960–1964 AND 1997–2006

FLAG OF ZAÏRE 1971–1997

Niger

Adopted November 23, 1959 | **Ratio** 2:3 | **Usage** National and Civil

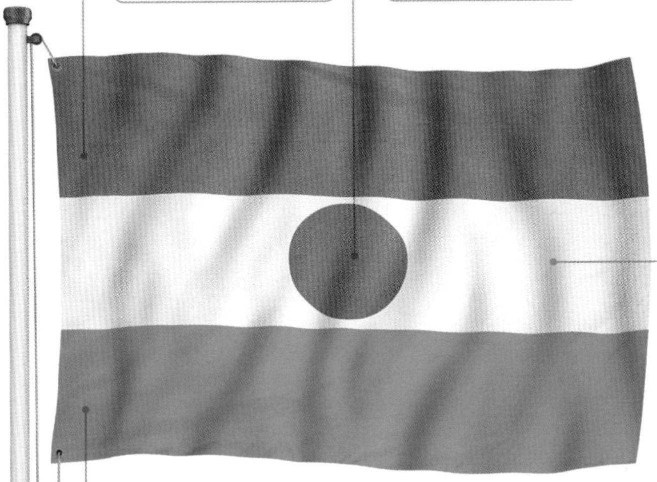
Orange represents the savanna grasslands
The orange disk is symbolic of the sun
White represents the Niger River
Green represents the country's rainforests

The flag was designed in 1958 along with the Ivory Coast, with which Niger was in an alliance of former French colonies, along with several other newly autonomous nations.

In the case of Niger, the orange is said to stand for the savanna and the green for both hope and the lush rainforest to the south, while the white strip stands for the Niger River, and the orange disk for the sun. The flag was retained when Niger gained full independence in 1960 and has remained unchanged ever since.

Four flags appear on the arms of Niger, surrounding a green or white shield. On the shield are weapons, the sun, a corncob, and a buffalo's head.

ARMS OF NIGER

Weapons represent military achievements
The title of the nation—in French—is placed on the scroll
Corn represents the country's agriculture
The buffalo's head reflects pastoral farming
REPUBLIQUE DU NIGER

Chad

Adopted June 11, 1959 | **Ratio** 2:3 | **Usage** National and Civil

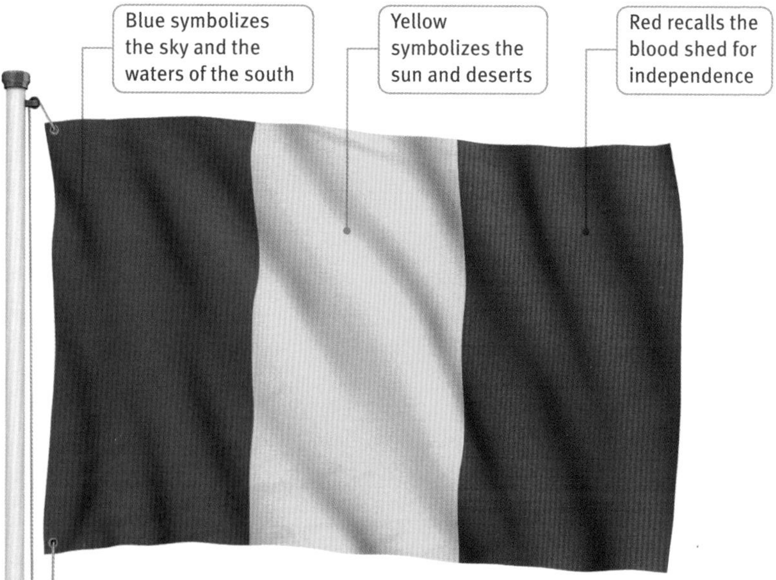
Blue symbolizes the sky and the waters of the south
Yellow symbolizes the sun and deserts
Red recalls the blood shed for independence

The flag is a combination of the Pan-African colors popularized by Ghana, and those of the French *Tricolore*, on which it is closely modeled. It was adopted for the autonomous republic and retained on gaining independence in 1960. Despite many upheavals since independence, the flag has not been changed.

THE NATIONAL ARMS

The coat of arms dates from 1970, although Chad also has a seal (like many former French colonies), adopted in 1959. The arms is in the colors of the national flag and is supported by a lion and a wild goat. The medal below the shield is the badge of the National Order of Chad.

ARMS OF CHAD

The red symbol is for salt, the country's main mineral
A mountain goat represents the north of Chad
UNITE
TRAVAIL
PROGRES
The wavy bars symbolize Lake Chad
The lion is symbolic of the south of the country
The national motto—*"Unité, Travail, Progrès"* ("Unity, Work, Progress")

Mauritania

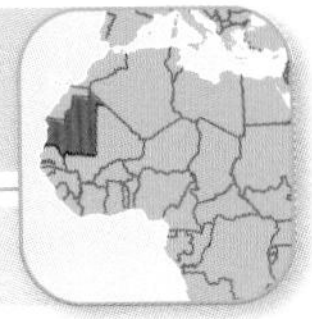

Adopted August 15, 2017 | **Ratio** 2:3 | **Usage** National and Civil

Green, representing the country's Islamic faith, and yellow are both Pan-African colors
The crescent and star of Islam
Red for sacrifice

The original flag was adopted in 1959 for the autonomous republic. It consisted simply of a yellow crescent and star, a classic symbol of Islam, on a green field, expressive of the country's full title—"Islamic Republic of Mauritania." In 2017, two red stripes were added at the top and bottom to represent the people's sacrifice.

Mauritania also has a seal, adopted in 1960. It bears the title of the state around the edge, and in the center are the Islamic crescent and star emblems, decorated with a palm branch and a millet plant, both important national plants.

SEAL OF MAURITANIA

The name of the country is given in both Arabic and French
A palm branch
The star and crescent of Islam
A millet plant
الجمهورية الإسلامية الموريتانية
RÉPUBLIQUE ISLAMIQUE DE MAURITANIE

Mali

Adopted March 1, 1961 | **Ratio** 2:3 | **Usage** National and Civil

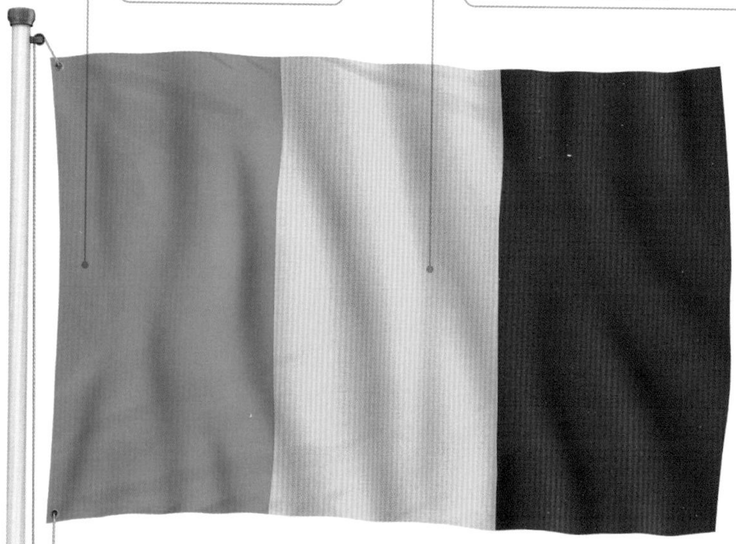
Green, yellow, and red are Pan-African colors
The style of the flag is modeled on the French *Tricolore*

The flag adopted in 1959 for the Confederation was an imitation of the flag of Ghana but following the style of the French *Tricolore*. It was charged with a black emblem known as a *kanaga*, a stylized human figure. The colors were intended to reflect a unity with other African nations. After the two countries split up in 1960, the flag was kept for use in Mali until March 1, 1961, when the black figure was dropped.

Mali also has a seal, like those of other former French colonies. Upon a light blue background, it displays the mosque of Djenné between two bows and arrows. Above the mosque is a dove of peace and below it is a rising sun in gold.

SEAL OF MALI

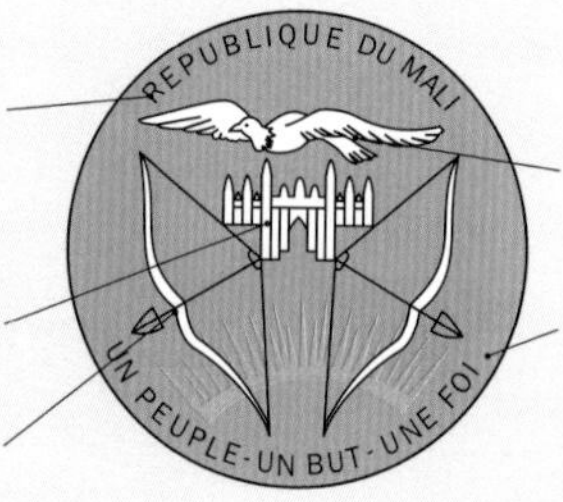
The title of the state
The Great Mosque of Djenné, central Mali
A bow and arrow
REPUBLIQUE DU MALI
UN PEUPLE-UN BUT-UNE FOI
The dove of peace
The national motto—"*Un Peuple, Un But, Une Foi*," meaning "One People, One Goal, One Faith"

Senegal

Adopted August 20, 1960 | **Ratio** 2:3 | **Usage** National and Civil

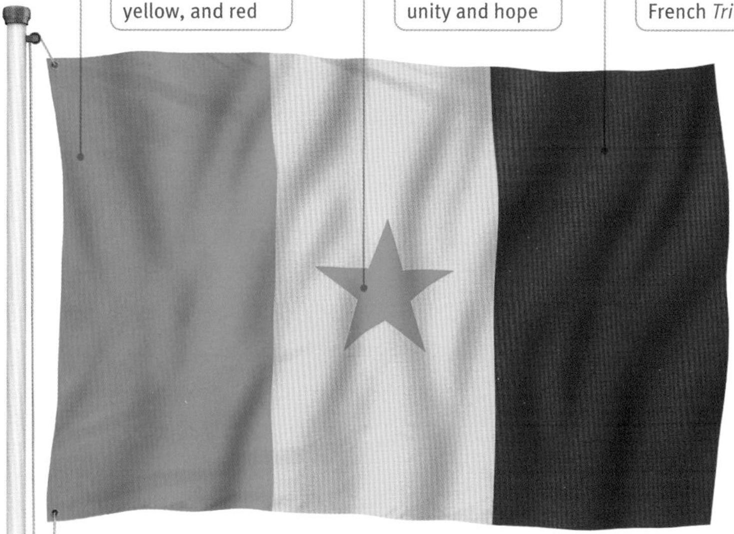
The Pan-African colors—green, yellow, and red
The star represents unity and hope
The design is modeled on a French *Tricolore*

The original flag for the Federation with Mali was adopted on April 4, 1959. It remained in use in Mali until March 1961.

A NEW NATIONAL FLAG

After the breakup of the Federation in 1960, Senegal adopted a new national flag, changing the black kanaga emblem on the original Federation flag to a green star representing unity and hope.

The coat of arms was designed by Suzanne Gauthier in 1965. It depicts a rampant lion and a baobab tree—emblems that had appeared on earlier badges of Senegal. The medal is the star of the National Order.

ARMS OF SENEGAL

The lion and baobab tree appeared on previous arms
A wreath of palm branches
The star of the National Order
The star is the same as that on the national flag
Motto is the same as Mali's—"*Un Peuple, Un But, Une Foi*" or "One People, One Goal, One Faith"

The Gambia

Adopted February 18, 1965 | **Ratio** 2:3 | **Usage** National and Civil

Red represents the savanna grasslands
The blue stripe symbolizes the Gambia River
Green symbolizes the forests

The flag of The Gambia has no political basis. The blue stripe of the flag is said to represent the Gambia River flowing between the green forest and the red savanna. The flag was adopted at independence in 1965.

The coat of arms was granted before independence, in 1964. It makes no reference to the previous colonial badge of The Gambia and follows traditional heraldry. The two tools represent the main ethnic groups—the Mandinka and the Fulani—and the crest above the helmet is a local oil palm.

The federation formed with Senegal from 1981–1989, but had no effect on the national symbols.

ARMS OF THE GAMBIA

The supporters are two lions, shown holding tools
The national motto— "Progress, Peace, Prosperity"
A crest of oil palm leaves
An ax and a hoe represent the Mandinka and the Fulani, the two main ethnic groups in The Gambia
PROGRESS
PEACE
PROSPERITY

Cape Verde

Adopted September 22, 1992 | **Ratio** 10:17 | **Usage** National and Civil

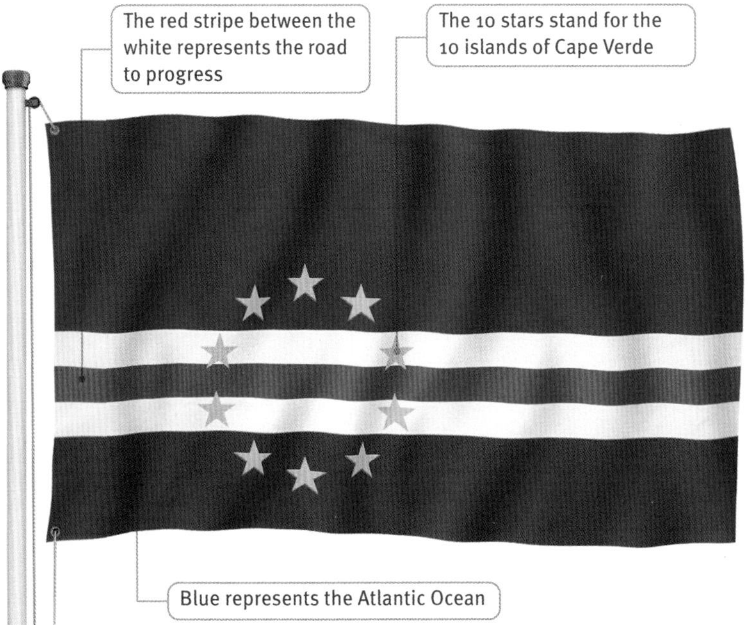
The red stripe between the white represents the road to progress
The 10 stars stand for the 10 islands of Cape Verde
Blue represents the Atlantic Ocean

The original flag, adopted in 1975, was very similar to that of Guinea-Bissau, born out of their mutual struggle for independence.

The current flag, adopted by the new government in 1992, depicts the ocean in blue, with the islands as a ring of stars on a line of red fimbriated in white, representing the road to progress. The stars may be derived from the arms of Praia, the capital.

The national arms depicts a torch on a triangle, symbolizing unity and freedom. It also includes the ring of stars and a plumb-bob signifying rectitude and virtue, which are the "keystones" of the Constitution.

ARMS OF CAPE VERDE

The title of the state
The stars represent the main islands of Cape Verde
REPÚBLICA DE CABO VERDE
The plumb-bob is symbolic of rectitude and virtue
The torch and triangle represent unity and freedom

Guinea-Bissau

Adopted September 24, 1973 | **Ratio** 1:2 | **Usage** National and Civil

The black star represents the unity of Africa
Yellow stands for the sun
Red stands for the blood shed during the struggle for independence
Green represents hope

The flag is based on that of the *Partido Africano para a Independencia da Guiné e Cabo Verde* (PAIGC), which achieved independence in 1973 after a bitter struggle and is still the dominant party in Guinea-Bissau.

THE GHANAIAN INFLUENCE

The party flag was derived from that of Ghana, which first used the Pan-African combination of red, yellow, green, and black in 1957. The black star stands for the unity of Africa. The colors are now said to stand for the blood that was shed for independence, hope, and the sun as the source of life.

The coat of arms is the PAIGC badge, a black star, and a scallop shell.

ARMS OF GUINEA-BISSAU

A star symbolizing African unity
As the PAIGC badge, the palm leaves represent Guinea-Bissau
The PAIGC motto—"*Unidade, Luta, Progresso,*" meaning "Unity, Struggle, Progress"
The scallop shell originally recalled the Cape Verde islands
UNIDADE
LUTA
PROGRESSO

Guinea

Adopted November 10, 1958 | **Ratio** 2:3 | **Usage** National and Civil

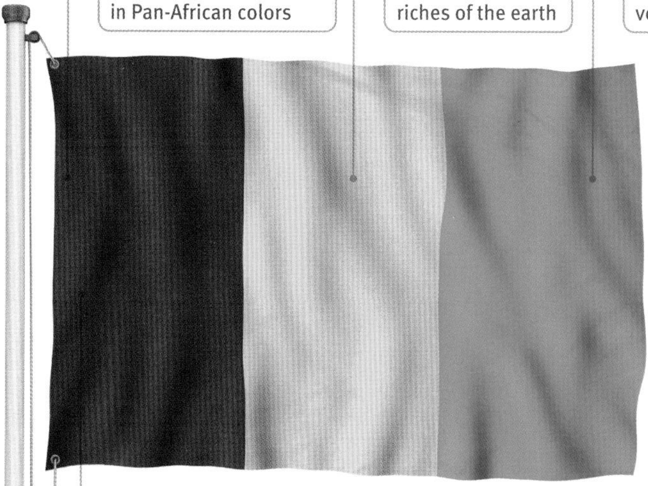
The flag is modeled on the French Tricolore, but in Pan-African colors
Yellow represents the sun and the riches of the earth
Green represents the country's vegetation
Red symbolizes the people's sacrifice

The colors of the flag were adapted from those of the *Rassemblement Démocratique Africaine*, the dominant movement at the time of independence. Their colors, first adopted in 1957, were, in turn, derived from those of Ghana. Sekou Touré, the first President of Guinea, was a close associate of Kwame Nkrumah, the former dictator of Ghana.

ARMS OF GUINEA
The coat of arms has been modified twice since the death of Sekou Touré in 1984. The elephant's head was dropped, as were the crossed weapons in 2011, and now it simply portrays a dove carrying an olive branch in its beak.

ARMS OF GUINEA

TRAVAIL
JUSTICE
SOLIDARITE
The dove is a symbol of peace
The olive branch symbolizes peace
The national motto—"*Travail, Justice, Solidarité*," meaning "Work, Justice, Solidarity"

Sierra Leone

Adopted April 27, 1961 | **Ratio** 2:3 | **Usage** National and Civil

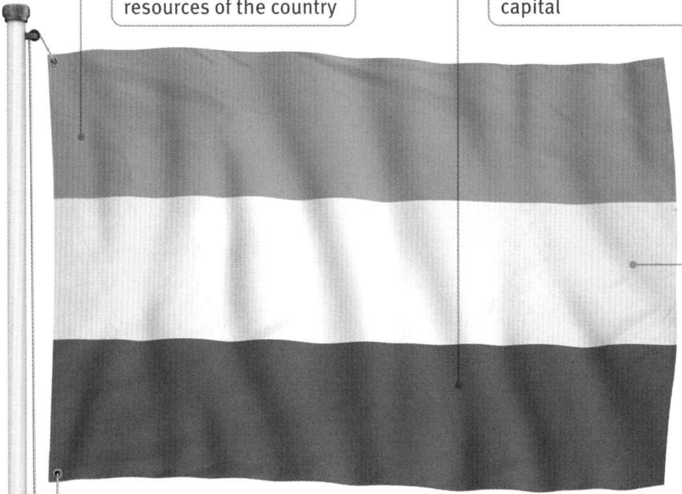
Green represents the agricultural and natural resources of the country
Blue recalls the natural harbor at Freetown, the capital
White stands for justice

The arms and flag of Sierra Leone, granted in 1960, were devised by the College of Arms in Britain.

ARMS OF SIERRA LEONE

The shield depicts a lion beneath a zigzag border, representing the Lion Mountains after which the territory was named, and three torches. At the base are wavy bars depicting the sea. The supporters are lions, which are similar to those on the colonial badge.

The three main colors from the shield—green, white, and blue—were used to form the flag. They represent agricultural and natural resources in green, unity and justice in white, and blue for the harbor at Freetown.

ARMS OF SIERRA LEONE

The lions holding oil palms are taken from the old colonial badge
National motto—"Unity, Freedom, Justice"
UNITY
FREEDOM
JUSTICE
The torches symbolize education and progress
The border represents the Lion Mountains
The wavy bars depict the sea

Liberia

Adopted August 24, 1847 | **Ratio** 10:19 | **Usage** National and Civil

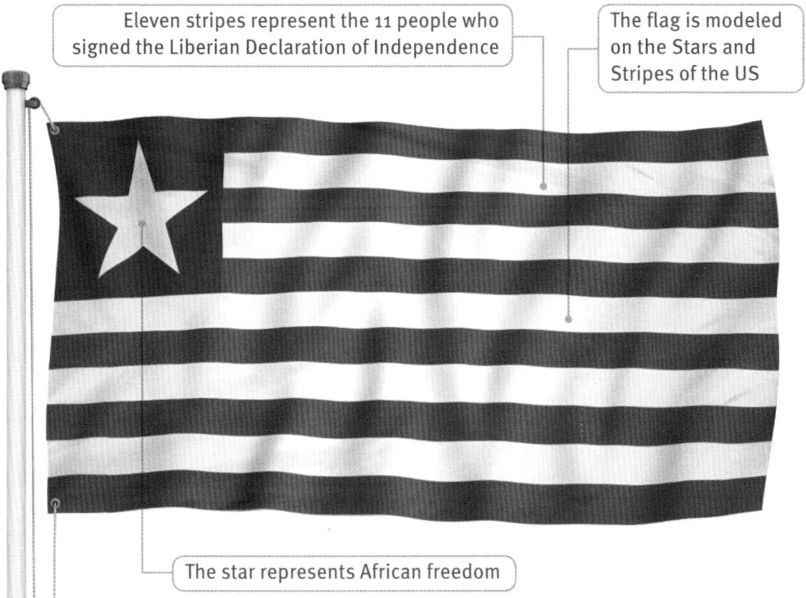
Eleven stripes represent the 11 people who signed the Liberian Declaration of Independence
The flag is modeled on the Stars and Stripes of the US
The star represents African freedom

The flag of Liberia is clearly based on that of the US, which was instrumental in the founding of this nation. The single white star in a blue canton stands for the freedom of the first independent republic in Africa, with the canton itself representing Africa. The 11 stripes symbolize the signatories of Liberia's Declaration of Independence.

Since 1915, August 24th has been known as National Flag Day and is celebrated with a public holiday.

ARMS OF LIBERIA

The shield depicts a ship bringing freed slaves from the US. The rising sun represents the birth of a nation, and a palm tree indicates prosperity. A white dove symbolizes peace.

ARMS OF LIBERIA

THE LOVE OF LIBERTY BROUGHT US HERE
REPUBLIC OF LIBERIA
White dove symbolizes peace
A plow indicates the value of hard work
The palm tree represents prosperity
The rising sun represents the birth of a nation

Ivory Coast

Adopted December 3, 1959 | **Ratio** 2:3 | **Usage** National and Civil

After independence in 1960, Ivory Coast formed a loose alliance of West African states. The flags of these states were influenced both by the Pan-African colors first used by Ghana and also by the model of the French *Tricolore*, the flag of the former colonial power.

ALLIANCE OF WEST AFRICAN STATES

The colors chosen for Ivory Coast's flag were also used by Niger, with which Ivory Coast had an alliance. They were intended to symbolize the following: orange represents the savanna grasslands, white the rivers, and green the coastal forests. Another interpretation is that they symbolize progress, peace, hope, and national unity. The flag was adopted in 1959, just prior to independence.

THE NATIONAL ARMS

The coat of arms, which has a green shield charged with an elephant's head, is based on the emblem of the *Rassemblement Démocratique Africaine*, the dominant political party at the time of independence. Originally the elephant's head was on a blue shield, but this was altered in 1964 to green to match the national flag. The shield is supported by two palm trees, behind which is a rising sun. On a scroll at the base of the arms is the title of the state, "*Republique de Côte d'Ivoire*."

Burkina Faso

Adopted August 4, 1984 | **Ratio** 2:3 | **Usage** National and Civil

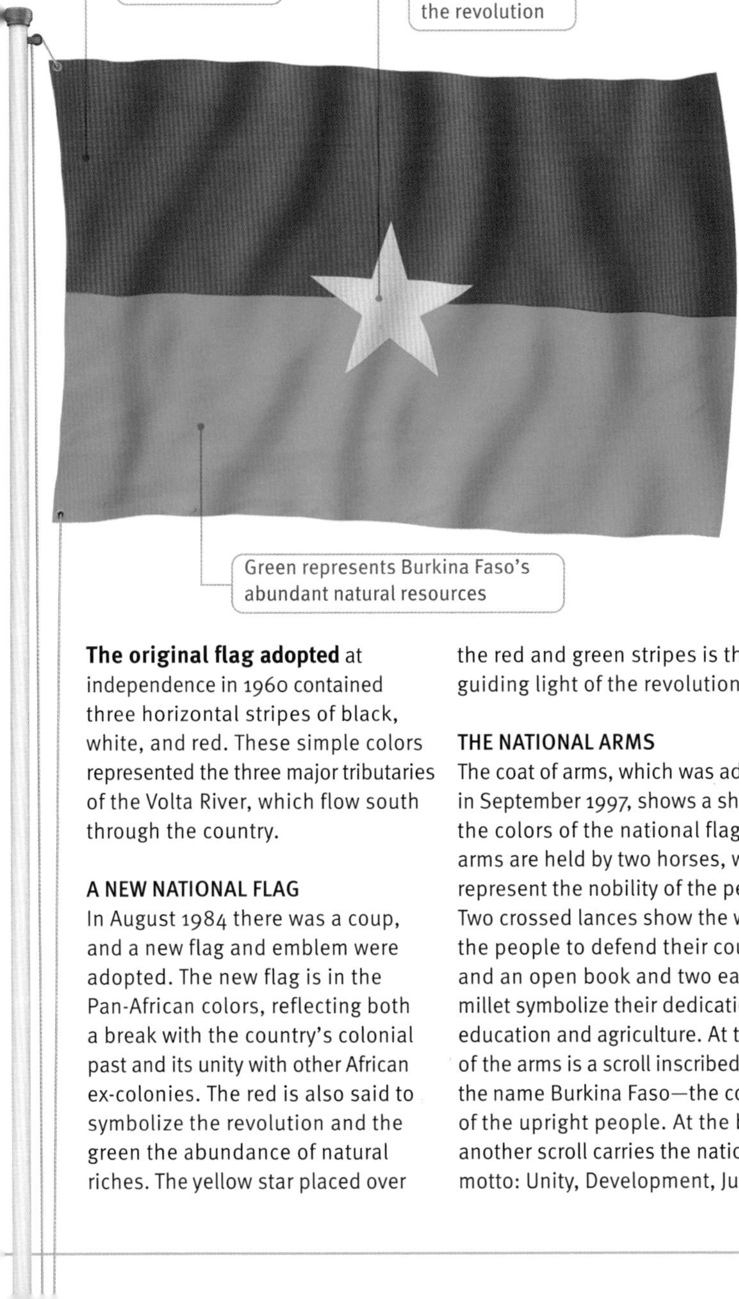
Red recalls the 1984 revolution
The star is the guiding light of the revolution
Green represents Burkina Faso's abundant natural resources

The original flag adopted at independence in 1960 contained three horizontal stripes of black, white, and red. These simple colors represented the three major tributaries of the Volta River, which flow south through the country.

A NEW NATIONAL FLAG

In August 1984 there was a coup, and a new flag and emblem were adopted. The new flag is in the Pan-African colors, reflecting both a break with the country's colonial past and its unity with other African ex-colonies. The red is also said to symbolize the revolution and the green the abundance of natural riches. The yellow star placed over the red and green stripes is the guiding light of the revolution.

THE NATIONAL ARMS

The coat of arms, which was adopted in September 1997, shows a shield in the colors of the national flag. The arms are held by two horses, which represent the nobility of the people. Two crossed lances show the will of the people to defend their country, and an open book and two ears of millet symbolize their dedication to education and agriculture. At the top of the arms is a scroll inscribed with the name Burkina Faso—the country of the upright people. At the base, another scroll carries the national motto: Unity, Development, Justice.

Ghana

Adopted March 6, 1957 | **Ratio** 2:3 | **Usage** National

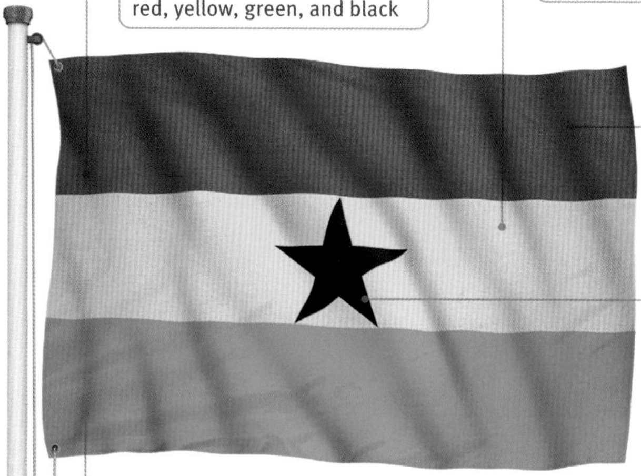
Ghana was the first country to use the Pan-African colors of red, yellow, green, and black
Yellow represents mineral wealth
Red recalls the blood shed by freedom fighters
The star of African freedom
Green is symbolic of the country's rich forests

Kwame Nkrumah, Ghana's first leader after independence in 1960, was the first to introduce the politically symbolic Pan-African colors—red, yellow, green, and black—into African flags. They were ultimately derived from the colors of Ethiopia, dating back to the 19th century, and have since become associated with the Rastafarian movement in the West Indies. The flag also became the inspiration for numerous other African flags during the period of decolonization.

Ghana followed the flag patterns established in the United Kingdom, and so has both a red ensign for use on civil vessels and a white ensign for naval vessels. This use of several flags sets it apart from other West African states, which normally have only one all-purpose flag.

GHANAIAN RED ENSIGN

The national flag is placed in the canton
The field is in the style of the British Red Ensign

Togo

Adopted April 27, 1960 | **Ratio** 2:3 | **Usage** National and Civil

Red symbolizes the blood shed during the struggle for independence
Yellow reflects Togo's mineral wealth
The star of hope
Green represents agricultural wealth

During 1956–1960, the period of autonomy, the flag was green with two yellow stars arranged diagonally. Between 1957–1958, the French *Tricolore* was in the canton.

On independence in 1960, the present flag was adopted. The five stripes stand for the regions of Togo and are in green and yellow to signify its agricultural and mineral resources. The red canton is for the blood of those who struggled for independence, while the white star is for hope, as on Liberia's flag. The national emblem contains two lions holding bows and arrows and a sun with the country's initials, with the national motto above it.

EMBLEM OF TOGO

PAIX
UNION
SOLIDARITÉ
RT
"RT" stands for the title of the state, *République Togolaise*
The national motto—"*Union, Paix, Solidarité*"—meaning "Unity, Peace, Solidarity"
Two lions are shown carrying bows and arrows to protect the homeland

Benin

Adopted November 16, 1959 | **Ratio** 2:3 | **Usage** National and Civil

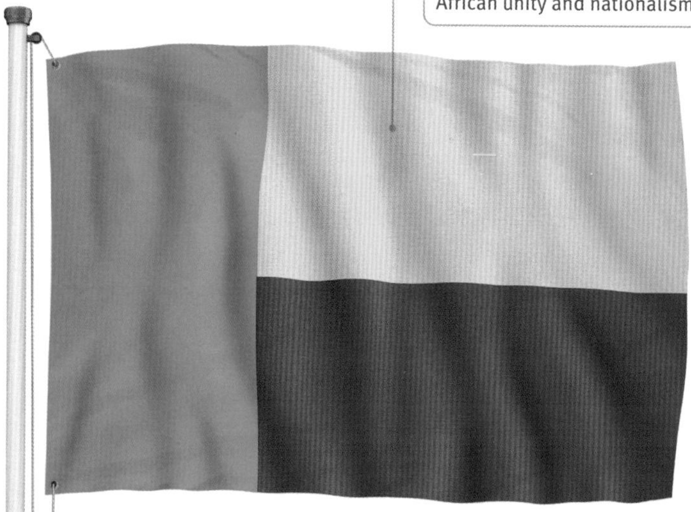
Red, yellow, and green symbolize
African unity and nationalism

The flag used today is the same as that adopted in 1959, although after the revolution of December 1975, a green flag with a red star in the canton was used. The original flag was restored in 1990, as was the original national emblem. The new name of the country was retained.

Benin has both a seal and a coat of arms. The seal depicts a *pirogue* or African canoe, with a bow and arrow, and two clubs. The arms consists of a quartered shield depicting a local Somba fortress, the medal of the Order of the Star of Benin, a palm tree, and a sailing ship. The motto is "*Fraternité, Justice, Travail*," meaning "Fraternity, Justice, Work."

ARMS OF BENIN

A Somba fortress
The national motto, meaning "Fraternity, Justice, Work"
FRATERNITE
JUSTICE
TRAVAIL
The Horns of Plenty spilling out ears of corn are symbolic of riches from the land
The Order of Star of Benin

Nigeria

Adopted October 1, 1960 | **Ratio** 1:2 | **Usage** National

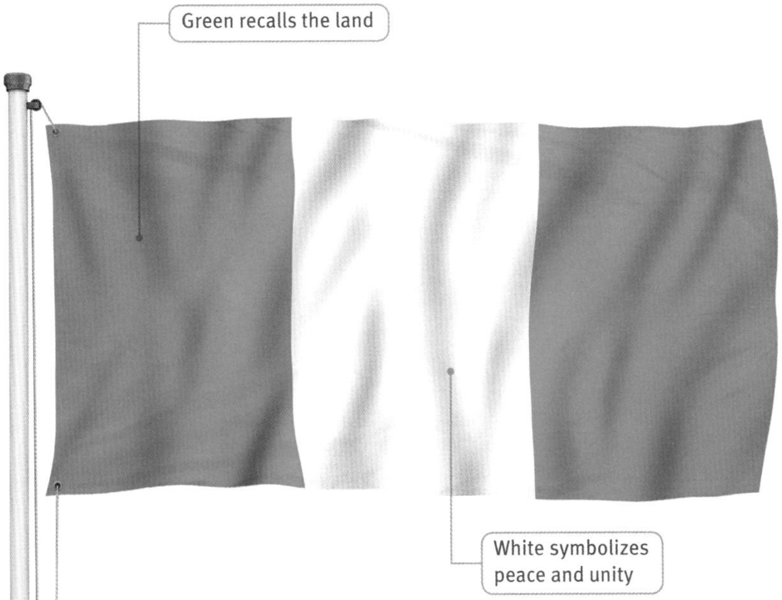
Green recalls the land
White symbolizes peace and unity

The national flag is an adaptation of the winning entry in a competition held in 1959. The original had a red sun with streaming rays placed at the top of the white stripe. This was removed by the judges and the flag has not been altered since.

Unusually for African nations, Nigeria has special flags for both civil and naval vessels.

The coat of arms was granted in 1960, but the motto has been altered since then to include the words "Peace and Progress." The shield represents the confluence of two rivers and the crest is a red eagle. It all stands on a green base strewn with the *Costus Spectabilis* flower.

ARMS OF NIGERIA

The confluence of the Niger and Benuë rivers
The *Costus Spectabilis* is the national flower
The national motto—"Unity and Faith, Peace, and Progress"
The red eagle, symbolizing strength, is the national badge
The two white horses symbolize dignity
UNITY AND FAITH, PEACE AND PROGRESS

Cameroon

Adopted May 20, 1975 | **Ratio** 2:3 | **Usage** National and Civil

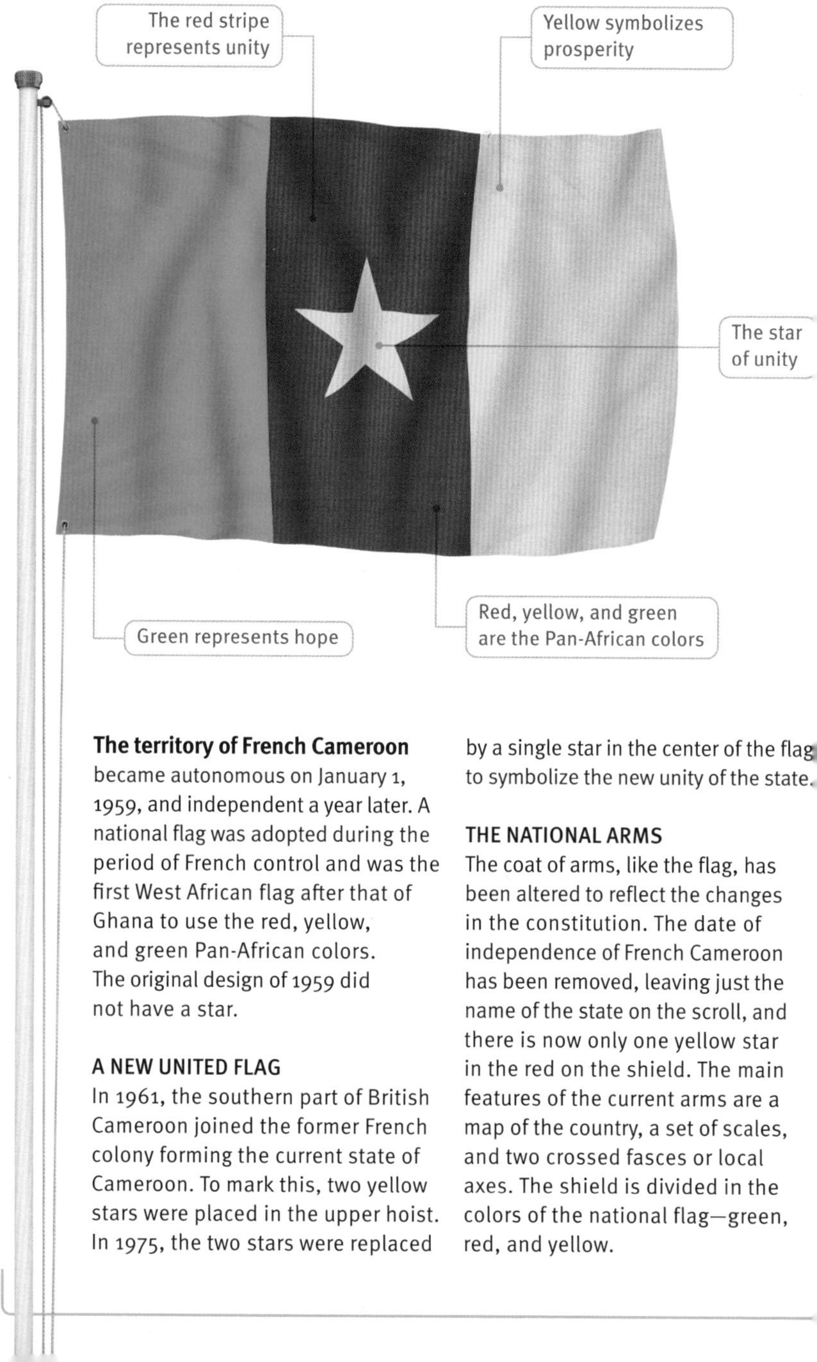
The red stripe represents unity
Yellow symbolizes prosperity
The star of unity
Green represents hope
Red, yellow, and green are the Pan-African colors

The territory of French Cameroon became autonomous on January 1, 1959, and independent a year later. A national flag was adopted during the period of French control and was the first West African flag after that of Ghana to use the red, yellow, and green Pan-African colors. The original design of 1959 did not have a star.

A NEW UNITED FLAG

In 1961, the southern part of British Cameroon joined the former French colony forming the current state of Cameroon. To mark this, two yellow stars were placed in the upper hoist. In 1975, the two stars were replaced by a single star in the center of the flag to symbolize the new unity of the state.

THE NATIONAL ARMS

The coat of arms, like the flag, has been altered to reflect the changes in the constitution. The date of independence of French Cameroon has been removed, leaving just the name of the state on the scroll, and there is now only one yellow star in the red on the shield. The main features of the current arms are a map of the country, a set of scales, and two crossed fasces or local axes. The shield is divided in the colors of the national flag—green, red, and yellow.

Equatorial Guinea

Adopted October 12, 1968 | **Ratio** 2:3 | **Usage** National and Civil

The blue triangle represents the sea
Green reflects the country's agricultural lands
The national arms have always appeared on the flag
UNIDAD PAZ JUSTICIA
Red symbolizes the country's independence
White stands for peace

The flag was first shown on the day of independence, October 12, 1968, and has always contained the national emblem in the center, although starting in 1972, a different national emblem appeared on the flag during the regime of Francisco Nguema. The original coat of arms was restored after he was deposed in August 1979.

ARMS OF EQUATORIAL GUINEA
The arms consists of a silver shield charged with a silk cotton tree, which was derived from the arms of Río Muni. Above the shield is an arc of six, six-pointed stars, which represent Río Muni and the offshore islands. Beneath the shield is a scroll bearing the national motto.

ARMS OF EQUATORIAL GUINEA

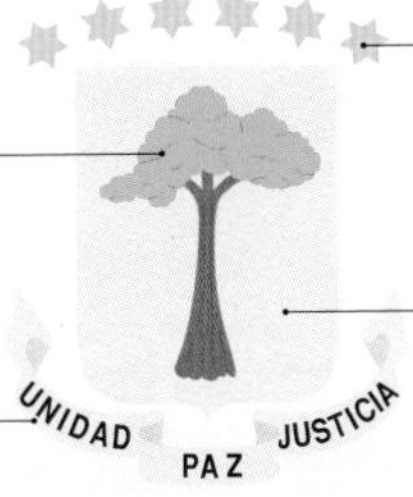
A silk cotton tree
The national motto—*"Unidad, Paz, Justicia"* ("Unity, Peace, Justice")
The six stars stand for the six parts of the state
A silver shield
UNIDAD PAZ JUSTICIA

São Tomé & Príncipe

Adopted November 5, 1975 | **Ratio** 1:2 | **Usage** National and Civil

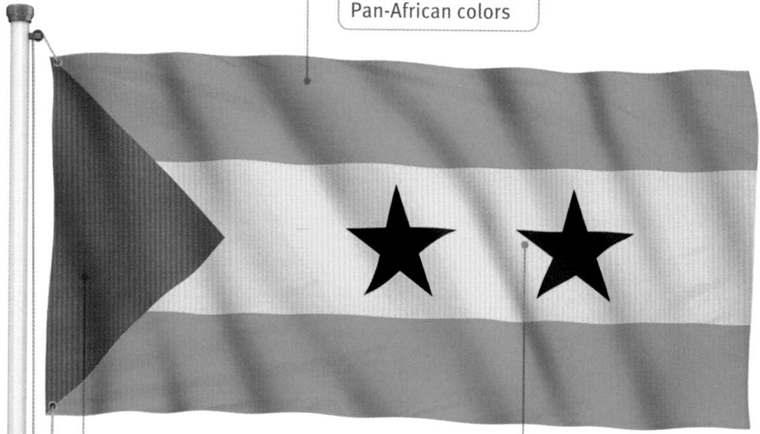
Green, red, yellow, and black are Pan-African colors
The red triangle recalls the struggle for independence, as on the flags of Ghana and Togo
The two stars stand for the two islands

The flag is based on the party flag of the Movement for the Liberation of São Tomé & Príncipe (MLSTP). It was retained even after the party lost its monopoly of power in 1990.

The combination of red, yellow, and green with black stars is clearly based on the flag of Ghana, with the stars representing the two islands.

The shield within the national arms is in the form of a cocoa pod, on which is depicted a cocoa palm, the country's main export. Above this is a star representing freedom. The supporters are two birds standing on a scroll with the national motto—"*Unidade, Disciplina, Trabalho*" ("Unity, Discipline, Work").

ARMS OF SÃO TOMÉ & PRÍNCIPE

The crest, a blue star, stands for African freedom
The shield is in the form of a cocoa pod
The upper scroll bears the title of the state
The shield is supported by a falcon on the left and a parrot on the right

Gabon

Adopted August 9, 1960 | **Ratio** 3:4 | **Usage** National and Civil

Yellow and green represent natural resources
Blue represents the sea

The original flag was adopted in 1959 and was similar to the present one, but with stripes of unequal width and the French *Tricolore* in the canton, which was dropped at independence in 1960. The flag's unusual proportions are laid down by law, and the colors symbolize the sea and the country's natural resources, especially its timber. The coat of arms is in European style and is the colors of the flag. The shield is supported by two black panthers and an okoumé tree, symbolic of the timber trade. The coat of arms has a Latin motto—"*Uniti Progrediamur*"—beneath the branches of the tree.

ARMS OF GABON

A Latin motto—"*Unite Progrediamur*"—meaning "We go forward in unity"
A second motto means "Union, Work, Justice"
The *okoumé* tree is symbolic of the timber trade
Two black panthers support the shield
The ship represents Gabon moving toward a brighter future

Congo

Adopted September 15, 1959 | **Ratio** 2:3 | **Usage** National and Civil

The Pan-African colors of green, yellow, and red
The distinctive diagonal pattern sets it apart from other Pan-African flags

The current flag was originally adopted for the autonomous republic, established on August 18, 1959. It is in the Pan-African colors used by many other West African flags. It was retained without change when full independence was achieved in 1960.

THE PEOPLE'S REPUBLIC 1970–1991

Following the Marxist revolution in 1964, no new national flag was officially adopted until the People's Republic was formed in 1970. This flag was red and contained the national emblem in the canton. The emblem depicted a wreath containing a crossed hoe and hammer and a gold star. This represented the communist regime that had taken power.

AN OLD FLAG FOR A NEW ERA

At the National Conference for the restoration of democracy in 1991, which restored a multiparty democracy, it was decided to readopt the original flag, arms and national anthem. This decision was made official on June 4, 1991.

ARMS OF CONGO

The coat of arms was originally adopted in 1963 and was designed by the European heraldist Louis Mühlemann, who also designed the arms of Gabon. It follows a traditional European heraldic style.

Angola

Adopted November 11, 1975 | **Ratio** 2:3 | **Usage** National and Civil

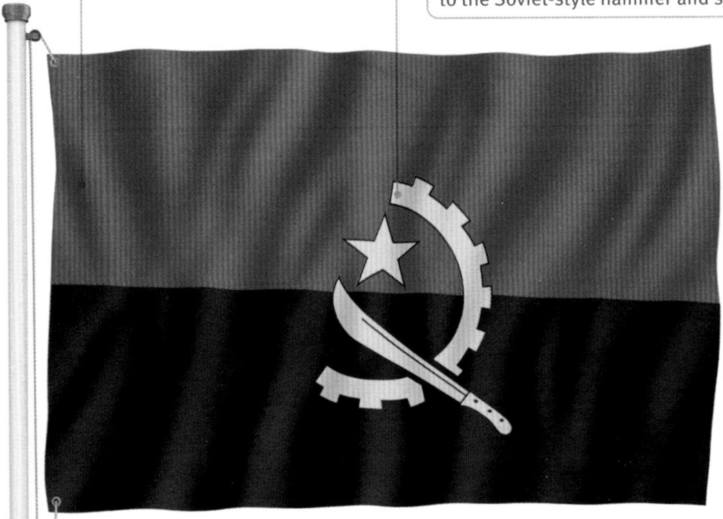
The design is based on flag of the MPLA
The cogwheel and machete represent agriculture and industry and are similar to the Soviet-style hammer and sickle

The flag of the People's Liberation Movement of Angola (MPLA) is like the present national flag but with a yellow star. The half cogwheel and machete on the national flag were added to create an emblem reminiscent of the hammer and sickle on the Soviet flag.

The national arms also features the cogwheel, star, and machete but includes a hoe. These symbols are on a background, which, like the emblem on the flag, is similar to the devices used in Soviet designs. The cogwheel is balanced by a wreath of cotton, coffee, and corn, and an open book. On the scroll is "Republic of Angola," the official country name.

ARMS OF ANGOLA

The tools are emblems of agriculture and of industry
The book is symbolic of the importance of education
The Soviet-style emblem is still in use
The state name, in Portuguese—*República de Angola*—is placed on the scroll
REPÚBLICA DE ANGOLA

Zambia

Adopted October 24, 1964 | **Ratio** 2:3 | **Usage** National and Civil

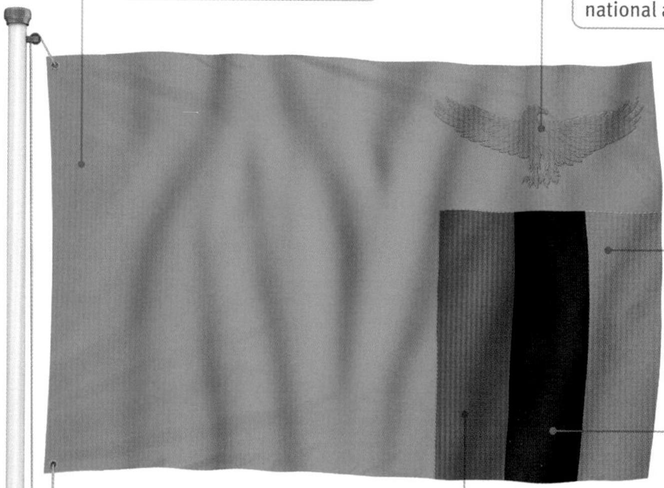
The green field represents Zambia's agriculture
The eagle is taken from the national arms
Orange represents the country's copper
Black stands for the people
Red recalls the struggle for independence

Although the United National Independence Party is no longer dominant in Zambia, the party's colors remain in the bottom corner of the flag, designed by graphic artists just prior to independence. The eagle is taken from the national arms, which are based on those of the former Northern Rhodesia.

In the arms, the eagle, which once appeared in the upper part of the shield, forms the crest, above a crossed pickax and hoe. White and black bars on the shield represent the famous Victoria Falls. The supporters are an African man and woman, and the motto on the base reads "One Zambia, One Nation."

ARMS OF ZAMBIA

The pickax and hoe are emblems of agriculture and industry
The eagle of liberty
The shield stands on an allegorical landscape
The shield represents the white waters of the Zambezi River flowing over black rock at the Victoria Falls
ONE ZAMBIA
ONE NATION

Tanzania

Adopted June 30, 1964 | **Ratio** 2:3 | **Usage** National and Civil

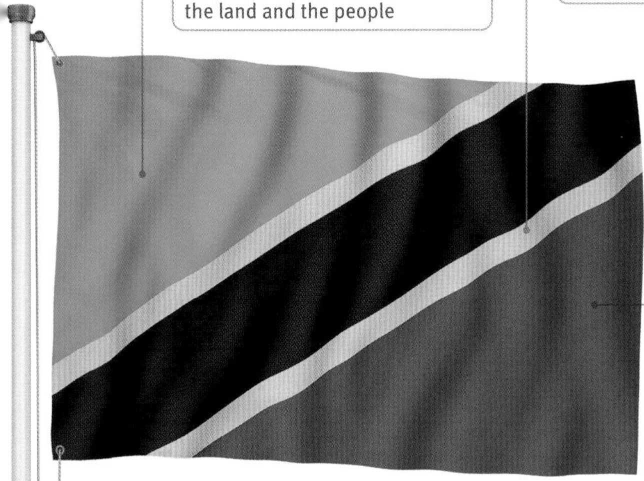
Green and black, taken from the old Tanganyikan flag, represent the land and the people
Yellow symbolizes mineral wealth
Blue, taken from the flag of Zanzibar, represents the sea

The original flag of independent Tanganyika featured horizontal stripes of green-black-green derived from the flag of Tanganyika African National Union, the dominant party at the time. For the national flag, yellow fimbriations were placed between the green and the black. Derived from the Afro-Shirazi Party, the flag of Zanzibar was green, black, and blue stripes, with a vertical white stripe along the hoist.

A NEW UNITED FLAG

When the two countries united to form Tanzania, a new national flag was created, which combined the colors of Tanganyika and Zanzibar. The country's coat of arms was also altered to include the new national flag in the shield, again to reflect the new union of the two countries.

FLAG OF ZANZIBAR

The national flag was added as a canton to the revolutionary flag of 1964
These are the colors of the Afro-Shirazi Party, which overthrew the ruling Sultan in 1964

Malawi

Adopted July 6, 1964 | **Ratio** 2:3 | **Usage** National and Civil

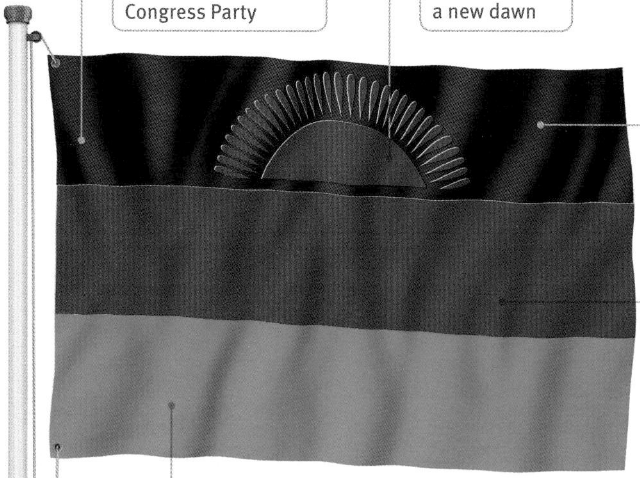
These are the colors of the Malawi Congress Party
The rising sun symbolizes a new dawn
Black is symbolic of Africa's indigenous people
Red represents the blood shed for freedom
Green represents the land

The colors of the flag are the same as those of Malawi Congress Party (MCP), which led the country to independence in 1964. The MCP flag was derived from the flag popularized by Marcus Garvey at the time of the First World War, as the flag of Africa, or "Ethiopia," symbolizing an African renaissance. For Malawi's national flag, the rising sun, or *kwacha*, was added in red.

In 2010, the design was altered to reflect the Pan-African layout, and a white sun was added to the center. A public outcry ensued, and the flag was finally changed back in 2012 by the new president.

THE PRESIDENT'S FLAG

The flag of the president has a bright red field. It uses the lion passant found in the center of the coat of arms.

THE PRESIDENT'S FLAG

MALAWI
The name of the state
The lion passant is taken from the coat of arms

Zimbabwe

Adopted April 18, 1980 | **Ratio** 1:2 | **Usage** National and Civil

The national bird of Zimbabwe
Green, yellow, red, and black are the colors of ZANU and Pan-Africanism
Black represents the new leaders, and white, their desire for peace

The Zimbabwe African National Union (ZANU) led the struggle for self-determination in the 1970s, and its flag was used as the basis for the new national flag. The ZANU flag is composed of concentric panels of green, yellow, red, with a central black panel—the colors of Pan-Africanism. The national flag has these colors simply arranged in stripes. Toward the hoist is a white triangle with a black edge, symbolizing new leaders and their desire for peace. Within this is the Zimbabwe bird on a red star.

THE ZIMBABWE BIRD

The bird is representative of birds found in the ruins of the ancient city of Zimbabwe and has been a local symbol since 1924. The star stands for an international outlook.

EMBLEM OF ZIMBABWE

The star represents the country's international outlook
The Zimbabwe bird
A representation of the ancient city of Zimbabwe

Mozambique

Adopted May 1, 1983 | **Ratio** 2:3 | **Usage** National and Civil

Red recalls the struggle for independence
Green symbolizes the riches of the land
Black recalls the African continent
Yellow symbolizes the country's minerals
The white fimbriations represent peace

The original flag of the *Frente da Libertação da Moçambique* (FRELIMO), the leading political party in Mozambique, also had green, black, and yellow horizontal stripes separated by white fimbriations. In the hoist was a red triangle. The black, green, and yellow were derived from the flag of the African National Congress, used in South Africa.

On independence in 1975, the colors were rearranged to form the national flag, in rays emanating from the upper hoist. Over this was a white cogwheel containing the hoe, rifle, book, and star, which appear on the present flag. The flag was altered in 1983—the colors were arranged in horizontal stripes, and the star of Marxism was made larger.

EMBLEM OF MOZAMBIQUE

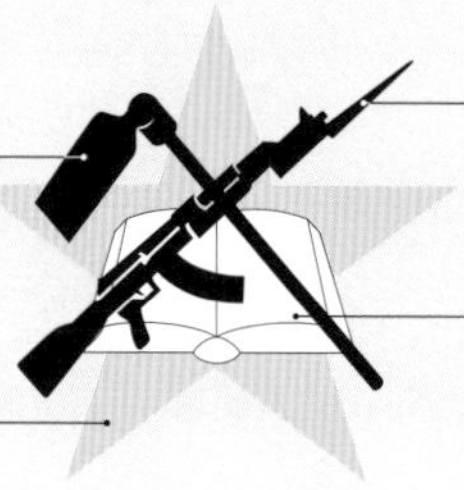
The hoe represents the country's agriculture
The star symbolizes Marxism and internationalism
The rifle stands for defense and vigilance
The open book symbolizes the importance of education

Namibia

Adopted March 21, 1990 | **Ratio** 2:3 | **Usage** National and Civil

The sun is the emblem of life and energy
Red, white, and blue were the colors of the Democratic Turnhalle Alliance
Blue, red, and green were the colors of SWAPO

The national flag combines the colors of the South West African People's Organization (SWAPO), which liberated Namibia in 1990, and those of the Democratic Turnhalle Alliance, another Namibian political party. The sun stands for life and energy and the red diagonal bar represents the strength of the people of Namibia.

ARMS OF NAMIBIA

The coat of arms, adopted with the flag, appears on the President's Flag. The shield is of the same pattern as the national flag and is supported by a pair of oryx. On a sand dune beneath is a *welwitschia* plant, found in the Namib Desert. The crest is a fish eagle on a chieftain's headring.

ARMS OF NAMIBIA

The shield is based on the national flag
The national motto—"Unity, Liberty, Justice"
The fish eagle stands on a chieftain's headring
Two oryx support the shield
The *welwitschia* plant is found in the Namib Desert
UNITY
LIBERTY
JUSTICE

Botswana

Adopted September 30, 1966 | **Ratio** 2:3 | **Usage** National and Civil

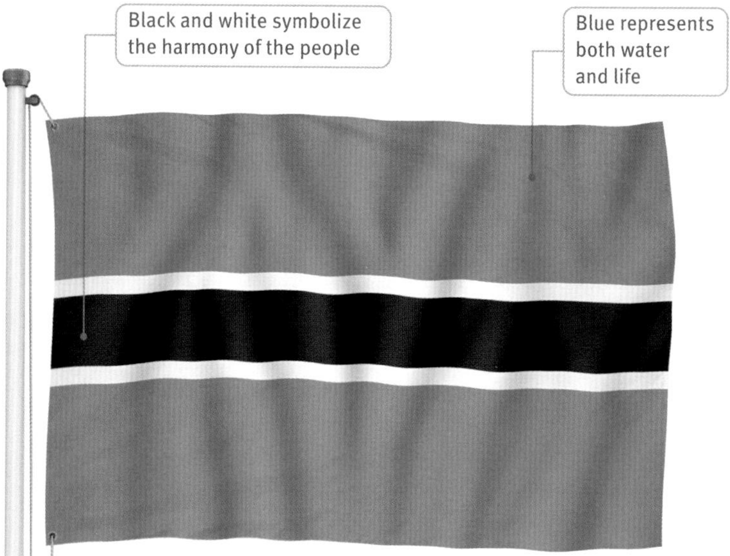
Black and white symbolize the harmony of the people
Blue represents both water and life

Prior to its independence, Botswana did not have its own distinctive flag. The flag was designed to contrast with the South African flag, in reaction to the neighboring country being ruled under an apartheid regime. As a result, the national flag of Botswana does not use the Pan-African colors. Neither is it derived from that of the dominant political party. The new flag was flown for the first time at midnight on September 30, 1966, the day independence was declared.

PULA—LIFE-GIVING RAIN

The flag is based on the idea of life-giving rain, an essential element in the drought-prone country. This is also reflected in the Setswana word *pula*, which forms the national motto. This means not only "water" and "rain" but also the life that is derived from it. This idea is manifested in the two horizontal blue stripes that represent rain and water. The black stripe fimbriated with white in the center of the flag represents the idea of the African and European populations of Botswana living together in harmony.

ARMS OF BOTSWANA

The coat of arms, which appears on the President's Flag, was adopted in 1966. The African shield depicts three cogwheels and a bull's head separated by three wavy bars of water The supporters are two zebras, holding an elephant tusk and the other a sorghum plant, the country's staple crop. Some also interpret the zebras, with their black and white stripes, as being symbolic of racial integration.

Lesotho

Adopted October 4, 2006 | **Ratio** 2:3 | **Usage** National and Civil

A black *mokorotlo* (Basotho hat) represents the people
Blue is symbolic of the importance of water and rain
White represents peace
Green represents plenty

The national flag was changed to commemorate the 40th anniversary of independence in 2006. The change from a shield to a black *mokorotlo*, a Basotho hat, reflects the hope for a peaceful future for the country.

ARMS OF LESOTHO

The central shield contains a crocodile, which is a symbol of King Moshoeshoe I, who founded the state in 1824. It stands on a representation of Mount Thaba Bosiu, the Mountain of Night, and is supported by two Basuto ponies. Behind the shield is a spear and a *knobkerrie*, which is a local club.

The national motto at the base reads *Khotso, Pula, Nala,* which translates as "Peace, Rain, Prosperity."

ARMS OF LESOTHO

The shield stands on a representation of Thaba Bosigo
A crocodile, symbol of King Moshoeshoe I
Two Basuto ponies support the shield
KHOTSO PULA NALA

Eswatini (formerly Swaziland)

Adopted October 1, 1968 | **Ratio** 2:3 | **Usage** National and Civil

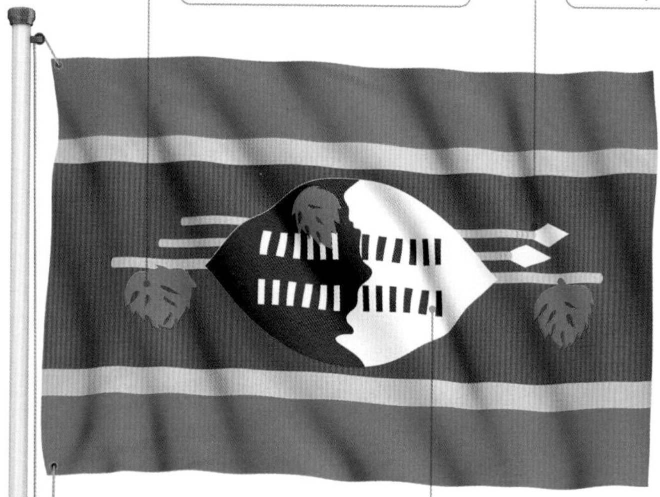
Injobo tassels, made from widowbird and lourie feathers
Assegais are Swazi spears
The pattern of the shield is taken from the Emasotsha Regiment

The flag is based on one given by the late King Sobhuza II to the Swazi Pioneer Corps in 1941. On it is an Emasotsha shield, laid horizontally. The shield is reinforced by a staff from which hang *injobo* tassels—bunches of feathers of the widowbird and the lourie. They also decorate the shield. Above the staff are two *assegais*—local spears. The shield and *assegais* appear on the national arms, which is supported by a lion and an elephant, symbolic of the King and of the Queen Mother. The crest is an otterskin headdress decorated with widowbird feathers, and the motto is *Siyinqaba,* meaning "We are the fortress."

ARMS OF ESWATINI

A lion, symbolic of the King
A headdress with widowbird feathers
The national motto—"We are the fortress"
SIYINQABA
An elephant, symbolic of the Queen Mother

South Africa

Adopted April 27, 1994 | **Ratio** 2:3 | **Usage** National and Civil

The overall design conveys convergence and unification
Green, black, and yellow are taken from the ANC flag
Red, white, and blue are taken from the colors of the Boer republics

South Africa had no distinctive flag until 1928 when a national flag was adopted based on the orange, white, and blue tricolor used by the first Dutch settlers, with three smaller flags in the center for Britain, Transvaal, and the Orange Free State.

A NEW FLAG FOR A NEW ERA

Following the end of apartheid and the onset of multiracial democracy in 1994, attempts were made to find a new flag and the present design, created by the Chief Herald of South Africa, was adopted.

The new flag combines the colors of the Boer republics with those of the African National Congress (ANC), whose flag was adopted in 1917. The Y-shape represents the convergence of old traditions with new and the progress of the state into the future.

ARMS OF SOUTH AFRICA

Tusks are for strength and eternity
Motto is in the Khoisan language; it translates as "Diverse People Unite"
The secretary bird spreads its wings to show the ascent of the nation
The weapons of war symbolize defense but are laid down, symbolizing peace
!KE E: /XARRA //KE

Seychelles

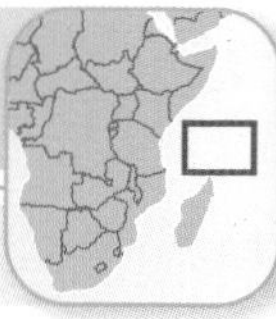

Adopted June 18, 1996 | **Ratio** 1:2 | **Usage** National and Civil

Blue and yellow are the colors of the Democratic Party

Red, white, and green are the colors of the SPUP

The Seychelles has had three flags since independence. After the coup of 1977, a new national flag, based on the party flag of the ruling SPUP, was adopted. This used their colors of red, white, and green.

Following the adoption of the Constitution of 1993, the existence of other parties was permitted and so the latest flag included the blue and yellow of the Democratic Party in a striking new design.

The coat of arms was adopted in 1976, and it has been only slightly altered since then. It is based on the old colonial badge and depicts the most famous inhabitant of the islands, the giant tortoise.

ARMS OF THE SEYCHELLES

Two sailfish support the arms

A Latin motto—*Finis Coronat Opus*, meaning "The end crowns the work," was chosen in the 19th century

The crest is a *paille-en-queue*—a native bird of the Seychelles

The giant tortoise and palm have been in use in the arms since the 19th century

Comoros

Adopted January 7, 2002 | **Ratio** 3:5 | **Usage** Government and Civil

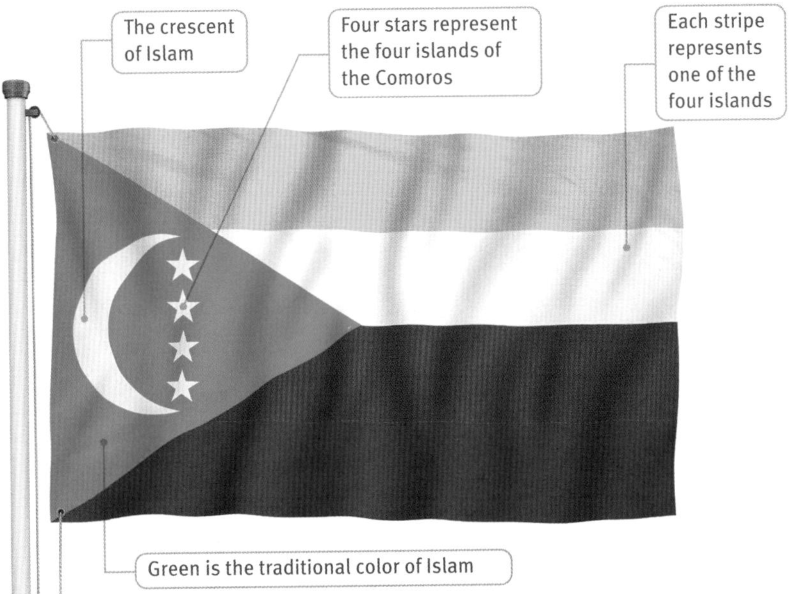
The crescent of Islam
Four stars represent the four islands of the Comoros
Each stripe represents one of the four islands
Green is the traditional color of Islam

The present flag is based on one adopted at independence, which included stars for the four main islands (including Mayotte) and a crescent to symbolize Islam.

The original flag was mainly red, to underline the socialist aspirations of the country. This was dropped in 1978 in favor of a green flag, with the crescent and stars in white. The Constitution of 1996 modified the flag to include the monograms of Allah and of Muhammad in the top right and bottom left corners.

Comoros adopted a new name, constitution, and flag in January 2002. The four stars, the crescent moon, and the green of Islam have been moved into a triangle. Each stripe of yellow, white, red, and blue represents one of the four islands.

THE NATIONAL FLAG 1996–2002

A monogram of Allah
A monogram of the Prophet Muhammad

Madagascar

Adopted October 14, 1958 | **Ratio** 2:3 | **Usage** National and Civil

White and red were the colors of the Kingdom of Madagascar

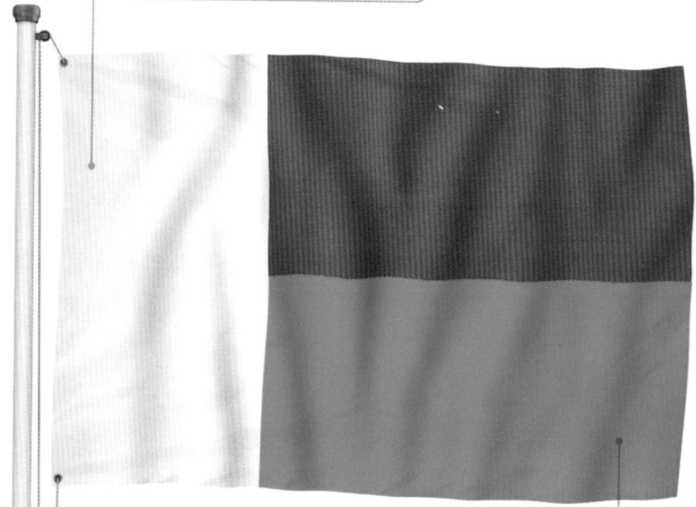

Green represents the Hova, the former peasant class

The flag was introduced when self-government was achieved in 1958 and was retained on independence. The red and white are said to symbolize the earlier Merina Kingdom, whose flags were all red and white, with the addition of green for the Hova, the former peasant class. The seal has changed several times since independence. That of the present republic, introduced in March 1993, shows a map of the island with a spray of leaves. Beneath these is a paddy field surmounted by the head of a zebu. The motto reads "Fatherland, Liberty, Justice." Above the design is the country's name.

SEAL OF MADAGASCAR

The leaves of the traveler's tree

The national motto—"Fatherland, Liberty, Justice"

The state title is in Malagasy, the local language

An outline of Madagascar

A stylized paddy field and a zebu—a local ox

Mauritius

Adopted January 9, 1968 | **Ratio** 2:3 | **Usage** National

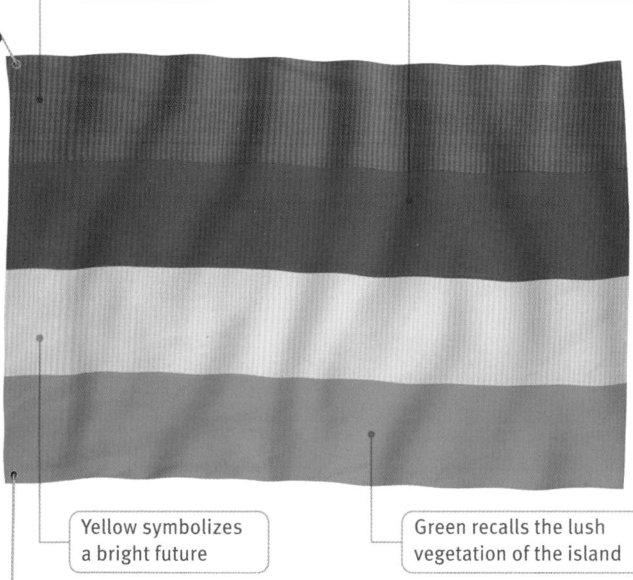
Red reflects independence
Blue is the color of the Indian Ocean
Yellow symbolizes a bright future
Green recalls the lush vegetation of the island

The flag was designed by the College of Arms in Britain prior to independence in 1968 and is a simple statement of the colors found in the coat of arms.

MAURITIUS'S COAT OF ARMS

The coat of arms was granted on August 25, 1906, and depicts various attributes of the island. In the lower right quarter is a key, and on the left-hand side is a white star, which are referred to in the Latin motto *Stella Clavisque Maris Indici* ("The star and the key of the Indian Ocean"). The supporters are a dodo and a deer each holding a sugar cane, the island's staple crop.

ARMS OF MAURITIUS

A dodo, extinct since the 18th century
A ship symbolizing colonization
The star and key are referred to in the motto
Palm trees represent the country's tropical vegetation
The national motto—"The star and the key of the Indian Ocean"
STELLA CLAVISQUE MARIS INDICI

18
19
46
11
30
5
15
25
14
43
23
34
41
2
28
37
20

Europe

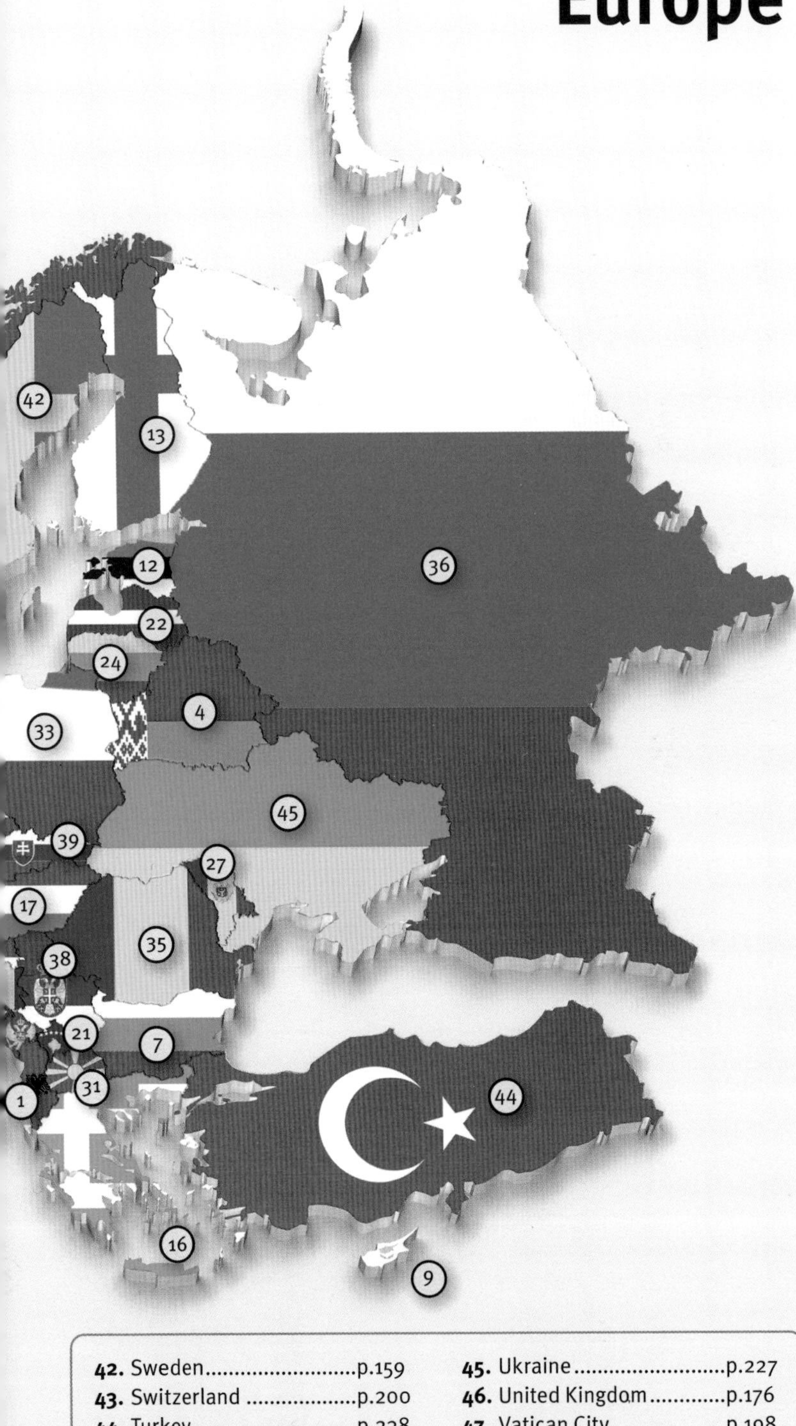

Iceland

Adopted June 19, 1915 | **Ratio** 18:25 | **Usage** National and Civil

White recalls the ice and snow that covers Iceland
Deep blue represents the Atlantic Ocean
Red represents the fire produced by the island's volcanoes

Iceland's first national flag was a white cross on a deep blue background. It was first paraded in 1897. The modern flag dates from 1915, when a red cross was inserted into the white cross of the original flag. It was adopted in 1918 and became the national flag when Iceland gained independence from Denmark in 1944.

The naval ensign is swallow-tailed, as are the naval ensigns of all the Scandinavian countries.

NAVAL ENSIGN

The swallow-tailed form is common in Scandinavia for government flags.

THE PRESIDENT'S FLAG

The shield is supported by a bull, an eagle, a dragon, and a giant, the mythical defenders of the island.

Norway

Adopted July 13, 1821 | **Ratio** 8:11 | **Usage** National and Civil

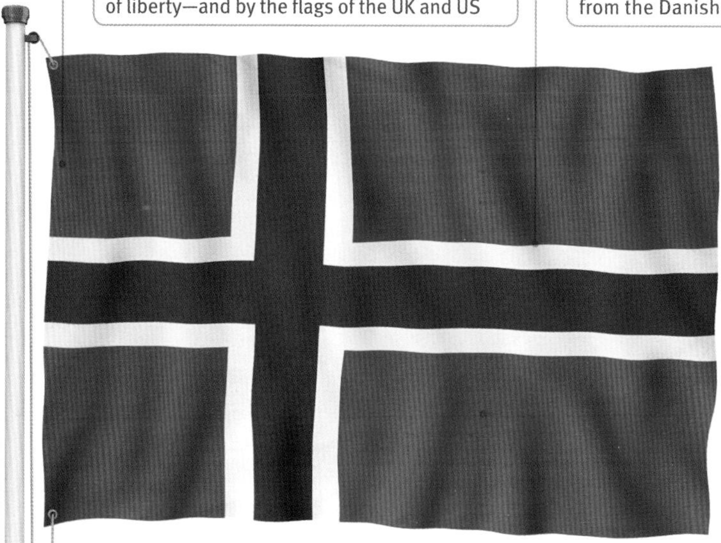
The red, white, and blue colors were influenced by the French *Tricolore*—a symbol of liberty—and by the flags of the UK and US
Off-centered white cross on a red field is taken from the Danish flag

Until 1814, the Norwegian flag bore the Danish red and white cross. The current flag was born in 1821, during the period when Norway was united with Sweden. The flag combines two influences—its red and white coloring was taken from the Danish flag, and a blue cross was added overall. These three colors were chosen in honor of the French *Tricolore*, a symbol of revolution and liberty. They were also the colors of the flags of the United States of America and the United Kingdom, two other countries that were not ruled by an absolute monarch.

The Royal Standard consists of a banner of the Royal Arms, dating back to the Middle Ages. It depicts a lion rampant on a red field.

THE ROYAL STANDARD

The standard dates back to the Middle Ages
A tall, slender lion bearing the ax of St. Olav II, the Eternal King of Norway

Denmark

Adopted 1821 | **Ratio** 28:37 | **Usage** National and Civil

According to legend, a red flag with a white cross "appeared as a sign from heaven"
The off-centered cross is the basis for other Scandinavian countries' flags

Besides being the oldest monarchy in Europe, Denmark also has the oldest flag, known as the *Dannebrog*, or Danish cloth. Legend says that a bloodred flag with a white cross appeared as a sign from heaven to King Valdemar II during the conquest of Estonia in 1219. In reality, the flag may have been a gi from the Pope during the Crusades.

THE SCANDINAVIAN CROSS

The flag was originally square, but it design was elongated and the arm c the cross in the fly was extended. It has become a model for other flags.

OVERSEAS TERRITORIES

FAROE ISLANDS

The Faroe Islands are a self-governing territory of Denmark. The flag has the Norwegian colors in a new arrangement. This recalls that they were once part of Norway.

GREENLAND

Greenland's flag was designed by a local artist and adopted in 1985. In the Danish colors, white represents the ice that covers most of the island and red is for the sun.

Sweden

Adopted June 22, 1906 | **Ratio** 5:8 | **Usage** National and Civil

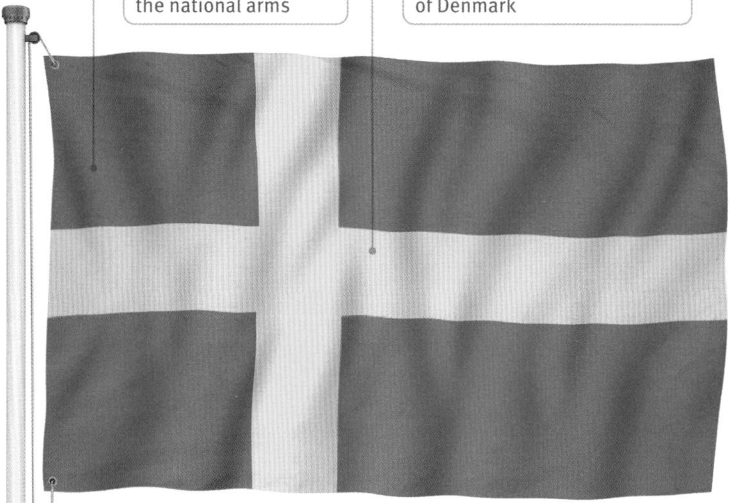
The blue and yellow colors are taken from the national arms
The distinctive Scandinavian cross is taken from the flag of Denmark

The present flag was adopted in 1906, but it was first used in a similar form almost four centuries before. The design is based on the Scandinavian cross. The flag's blue and yellow colors are thought to come from the national coat of arms—three gold crowns in a blue field—which originated in the 14th century. A national flag day is celebrated each year on June 6. On this day in 1523, King Gustav Vasa was elected and, on the same date in 1809, Sweden adopted a new constitution.

SWEDISH ROYAL STANDARD
The coat of arms is placed in the center of the Royal Standard, which is used on special occasions by Parliament and dates from the 1440s.

THE ROYAL STANDARD

The shield is supported by two golden lions
The triple crown symbolizes the "Three Wise Men," a Swedish emblem since 1336

Finland

Adopted May 29, 1918 | **Ratio** 11:18 | **Usage** National and Civil

The overall design is based on the Scandinavian cross
Blue represents Finland's blue skies and its thousands of lakes
White recalls the snows of winter

Finland's national flag, like others in the region, is based on the distinctive Scandinavian cross.

It was adopted after independence from Russia, when many patriotic Finns wanted a special flag for their country, but its design dates back to the 19th century. The blue coloring represents the country's thousands of lakes and the sky, with white for the snow that covers the land in winter. This color combination has also been used over the centuries in various Finnish provincial, military, and town flags.

THE ÅLAND ISLANDS

The Åland Islands are an autonomous group of Finnish islands with their own flag since 1954. The design incorporates a Scandinavian cross.

THE FLAG OF THE ÅLAND ISLANDS

Red and yellow are taken from the arms of Finland, while blue and yellow represent Sweden; the islands have a large Swedish population

Estonia

Adopted May 8, 1990 | **Ratio** 7:11 | **Usage** National and Civil

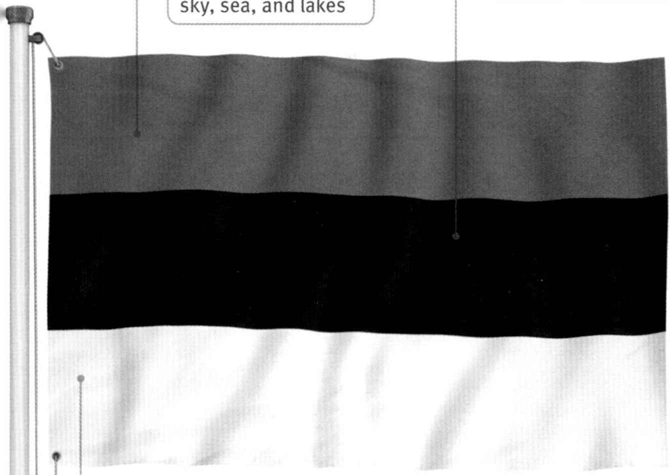
Blue represents loyalty and Estonia's sky, sea, and lakes
Black is symbolic of past oppression and the soil
White represents virtue, the snow, and Estonia's struggle for freedom

The tricolor was first adopted by students in 1881 during uprisings against occupying Russian Czarist forces. It was readopted as the national flag in 1990 just prior to independence. The colors represent Estonian history, folk costumes, and landscape. Blue is the color of loyalty and also represents the sky, sea, and lakes. Black symbolizes the past suffering of the people, the soil, and the traditional black peasant's jacket. White represents virtue and the struggle for freedom. It is also the color of birch bark and snow.

The great coat of arms was originally the emblem of 13th-century Danish King, Valdemar II.

GREAT ARMS OF ESTONIA

The shield is surrounded by golden branches of oak
Three blue lions are ranged on a gold shield, derived from the arms of Danish King Valdemar II

Latvia

Adopted February 27, 1990 | **Ratio** 1:2 | **Usage** National and Civil

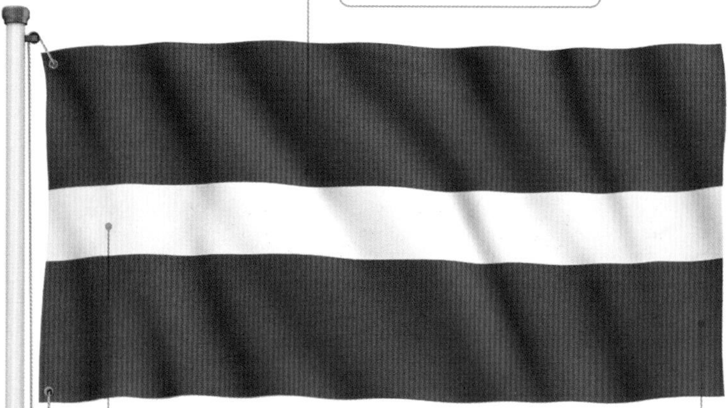
Red recalls the blood shed by the wounded leader
White may stand for the sheet used to wrap the wounded Latvian leader
Red also represents Latvians' willingness to defend their liberty

Though officially adopted in 1922, the Latvian flag was in use from as early as the 13th century, but its use was suppressed during Soviet rule.

The red color has been described as symbolizing the readiness of the Latvians to give the blood from their hearts for freedom. An alternative interpretation, according to one legend, is that a Latvian leader was wounded in battle, and the edges of the white sheet in which he was wrapped were stained by his blood.

The coat of arms depicts a tripartite shield, recalling the three reunited duchies of Latvia. The shield is held by a red lion and a silver griffin.

ARMS OF LATVIA

Rising sun represents the Duchy of Latgale
The red lion represents the Duchy of Kurzeme
Three stars for the reunited duchies
The silver griffin recalls the Duchy of Vidzeme

Lithuania

Adopted March 20, 1989 | **Ratio** 3:5 | **Usage** National and Civil

Yellow represents wheat and freedom from want
Green symbolizes the forests and renewed hope
Red symbolizes patriotism and courage

The national flag dates from the independent republic of 1918–1940. It was suppressed under the Soviet regime but was readopted in 1990. Yellow stands for ripening wheat, green for the forests, and red for love of the country, or alternatively for the blood shed in defense of the nation. Red also refers to the color of the medieval banners of the kingdom of Lithuania. Together, the colors stand for hope, courage, and freedom from want.

ARMS OF LITHUANIA

The coat of arms' red shield dates from the 14th century. It was readopted in 1991 after Lithuania declared independence from the Soviet Union.

ARMS OF LITHUANIA

A white knight on his charger
The double-barred cross commemorates the conversion of Grand Duke Jaggelon of Lithuania to Catholicism in 1386, at the time of his marriage to Queen Hedwig of Poland

Poland

Adopted August 1, 1919 | **Ratio** 5:8 | **Usage** National

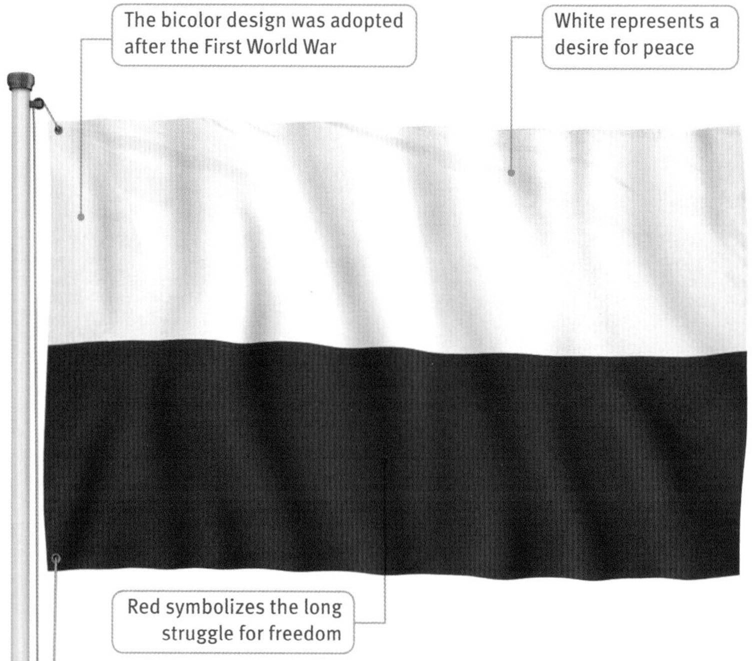

The red and white colors of the flag have been used since the 13th century, although they did not become the official national colors until 1831. The bicolor design was adopted after the First World War.

White represents the desire for peace, while red symbolizes the long stuggle for freedom.

MODERN POLAND

Following a period of communist rule from 1945–1989 the original 1919 design was reconfirmed as the national flag by the new government in 1992.

The plain bicolored flag is used for general purposes on land. When at sea, the flag is charged with the state arms in the center.

The people of Poland are obliged by law to treat the flag with respect. The country also has four flag flying days each year when certain institutions are legally required to fly the flag to celebrate significant events in Polish history.

THE NATIONAL ARMS

The coat of arms traditionally shows a white eagle on a red field. This emblem has remained more or less unchanged throughout Poland's turbulent history. The coat of arms was used by the Kingdom of Poland until its fall in 1795 and was readopted by the newly declared republic around 1918/19.

Germany

Adopted May 23, 1949 | **Ratio** 3:5 | **Usage** National and Civil

The colors of the German flag were taken from the uniforms of German soldiers during the Napoleonic Wars

First adopted in 1848, the flag was officially adopted for the republic in 1919

Until the 19th century, Germany was a collection of feudal states. In 1848, an attempt was made to unite them, and although no union was established, a flag was produced. This was a black, red, and gold horizontal tricolor. The colors were taken from the uniforms of the German soldiers in the Napoleonic Wars in the late 18th century.

THE GERMAN EMPIRE

Most of the states finally united into the German Empire in 1871, but instead of retaining the black, red, and gold flag, the rival Bismarck tricolor of black, white, and red was adopted. This was a combination of the red of the Hanseatic League and the black and white of Prussia, of which Bismarck was Chancellor.

THE *WEIMAR* REPUBLIC

After Germany's defeat in the First World War, a republic was declared in 1919 and the black, red, and gold flag returned. Its revival was short-lived, and in 1933, when the Nazi government came to power, they restored the imperial colors and made their party flag, the *Hakenkreuz*, the national flag.

After the Second World War, both German states reverted to using the black, red, and gold tricolor, but East Germany added its coat of arms. Since reunification, the plain tricolor has been used.

Germany: Länder flags

On German regional flags, the arms appear only on the official versions (except Lower Saxony, Saarland, and Rhineland Palatinate).

Baden-Württemburg

The flag was adopted in 1953. Its colors derive from the arms of Duke Frederick V of Swabia; the coat of arms dates back to 1265. It was adopted as the state arms in 1954.

Bavaria

Bavaria's flag was adopted in 1950, but blue and white have been Bavarian colors since 1330, and the lozenge shapes first appeared on banners in the 15th century.

Berlin

The flag was first adopted for West Berlin in 1950 and extended to the whole city in 1991. The bear, a pun on the name Berlin, dates from 1338 and the colors from 1861.

Brandenburg

The colors of the flag are derived from the central shield, dating from 1170, although red and white were also the colors of the medieval Hanseatic League. The flag was adopted in 1990.

Bremen

The flag of Bremen predates its coat of arms, which was adopted in 1891. Prior to this, Bremen was a member of the Hanseatic League, where the flag originated.

Hamburg

Used since 1325, red and white are the Hanseatic colors. The castle is for Hamburg; the three towers for the Trinity; the cross for Christ; the stars for the Father and Holy Spirit.

Hessen

The flag of Hessen was adopted in 1948. The coat of arms was that of Ludwig III of Thuringia in 1182. The red and white colors of the flag are taken from the lion in the arms.

Lower Saxony

This flag uses the national flag with Lower Saxony's local arms in the center. It was adopted in 1946, but the arms dates from around the 12th century when it first became associated with the Duke of Saxony.

Länder flags (continued)

Mecklenburg-Vorpommern

This flag, adopted in 1991, combines blue and white of Pomerania with the blue, yellow, and red of Mecklenburg. The bull and the griffin are also local emblems. Red and white recall the Hanseatic League.

North-Rhine-Westphalia

The coat of arms depicts the Rhine River of the Rhineland, the horse of Westphalia, and the rose of Lippe—the three territories that united to form the state. The colors of the flag are from the arms.

Rhineland-Palatinate

The flag was adopted in 1948 when the arms were placed on the national flag. The coat of arms depicts the lion of the Palatinate dating from 1229, the cross of Trier from 1273, and the wheel of Mainz from 1335.

Saarland

Adopted in 1957, the flag of Saarland recalls the different parts of the state. Depicted on the shield is the lion of Saarbrücken, the cross of Trier, the eagles of Lorraine, and the lion of Pfalz-Zweibrücken.

Saxony

The flag was adopted in 1991, but the coat of arms is the traditional symbol of the rulers of Saxony: black and yellow bands and the green crown of rue. The white and green flag dates from the 19th century.

Saxony-Anhalt

This flag was the same as Baden-Württemberg until 1991, when the colors were reversed. The eagle recalls Prussi; the bicolored bands and rue crown, Saxony; and the bear and wall are the arms of Anhalt.

Schleswig-Holstein

The shield depicts two lions from the arms of Schleswig and a nettle leaf from those of Holstein. The colors of the flag, adopted in 1957, are taken from the arms.

Thuringia

Another flag whose colors are based on the state arms, it was adopted in 1991. The red and white lion was the arms of the Counts of Thuringia in the 12th century.

The Netherlands

Adopted February 19, 1937 | **Ratio** 2:3 | **Usage** National and Civil

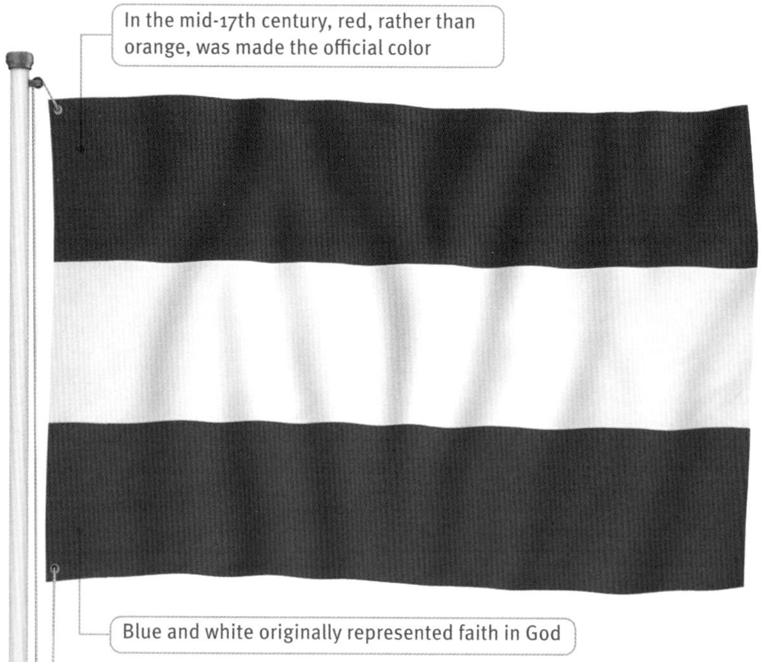
In the mid-17th century, red, rather than orange, was made the official color
Blue and white originally represented faith in God

The first *stadtholder,* or ruler, of the Dutch Republic was William of Orange, who joined with Dutch nationalists and led the struggle for independence from Spain.

THE PRINSVLAG

Partly out of respect for him, the first flag adopted by the Dutch was a horizontal tricolor of orange, white, and blue (see p.20). It became known as the *Prinsenvlag* and was based on the livery of William of Orange. The orange dye was particularly unstable and tended to turn red after a while, so in the mid-17th century, red was made the official color. The flag has flown since then, but was only confirmed by Royal Decree in 1937. As perhaps the first revolutionary flag, it has had a seminal influence throughout the world, particularly on the Pan-Slavic colors of Russia.

Until about 1800, in the case of both the orange- and red-striped versions, the number of stripes and their order frequently varied.

ARMS OF THE NETHERLANDS

The Dutch coat of arms depicts a golden lion on a blue shield, holding a sword and a sheaf of arrows. It is a combination of the coat of arms of the Dutch Republic and that of the House of Orange. The seven arrows represent the seven original provinces in the Netherlands.

Provincial flags

Except for South Holland and North Brabant, all the Dutch provincial flags are modern creations.

Drenthe

White and red are the colors of the Archbishops of Utrecht, former rulers of Drenthe. The black castle and stars recall the uprising of Coevorden against the archbishop.

Flevoland

Blue is for the Lake Ijssel from which the province was reclaimed. Green is for vegetation, and yellow for the cornfields. The lily device is a pun on the name of Cornelis Lely, the engineer of the reclamation project.

Friesland

The flag is based on that of the 15th-century kings of Friesland. The colors are those of the Dutch flag. The stripes and pompblêden (the leaves of the yellow water lily) represent the seven districts of Friesland.

Gelderland

In 1371, the dukedoms of Gelre and Gulik were united and combined their arms. The new arms was blue, yellow, and black. These colors also appear in the flag, which was hoisted in 1953.

Groningen

The flag, adopted in 1950, combines green and white from the town of Groningen, surrounded by red, white, and blue of Ommeland, reflecting the town's position.

Provincial flags (continued)

Limburg

The red lion is from Limburg's arms. White and yellow are from local coats of arms, while the narrow blue stripe is for the Maas River, which crosses the province.

North Brabant

The design, adopted in 1959, originated in Antwerp where red and white checked coats of arms were popular. It was associated with the area from the 17th century.

North Holland

Adopted in 1958, this flag unites the colors of Holland—yellow and red—with the blue and yellow of West Friesland. Yellow, the common color, is placed at the top.

Overijssel

The yellow and red stripes recall the ancient association of the province with Holland. The wavy blue stripe running across the center is for the Ijssel River, after which the province is named.

South Holland

The flag is a banner of the arms of Holland and was adopted in this form in 1986, replacing the previous simple triband of yellow-red-yellow, which was also based on the colors of the arms.

Provincial/overseas territory flags

Utrecht

The Archbishop of Utrecht used a red flag with a white cross from 1528. The Archbishop's flag remains in the canton of the modern flag, adopted in 1952. The field is in the traditional colors of the province.

Zeeland

The flag of Zeeland, adopted in 1949, shows its full coat of arms. The wavy blue and white stripes represent the sea and the constant struggle to control it. From the water, the Dutch lion rises in triumph.

Aruba

The flag of Aruba was adopted in 1976 when it was still administered as part of the Netherlands Antilles. The flag was retained when Aruba became autonomous in 1986.

Curaçao

Curaçao's flag was adopted in 1984, designed by Martin Den Dulk. The blue symbolizes the sky and sea, and the yellow stripe, the sunshine that bathes the island. The two stars represent Curaçao and Klein Curaçao.

Bonaire

The flag of Bonaire, adopted in 1984, consists of yellow and blue triangles that represent the sun and the sea, while the white represents the sky. The six-pointed red star represents the six original villages that made up the territory.

Sint Maarten

Introduced in 1985, the Sint Maarten flag has two horizontal bands of red and blue, with a white triangle, representing its past association with the Netherlands and France. Its coat of arms depicts the distinctive courthouse in Philipsburg, the capital.

Belgium

Adopted January 23, 1831 | **Ratio** 13:15 | **Usage** National and Civil

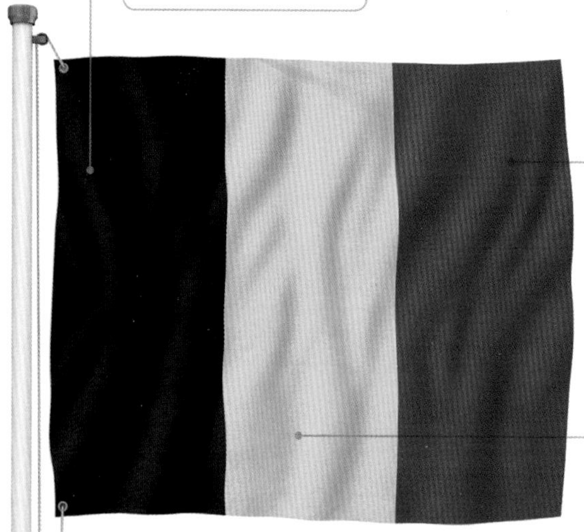
Black is taken from the shield of the arms
Red is adapted from the lion's claws and tongue
Gold is the color of the lion in the arms

The Belgian colors black, yellow, and red derive from the arms of Brabant, a black shield with a gold lion having red tongue and claws. The first flag in these colors, but with horizontal stripes, appeared in 1792 in a revolt against Austrian rule.

Upon gaining independence in 1831, they were changed to a vertical arrangement in imitation of the French *Tricolore*.

BELGIAN REGIONAL FLAGS

Brussels

Adopted in 1991, the lily was widespread in the area that later became Brussels.

German-speaking Community

Adopted in 1990, the lion recalls the Duchy of Limburg; nine roses are for the nine communes.

Flanders

Adopted in 1985, it is based on the arms, and the colors are taken from the national flag.

Wallonia

The cockerel is derived from the Gallic rooster, recalling the cultural links with France.

Ireland

Adopted January 21, 1919 | **Ratio** 1:2 | **Usage** National and Civil

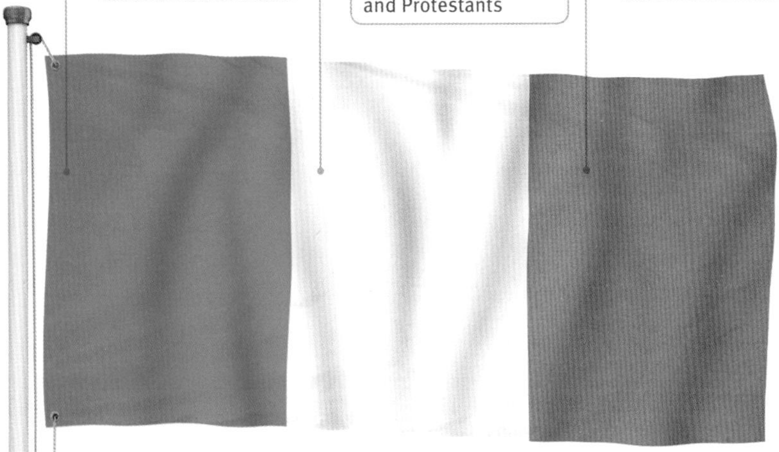
Green represents the Catholic people
White is for the union between Catholics and Protestants
Orange is for the Protestant people

The Irish flag is modeled on that of the French *Tricolore*. It was first flown by nationalists during their struggle for freedom from Britain in 1848, a year of Europe-wide revolution. However, it was not until the Easter Rising of 1916 that it came to be regarded as the national flag. It was officially confirmed in 1919 and was written into the Constitution in 1937. The green coloring on the flag represents the Catholic majority; orange is for the Protestant minority (originally supporters of William of Orange), and white is for peace between the two faiths.

THE PRESIDENT'S STANDARD

The flag of the president was introduced in 1945 and is based on the ancient "Green Flag," a traditional symbol of Irish nationalism.

THE PRESIDENT'S STANDARD

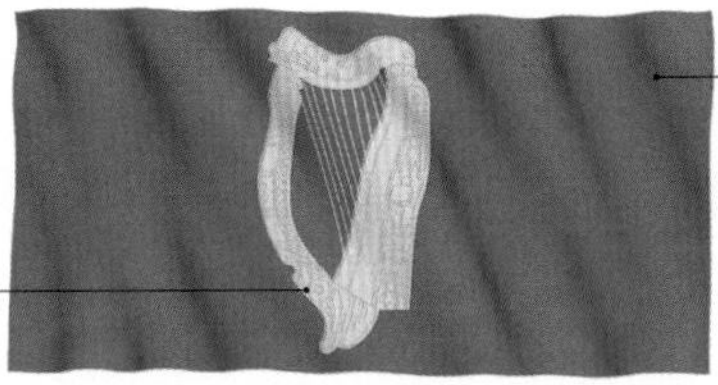
The harp has been a symbol of Ireland for centuries
The flag is similar to the quartering for Ireland on the Royal Arms of the United Kingdom

United Kingdom

Adopted January 1, 1801 | **Ratio** 3:5 | **Usage** National and Civil

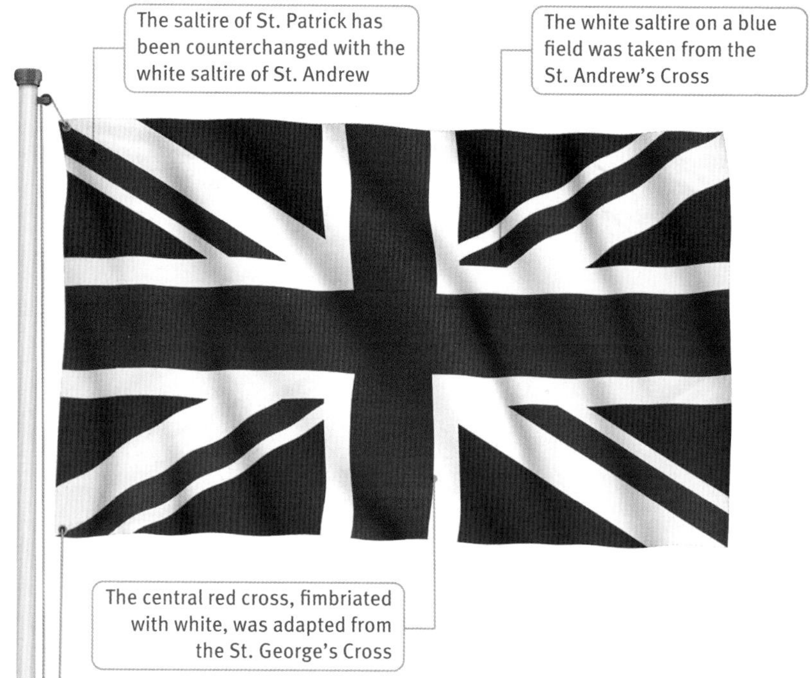
The saltire of St. Patrick has been counterchanged with the white saltire of St. Andrew
The white saltire on a blue field was taken from the St. Andrew's Cross
The central red cross, fimbriated with white, was adapted from the St. George's Cross

The Union Flag reflects the complex history of the British Isles. The distinctive design has evolved over the centuries to encompass the growth of the Union between England, Scotland, and Ireland.

THE FIRST UNION FLAG

When King James of Scotland became King of England in 1603, both countries retained their own flags. Even today, the St. George's Cross and St. Andrew's Cross remain the flags of England and Scotland, respectively. In 1606, King James considered it necessary to have a flag reflecting the new union of Scotland and England, and ordered that a Union Flag, more commonly known as the Union Jack, be flown on British ships, combining the English Cross of St. George with the Scottish Cross of St. Andrew.

A NEW UNION FLAG

In 1801, when Ireland joined the Union, the Cross of St. Patrick was added to form the present flag but was counterchanged with the Cross of St. Andrew.

A ROYAL FLAG

The Union Flag was established as a maritime flag and it remains a royal flag, not officially a national flag. In 1915, King George V gave permission for British citizens to use the flag on land.

UK: Subnational flags

Most regional flags are older than the Union Flag, except those based on the St. George's Cross, which date from the 20th century.

England

Originally used in 1191, the flag of St. George became the flag of England after 1277. The white flag has a red upright cross throughout. At sea, it is the flag of an Admiral.

Scotland (National flag)

In use since 1512, the Scottish flag is the Cross of St. Andrew. As James was King of Scotland before he was King of England, this flag formed the basis of the Union Flag.

Wales

Approved in 1959 as the Welsh national flag, the Red Dragon is an ancient emblem of Wales. For a time it appeared on a green hill, but the horizontal division is traditional.

Northern Ireland

The official flag of Northern Ireland is the Union Flag of the United Kingdom (see left) which is flown over certain public buildings on a number of specific dates each year.

State flags

Scotland "The Lion Rampant"

The red lion on gold is the traditional royal flag of Scotland. Dating from the late 13th century, the *fleur-de-lis* on the border recall the "auld alliance" with France. It is used by representatives of the crown, such as lord lieutenants, the first minister and the Lord Lyon.

Guernsey

Guernsey formerly used only the Cross of St. George. In 1985, a gold cross taken from the flag of William the Conqueror at the Battle of Hastings was added to the flag.

Isle of Man

This is a traditional design, which was adopted in 1968. The *Trinacria*, three legs of Man, has been used for several centuries in varying forms, but its origin is uncertain.

Jersey

Prior to the adoption of its current flag, Jersey used a red diagonal cross on white, which is the same as the saltire of St. Patrick. The arms were added in 1981.

Royal Standards

Like other monarchies, the UK has a wide range of flags that are armorial or semi-armorial, for the leading members of its royal family. In the case of HM Queen, it is necessary to distinguish between her role as Queen of the United Kingdom and her other Realms, and as Head of the Commonwealth. In addition to her British Royal Standard, she has standards for other Realms.

Royal Standard of the United Kingdom

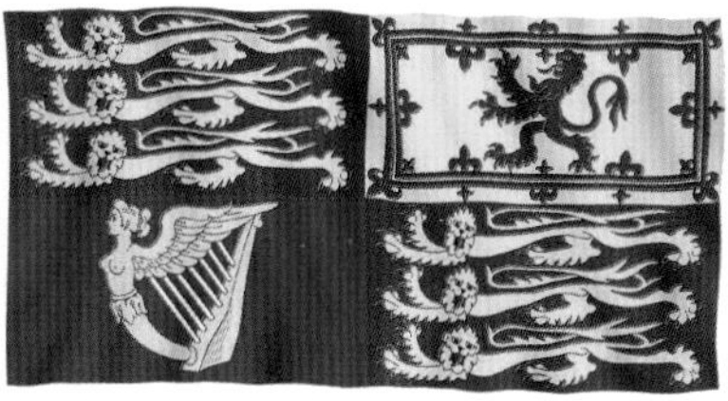

This form has been in use since the accession of Queen Victoria in 1837 and depicts the three areas united to form the United Kingdom (England, Scotland, and Northern Ireland). Strictly, flags of this kind are armorial banners rather than "standards."

Queen as Head of the Commonwealth

This is used when the Queen is not in a "Queen's Realm" (i.e., a country of which she is directly the Head of State) or in one that does not have a local Royal Standard. It is a banner with Her Majesty's initial "E," a gold crown, and chaplet of roses.

HRH Prince Charles Prince of Wales

The banner is an adaptation of the Royal Standard, with a "label" for the eldest son: a white bar with three points, and the quartered arms of the Principality of Wales in the center. Labels are used for children and grandchildren of the Queen.

Royal Standards (continued)

HRH Prince Charles for use in Wales

For personal visits to Wales and as his own flag, the Prince uses the banner of the Principality of Wales with his crown on a green shield in the center. The Prince also has a banner for his title as Duke of Cornwall.

HRH Prince Charles Duke of Rothesay

The Prince's Scottish titles are Duke of Rothesay, Lord High Steward and Lord of the Isles. His Scottish banner quarters the emblems of the Stewards and Lord of the Isles, with the Royal Arms in a shield in the center with a blue "label" to show he is the heir.

HRH Prince William Duke of Cambridge

Prince William is directly after his father in the line of succession, so he also uses a three-pointed label, but in his case, the central point carries a red escallop (shell). William chose this emblem from his mother's coat of arms.

Other Royal Standards

Other members of the Queen's family who have standards based on the Royal Standard are the Princess Royal, the Duke of York, Earl of Wessex, and the Queen's royal cousins. There is a general banner for those members of the royal family not entitled to an individual standard.

Overseas territories

Official flags for British Overseas Territories are generally based on the British blue or government ensign with a local badge in the fly.

Anguilla

The flag of Anguilla was adopted in 1990. It is a blue ensign with the badge of the island. This derives from the unofficial flag used locally on land only.

Ascension Island

The arms of Acension Island feature local fauna and flora. The green chevron represents Green Mountain and is surrounded by three wideawake birds. The shield is held up by two green turtles. It was officially introduced in 2013.

Bermuda

Unusually, Bermuda uses a red ensign. The badge shows a lion holding a shield on which appears the 1609 wreck of a ship, which struck a reef, not a cliff as is shown.

British Virgin Islands

The badge dates from 1909, and the flag from 1956. It shows St. Ursula, the namesake of the islands, with a lamp. She was martyred with 11,000 virgins, which are represented by 11 lamps.

Overseas territories (continued)

British Antarctic Territory

The white field of the new flag, approved in 1998, symbolizes the snow that covers the Antarctic continent. It is used by research stations within the territory.

British Indian Ocean Territory

The flag was adopted in 1990. Blue and white wavy lines represent the ocean, and the palm recalls the natural vegetation of the islands. The crown shows British possession of the territory.

Cayman Islands

Blue and white lines recall the sea and the three stars, the three main islands. The lion of England appears above: the crest is a turtle, and a pineapple is representative of the fauna and flora.

Falkland Islands

The badge shows a ram for the sheep industry of the islands. The ship is the *Desire*, the ship of John Davies who discovered the islands in 1592. The flag was hoisted in 1948.

Tristan da Cunha

The flag was adopted in 2002. It shows a stylistic image of the main island in the sea surrounded by four albatrosses. The arms show a Tristan longboat above a Naval Crown, with a central shield decorated with four albatrosses. The supporters are Tristan lobsters, the island's main export.

Gibraltar (City)

The local flag of Gibraltar City is a banner of the arms officially granted in 1926. It is based on the original arms granted by Spain in 1502. The banner was granted for use exclusively on land in 1983. Like the badge, it depicts a red fortress with a gold key. The red and white field is derived from the arms.

Montserrat

The coat of arms dates from 1909, although its origin is unknown. It shows a woman in green holding a cross and a harp. The cross is for Christianity, and the woman and harp recall Irish immigrants who settled on the island in 1632. The arms was readopted in 1962, when the West Indies Federation was dissolved.

Overseas territories (continued)

Pitcairn Islands

Adopted for the Pitcairn Islands in 1984, the badge commemorates the island's earliest settlers, the infamous crew of *HMS Bounty*, who mutinied in 1790. The badge is blue to represent the Pacific Ocean, with a green triangle symbolizing the island. The shield is charged with the Bible and the anchor of *HMS Bounty*.

Saint Helena

The current badge was made into a coat of arms in 1984. It depicts a ship flying the Cross of St. George sailing between two cliffs. Above is a wirebird representing the local fauna. The flag is also flown in the Ascension Islands and Tristan da Cunha, dependencies administered by Saint Helena.

South Georgia and South Sandwich Islands

Two of the four animals that appear on South Georgia's 1992 flag were not native: the lion, representing Britain, and the reindeer that were introduced by Norwegian whalers. The fur seal and macaroni penguin are native.

Turks and Caicos Islands

The blue ensign was granted in 1968, three years after the arms. The shield from the arms shows a conch shell and a crayfish representing fishing (the islands' main industry) and a cactus for their flora. The Turks and Caicos became a separate colony after the Bahamas achieved independence.

Military flags

Royal Navy 1864

The flag incorporates the cross of St. George and includes the Union Jack in the canton. It is flown by the British Navy and is also used by the Royal Yacht Squadron and by ships escorting the reigning British monarch.

British Army 1938

The Union Jack is the British Army's official flag, but this non-ceremonial version bearing the Monarch's insignia is used at military events and exhibitions. Sometimes the word "army" appears below the badge.

Royal Air Force 1921

The Blue Ensign bears the Royal Air Force roundel in the middle of the fly. The flag is hoisted from the flagpole of every Royal Air Force station during daylight hours and is one of the flags on permanent display at the Cenotaph war memorial in London, UK.

Royal Fleet Auxiliary 1864

The Royal Fleet Auxiliary is an amalgam of the supply and support vessels that provide logistical assistance to the Royal Navy. Its flag uses the Blue Ensign with the symbol of an anchor in the middle of the fly.

France

Adopted February 15, 1794 | **Ratio** 2:3 | **Usage** National and Civil

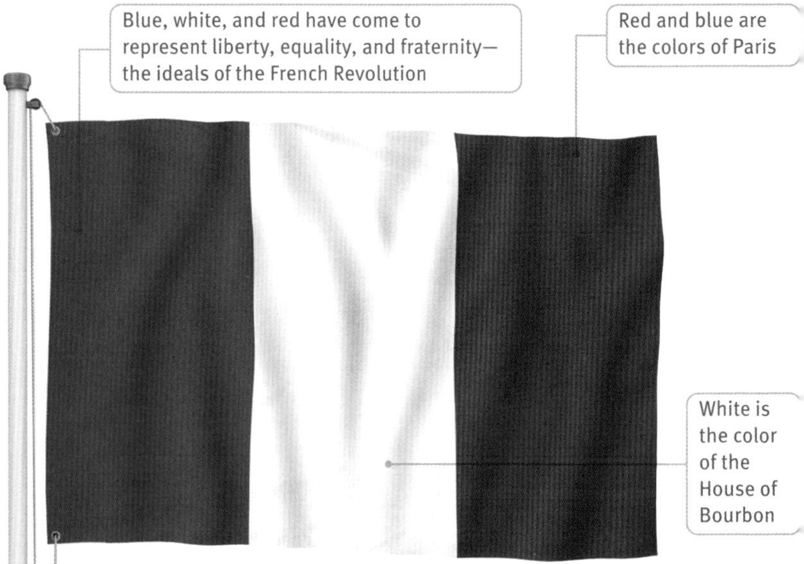
Blue, white, and red have come to represent liberty, equality, and fraternity—the ideals of the French Revolution
Red and blue are the colors of Paris
White is the color of the House of Bourbon

The traditional emblem of France was the *fleur-de-lis*, or lily, which first appeared on the arms in the 12th century.

The *Tricolore* was used during the French Revolution at the end of the 18th century and has since become a symbol of liberty around the world. Other nations have also adopted the design. Because France has no arms, the *Tricolore* is also the national emblem.

The colors are probably derived from the traditional blue and red of Paris, combined with those of the Bourbon Dynasty, though they are usually associated with liberty, equality, and fraternity.

OVERSEAS TERRITORIES

ST. PIERRE & MIQUELON

These islands lie just south of Canada's Newfoundland. The flag features the emblems of the Basques, Bretons, and Normans who settled the islands.

FRENCH POLYNESIA

Red and white are local colors. The emblem depicts a *pirogue*—a local canoe—below a rising sun. The five crew members recall the five island groups.

Luxembourg

Adopted 1848 | **Ratio** 3:5 | **Usage** National

The colors date back to the 13th century
The blue stripe is paler than that of the Netherlands

Luxembourg had no flag until 1830, when patriots were urged to display the national colors. The flag was defined as a horizontal tricolor of red, white, and blue in 1848, but it was not officially adopted until 1972. The tricolor flag is almost identical to that of the Netherlands, except that it is longer and its blue stripe is a lighter shade. The red, white, and blue coloring was derived from the Grand Duke's coat of arms, which dates from the 13th century.

THE CIVIL ENSIGN

Since 1972 a banner of the Grand Duke's arms has been used as a civil ensign for use at sea. This is a blue-and-white striped field with a lion rampant in the center.

LUXEMBOURG CIVIL ENSIGN

Red, white, and blue coloring gave rise to colors of national flag
A crowned two-tailed rampant lion

Monaco

Adopted April 4, 1881 | **Ratio** 4:5 | **Usage** National and Civil

The bicolor design is common on other national flags and is often used as a background for heraldic livery
Red and white are the heraldic colors of the Grimaldi family

The present bicolor design was adopted in 1881 under Prince Charles III. It is identical to the far younger Indonesian national flag except in its statutory proportions, which are 4:5, compared to 2:3.

The Grimaldi coat of arms, which appears on the state flag, is the traditional one of the princely family and consists of a shield supported by two monks bearing swords. The device alludes to the legend of 1297, in which the Grimaldis conquered Monaco after entering the city with soldiers disguised as monks. Earlier Monegasque flags incorporated the Grimaldi shield and crown on a white field.

ARMS OF GRIMALDIS

A princely crown
The Grimaldi motto—"*Deo Juvante*" ("With God's Help")
The collar of the Order of St. Charles surrounds a shield of red and white (or silver)
DEO JUVANTE

Andorra

Adopted August 27, 1971 | **Ratio** 7:10 | **Usage** National and Civil

The colors reflect Andorra's reliance upon France and Spain for its national security
Red and blue taken from the colors of France
Red and yellow are taken from the colors of Spain
Andorran coat of arms
VIRTVS VNITA FORTIOR

The principality of Andorra has been under Franco-Spanish protection since 1278, governed by the Counts of Foix and the Bishops of Urgel. The colors of its national flag reflect both France (blue and red) and Spain (yellow and red). The Andorran coat of arms is placed in the middle of the yellow stripe.

ARMS OF ANDORRA

Like the colors of the flag, the coat of arms also depicts the areas on which Andorra has been traditionally reliant. The quartered shield represents Urgel by the crozier and miter, Foix by the three vertical red stripes, Catalonia by the four vertical red stripes, and Béarn by the two cows.

ARMS OF ANDORRA

The crozier and miter symbolize the Bishops of Urgel
The four red stripes are taken from the arms of Catalonia
The three red stripes recall the Counts of Foix
The two cows are taken from the arms of Béarn
The motto is, "*Virtus Unita Fortior*"—"Strength united is stronger"
VIRTVS VNITA FORTIOR

Portugal

Adopted June 30, 1911 | **Ratio** 2:3 | **Usage** National and Civil

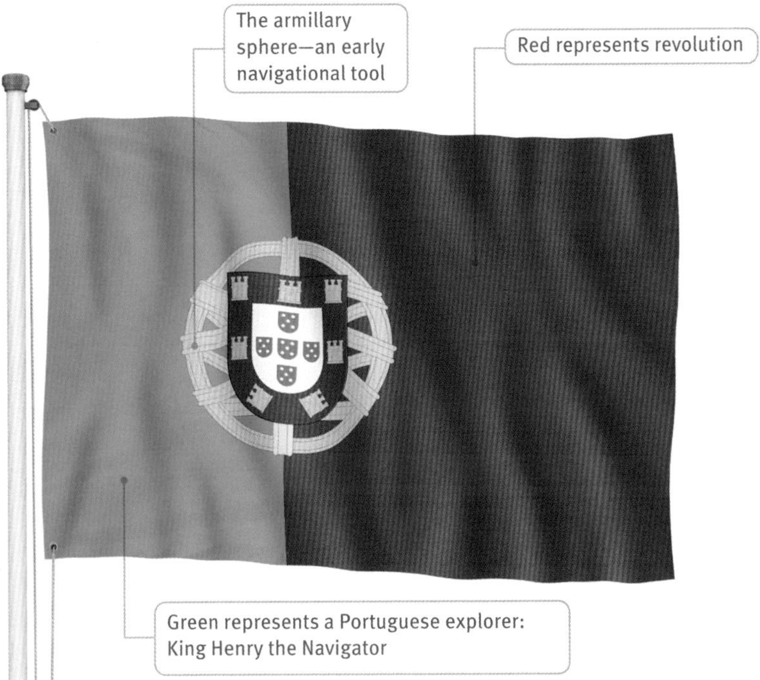
The armillary sphere—an early navigational tool
Red represents revolution
Green represents a Portuguese explorer: King Henry the Navigator

The present flag with red for revolution and green for Portuguese exploration dates from 1910. The central emblem is an armillary sphere, an early navigational instrument, on which is the former royal arms of Portugal. The white shield was first used by King Sancho I. The five blue shields recall the victory of King Afonso Henriques over five Muslim princes. The red edge and castles are representative of the marriage of King Alfonso III to Beatrice of Castile in 1252.

EMBLEM OF PORTUGAL

Five blue shields recall the victory of King Afonso Henriques
Gold castles on red recall the marriage of King Alfonso III to Beatrice of Castile
This armillary sphere and shields appear in the center of the Portuguese coat of arms
The armillary sphere recalls the importance of Portuguese exploration of the globe

Spain

Adopted July 19, 1927 | **Ratio** 2:3 | **Usage** National and Civil

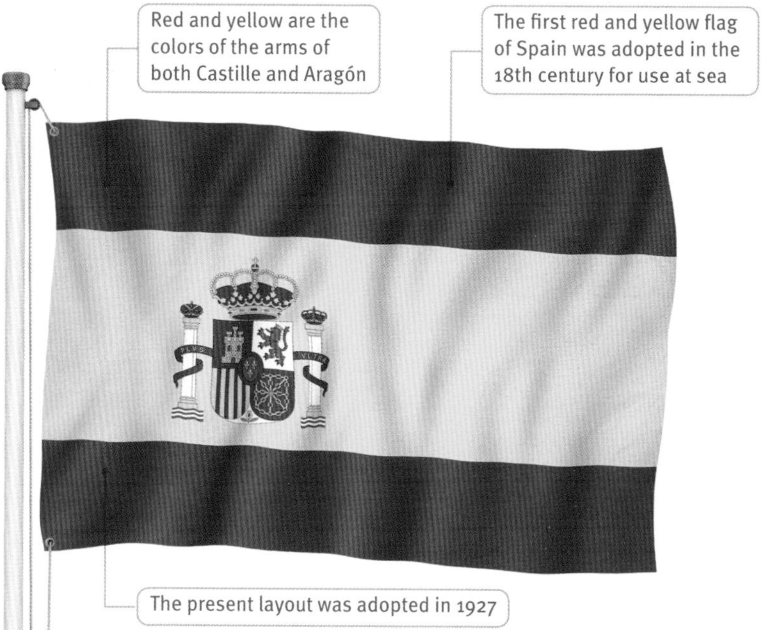
Red and yellow are the colors of the arms of both Castille and Aragón
The first red and yellow flag of Spain was adopted in the 18th century for use at sea
PLVS
VLTRA
The present layout was adopted in 1927

Early Spanish flags were mostly heraldic; some, like the flag of Castilla y León (see p.194), survive today.

In 1785 the King of Spain adopted red and yellow, a bold combination of colors then used by no other country, to distinguish Spanish ships. The present pattern was finally established in 1927.

THE SPANISH REPUBLIC

When Spain became a republic in 1931, an equal horizontal tricolor in red, yellow, and purple became the new flag. Purple was from the arms of León. At the end of the Spanish Civil War (1936–1939) the original flag was restored.

The state flag has the national arms set toward the hoist.

ARMS OF SPAIN

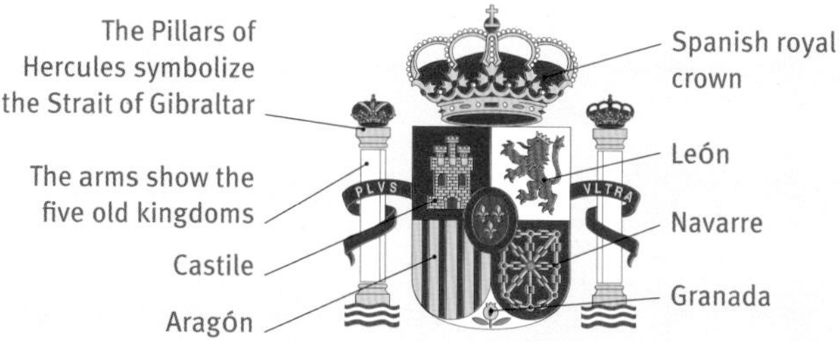
The Pillars of Hercules symbolize the Strait of Gibraltar
The arms show the five old kingdoms
Castile
Aragón
PLVS
VLTRA
Spanish royal crown
León
Navarre
Granada

Spain: Regional flags

Although most of the flags were adopted recently, all are based on older models, or traditional arms, reflecting continuity with the past.

Andalusia

Adopted in 1918, but not confirmed until 1983, the colors were those used during the Napoleonic Wars. The coat of arms depicts the Pillars of Hercules and the lions of Cadiz.

Aragón

The stripes of Aragón date from the 14th century. Legend states that a King of Aragón drew bloodstained fingers over a gold shield. The flag was adopted in 1981.

Asturias

Blue is the color of the Virgin Mary. The cross is the Cross of Victory, a traditional Asturian emblem. From it hang Greek letters, symbolizing Christ, the Beginning, and the End.

Baleares

The field is the same as the flag of Aragón, to which the islands belonged in medieval times. The canton is the emblem of Palma de Majorca, the islands' capital.

The Basque Country (País Vasco)

This flag was first adopted in 1931 and readopted in 1979. It is based on the Union Jack. Red recalls bloodshed, white the Catholic faith, and green the Oak of Guérnica.

Canary Islands (Islas Canarias)

The colors symbolize those of the Virgin Mary and the Papacy. They are also thought to evoke the blue sea, the white beaches, and the golden sun. It was adopted in 1989.

Cantabria

White and red are the traditional colors of the area. The arms allude to the seafaring customs of the people and include an ancient seal. The flag was adopted in 1981.

Castilla-la Mancha

Adopted in 1989, the deep red stripe and the castle are the emblem of Castile. The white panel is intended to recall the surcoats worn by the soldiers in the Crusades.

Regional flags (continued)

Castilla y León

This flag has been used by Castilla y León since 1248. It depicts the union of Castilla (castle) and León (lion). It was adopted for the region in 1989.

Catalonia (Catalunya)

The flag, adopted in 1932, has been used since the 13th century and has the same origin as that of Aragón. It was outlawed for political reasons from 1939 to 1975.

Extremadura

This flag was adopted in 1985, but the colors are traditional regional colors. Green is for fidelity, white for truth, and black for courage.

Galicia

Based on a traditional Galician design, white and blue are the colors of the Virgin Mary. The arms reflects loyalty to the Catholic Church.

La Rioja

The upper red stripe was originally to be in the color of Rioja wine but is now simply red. The colors are taken from the arms.

Madrid

The flag, adopted in 1983, is in the traditional color of Castilla. The seven white stars, from the arms, represent the seven districts of the region.

Murcia

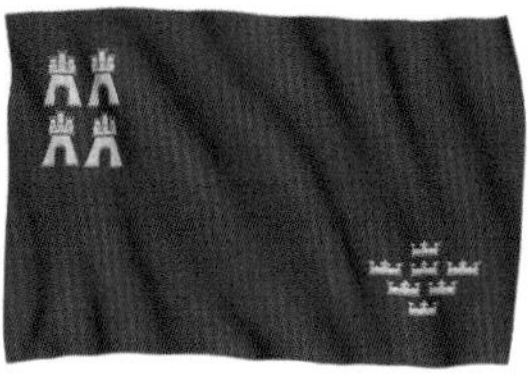

The four castles recall Murcia's links with Castilla: the seven crowns, the seven regions of the province.

Navarre

The red field and golden chains of Navarre date from the 14th century. The current flag was adopted in 1982.

Valencia

The stripes recall Valencia's links with Catalonia. The blue decorative band on the hoist side is representative of its own unique identity.

Italy

Adopted January 1, 1948 | **Ratio** 2:3 | **Usage** National

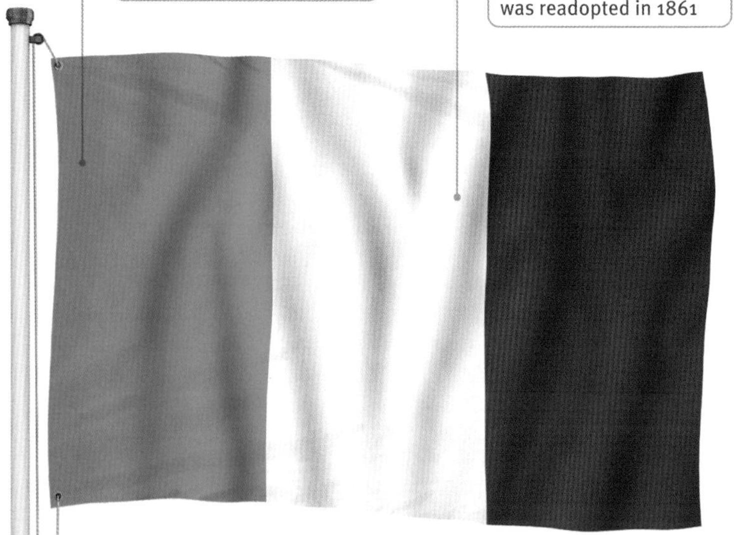
Green was said to be Napoleon's favorite color
The first vertical tricolor was used until 1814 and was readopted in 1861

The Italian tricolor comes from the standard designed by Napoleon during the Italian campaign of 1796. The coloring was influenced by the French *Tricolore*, at first appearing in horizontal bands. The vertical tricolor was introduced in 1798 but was used only until 1814. It was reintroduced when the new Kingdom of Italy was formed in 1861. When the monarchy ended in 1946, the coat of arms of the House of Savoy was removed from the flag. The present flag was officially adopted in 1948.

ITALIAN CIVIL ENSIGN

The most famous seafaring states of ancient Italy are commemorated in the quarters of the civil ensign.

ITALIAN CIVIL ENSIGN

The winged lion of St. Mark represents Venice
The Maltese cross recalls Amalfi
The Cross of St. George represents Genoa
The Pisan cross stands for Pisa

Malta

Adopted September 21, 1964 | **Ratio** 2:3 | **Usage** National

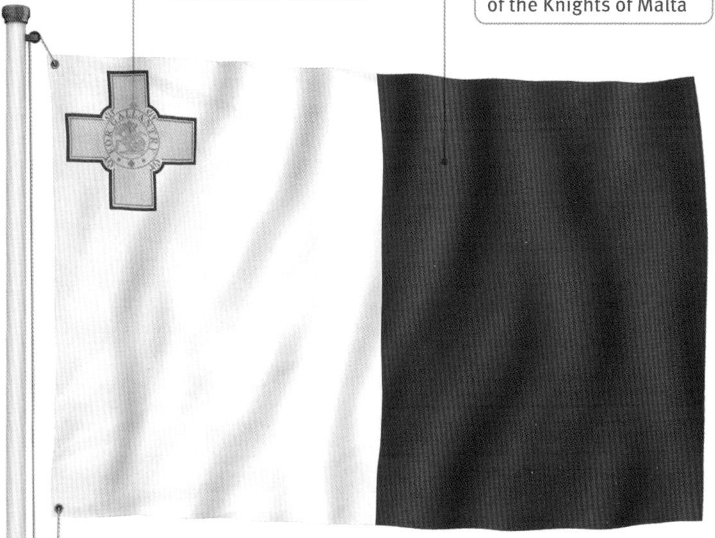
The George Cross is fimbriated with red
Red and white were adapted from the badge of the Knights of Malta

A key stronghold during the Crusades, much of the heraldry of Malta is influenced by the colors and devices of the Knights of Malta. Their badge was the characteristic Maltese cross and their arms was a white cross on a red field. From these colors came the red and white shield that was used during the colonial period. The George Cross medal was added to the shield in 1943. It was awarded to the islanders by King George VI of Britain for heroism in World War II. In 1964, the blue canton on which the cross was originally placed was replaced by a red fimbriation.

The president's flag, introduced in 1988, has the shield on a blue field with a Maltese cross in each corner.

THE PRESIDENT'S FLAG

The wreath of olive and palm branches represents peace
A gold mural crown with a sally port and eight turrets represents fortifications of Valetta
The Maltese cross
The Shield of Malta

Vatican City

Adopted June 7, 1929 | **Ratio** 1:1 | **Usage** Civil

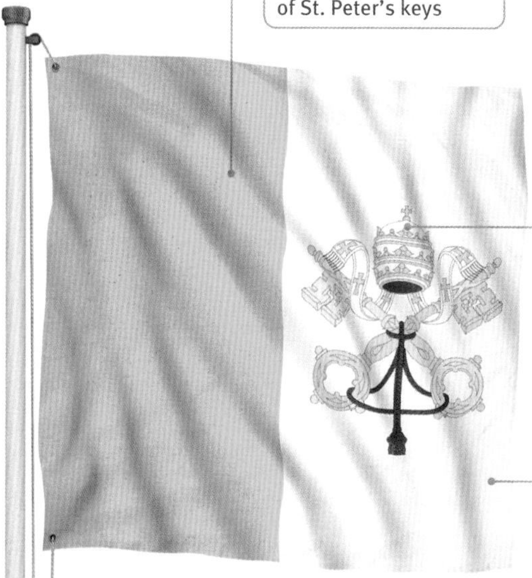
Yellow (gold) and white (iron) are the colors of St. Peter's keys
The emblem features St. Peter's keys supporting the papal crown
White and yellow were adopted as the papal colors in 1808

The modern Vatican colors were first adopted as the papal colors in 1808. The flag was used until 1870 when the Papal States were incorporated into a new unified Italy. In 1929, the Papal States were granted independent status, but their authority was confined to Vatican City. Gold and iron, represented in the flag as yellow and white, are the colors of the keys of St. Peter, which have accompanied papal arms since the Middle Ages. The flag's white stripe bears an emblem used since the 13th century to represent the Vatican's role as the headquarters of the Roman Catholic Church.

EMBLEM OF VATICAN CITY

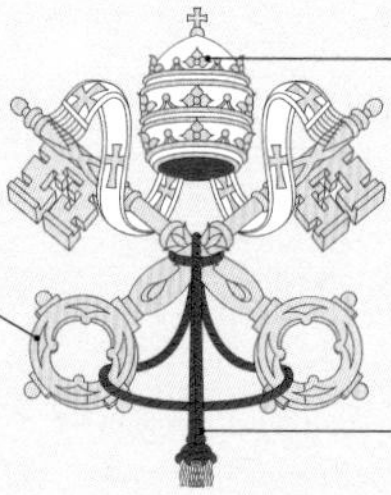
The crossed keys represent the keys to the Kingdom of Heaven bestowed by Christ on St. Peter
The triple crown signifies the three types of temporal power—legislative, executive, and judicial—vested in the Pope
A red rope binds the keys

San Marino

Adopted April 6, 1862 | **Ratio** 3:4 | **Usage** National and Civil

The colors are taken from the traditional arms, which is placed at the center of the flag for official purposes only
White represents the snow on Mt. Titano and the clouds above it
LIBERTAS
Blue recalls the sky

The flag of San Marino dates back to 1797 and was recognized by Napoleon as that of an independent state in 1799. The colors were taken from the coat of arms and were introduced in the 18th century. Blue is said to represent the sky over San Marino, and white the clouds and snow on Mt. Titano.

The traditional coat of arms is placed in the center of the flag for official purposes only. It depicts three white towers crowned with ostrich plumes, representing three citadels resting on the peak of Mt. Titano, which was once vaned with ostrich feathers. They symbolize the state's ability to defend itself.

ARMS OF SAN MARINO

A laurel wreath
The motto "*Libertas*," meaning "Liberty", also dates back to the 4th century, when the state was established as a refuge for those fleeing religious persecution
LIBERTAS
A wreath of oak
The towers represent the three citadels, Guaita, Cesta, and Montale, situated on Mt. Titano

Switzerland

Adopted December 12, 1889 | **Ratio** 1:1 | **Usage** National and Civil

The red field with a white cross was adapted from the flag of Schwyz, one of the original three cantons
The Swiss and Vatican flags are the only square national flags
A white couped cross

The flag of Switzerland is one of the most iconic European flags. In the medieval era, many European states used a plain flag with a cross.

A FLAG FOR THE CONFEDERATION

For many years, the separate cantons of Switzerland had no one common flag but were each represented by its own flag. The present flag of Switzerland, a white couped cross on a red field, was based on that of Schwyz, one of the three original provinces that united into a confederation against the Holy Roman Empire in 1291. It became accepted as the common badge of the Confederation in 1339 at the Battle of Laupen, when it was used to distinguish the soldiers of the Confederation from other soldiers and became the accepted flag of the Confederation in 1480. It was not officially confirmed as the flag of Switzerland until 1848, and it was last regulated in 1889.

Apart from that of the Vatican, the Swiss flag is the only totally square national flag. However, when used on the Swiss lakes, it has the ratio of 2:3—a practice adopted in 1941.

THE NATIONAL ARMS

The coat of arms is simply a shield in the form of the flag. It was officially adopted in 1889. Every town or commune in Switzerland has its own flag and coat of arms.

Switzerland: Canton flags

In every case, the flags are based on the arms of the canton, some of which predate the canton's joining the Swiss Confederation.

Aargau

Adopted in 1803, the white waves on black represent the River Aare, and the white stars on blue, the districts of Baden, the Free Areas, and Fricktal, which came together to form the canton. In 1963, it was decreed that the stars should be arranged two on top and one below.

Appenzell Ausser-Rhoden

Adopted in 1597, when the canton separated from the Inner-Rhoden, the flag retained the bear but added the initials VR (for Ussroden). The bear dates back to medieval banners. It was used from 1403 in battles against feudal landlords.

Appenzell Inner-Rhoden

This is the original form of the flag before the partition from Appenzell Ausser-Rhoden in 1597. The bear emblem was widely used locally in the Middle Ages and was taken by the Appenzellers from the arms of the abbey of Sankt Gallen.

Basel-Land

Basel-Land separated from the City in 1832. The arms and flag were adopted in 1834, based on the form of crosier used in Liestal, with the crook turned to the right and decorated with small spheres. This was made official in 1947.

Canton flags (continued)

Basel-Stadt

The emblem of Basel-Stadt is the headpiece of a bishop's crosier. The emblem dates back to the earliest days of heraldry. Since the 15th century, it has been depicted as black on white. It was kept in this form when the canton was divided in 1832.

Bern

The coat of arms dates back to the 12th century. Soon after, the arms, which depict a bear on a red field with a yellow diagonal, became the canton's banner. There have, however, been many variant forms through the ages. The bear represents the name of the canton.

Fribourg

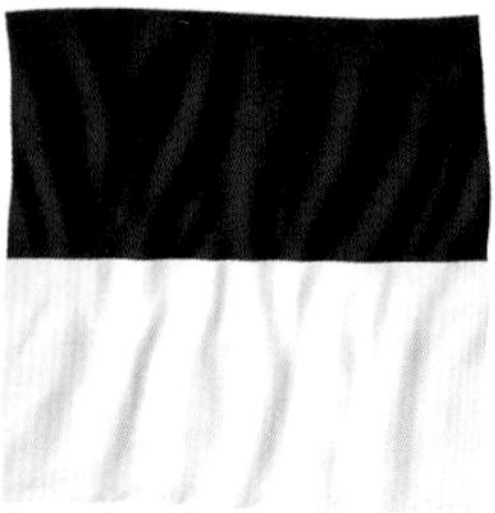

The original colors of Fribourg, black and white, were readopted when it joined the Confederation in 1831, but the colors actually date back to 1410 and are related to the coat of arms.

Geneva

The eagle recalls the former Holy Roman Empire. The key is the Key of St. Peter and shows Geneva as the key to western Switzerland. The flag was adopted in 1815.

Glarus

The flag of Glarus depicts the figure of St. Fridolin, the patron saint of the canton, on a red field. The flag was adopted when the canton joined the Confederation in 1352.

Graubunden

The flag includes symbols for the three original parts of the canton that united in the 15th century: Graubunden, Zehgerichtenbund, and the Gotteshausbund.

Jura

This flag was adopted 1978, when Jura became a separate canton. It was formerly part of Basel-Land—recalled by the crosier—and Bern. The stripes are from the arms of Jura.

Lucerne

Lucerne was the first canton, after the original three, to join the Confederation in 1332. Its flag has the colors of its shield arranged horizontally instead of vertically.

Canton flags (continued)

Neuchâtel

The tricolor was used as a revolutionary banner before being adopted in 1848. The white cross was added to show the canton's association with Switzerland.

Nidwalden

The key with two wards is the emblem of St. Peter and was used in the 15th century. It was retained when the canton divided in 1815.

Obwalden

The red and white flag was used in Obwalden from the 13th century, and it was adopted when the separate canton was formed in 1815. Moreover, a key was added in 1816.

Sankt Gallen

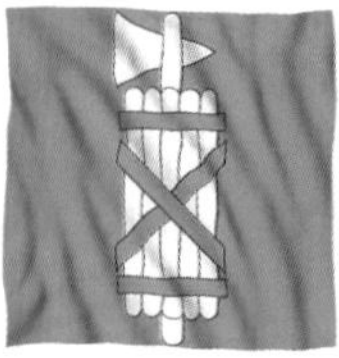

The emblems of Sankt Gallen—an ax and a fasces—were adopted in 1803 when the canton was formed under French influence. They are both symbols of republicanism.

Schaffhausen

The emblem has been in use since the 14th century. It depicts a ram (the "sheep" of the town's name) on a yellow field. The flag's existence was first recorded as early as 1386.

Schwyz

Schwyz was one of the first three cantons, and the one from which the country takes its name. Its solid red design existed before the Confederation was formed in 1291.

Solothurn

The coat of arms dates back to 1394 and has colors derived from those of the Confederation. The flag was originally red with a white cross but was simplified into its current form.

Thurgau

The flag of Thurgau, adopted in 1803, depicts two gold lions arranged diagonally. They are taken from the coat of arms, which dates from the medieval era.

Ticino

The colors of Ticino's flag may be derived from the French *Tricolore*, or from the main colors of the arms of the united townships.

Uri

The emblem is an auroch's head (linked to the canton's name). It dates from the 13th century, but the nose ring was added later.

Canton flags (continued)

Valais

The modern flag of Valais is derived from that of the original republic, which had seven stars for its component townships. These were increased to 12 in 1802 and retained when the state joined the Confederation in 1814.

Vaud

The colors date from 1798 when the Léman Republic was formed, and stand for freedom. They were retained when the state entered the Confederation in 1803. The motto is "*Liberté et Patrie*" ("Freedom and Fatherland").

Zug

Zug joined the Confederation in 1352 and again in 1364, after a brief return to Habsburg rule. The colors of the flag were originally red-white-red of Austria but were altered to the blue and white from the arms of the Counts of Lenzburg in 1352.

Zürich

The flag in this case preceded the arms and dates back to the 13th century. It was adopted in 1351 when Zürich joined the Confederation. However, since 1957, it has been compulsory to depict the flag in the same format as the shield.

Liechtenstein

Adopted June 24, 1937 | **Ratio** 3:5 | **Usage** National and Civil

The yellow crown was introduced to distinguish Liechtenstein as a principality
Royal blue and red have been used to represent the country of Liechtenstein since the 18th century

The red and blue of Liechtenstein's flag date from the mid-19th century but were formalized into the constitution only in 1921. In 1937, the crown was introduced to the flag, both to establish Liechtenstein's status as a principality and to distinguish it from the flag of Haiti, which uses the same colors. The flag can be hung vertically or horizontally, but the crown always remains upright.

THE PRINCE'S FLAG

The arms of Silesia, Künringen, Troppau, and East Friesland and Rietburg make up the four quarters of the shield of the Prince's arms, in the center of his flag. They represent the noble ancestors of the prince.

THE FLAG OF PRINCE OF LIECHTENSTEIN

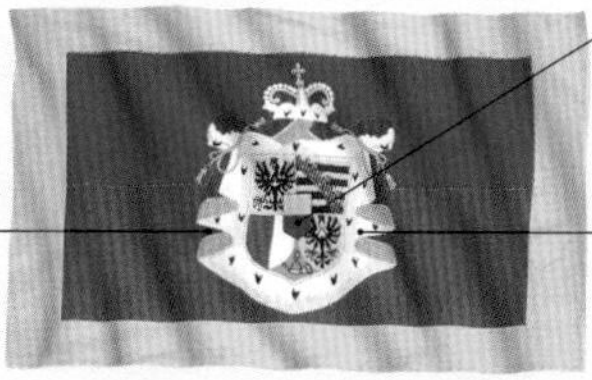
The inner shield represents the ancient princely family
Red and yellow are the Prince's colors
The four arms within the Prince's Arms represent his noble ancestors

Austria

Adopted Circa 1230 | **Ratio** 2:3 | **Usage** National and Civil

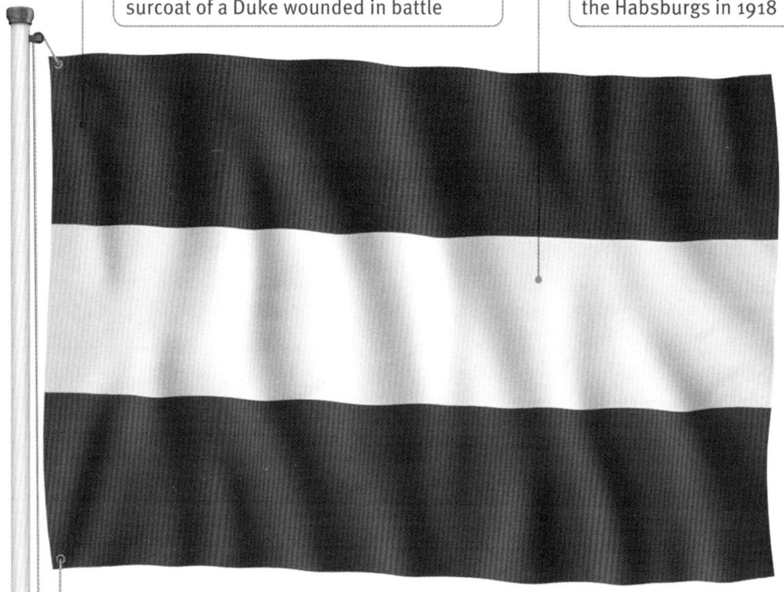
According to legend, the red-and-white flag was modeled after the bloodstained surcoat of a Duke wounded in battle
The traditional flag, retained after the fall of the Habsburgs in 1918

Legend states that Duke Leopold V of Austria once fought so fiercely in battle that the white surcoat he wore was soaked in blood, except for the part covered by his sword belt. So he adopted red, with a white band across the center, as his colors.

ONE OF THE WORLD'S OLDEST FLAGS

The story is probably apocryphal, but stripes of red-white-red have been an emblem of Austria for over 800 years. Their use on a flag was recorded in 1191, making the Austrian flag one of the world's oldest flags. It was officially adopted as the national flag after the fall of the Habsburg Dynasty, and the formation of a republic in 1918. During the Second World War, the Austrian flag and arms were banned; they were restored in 1945.

ARMS OF AUSTRIA

The coat of arms depicts an imperial black eagle, an emblem used by the Habsburgs. It originally had two heads, but they were changed to one when the Habsburg Empire disintegrated. On the eagle's chest is a shield in the national colors. The eagle holds a hammer and sickle recalling agricultural and industrial workers. Its crown, with three turrets, also represents agriculture, industry, and commerce. The broken chains on the eagle's feet symbolize the restoration of freedom.

Austria: State flags

Most provincial flags in Austria are based on the local arms. In many cases, they existed before their official adoption.

Burgenland

The colors of the flag, officially hoisted in 1971, are based on the red eagle and yellow shield of the arms.

Carinthia

Adopted in 1946, the colors are derived from those of the Austrian flag and the yellow state shield.

Lower Austria

Adopted in 1954, the colors are based on the arms that contains a blue shield and five gold eagles.

Salzburg

The flag, adopted in 1921, uses the traditional colors of the state, which are the national colors.

Styria

The coat of arms of Styria is a green shield bearing a white lion. The flag, adopted in 1960, uses these colors.

State flags (continued)

Tyrol

The bicolored flag is derived from the arms that depicts a red eagle on a white disc. It was adopted in 1945.

Upper Austria

Upper Austria's flag, adopted in 1949, is derived from the national colors and the arms of the province.

Vienna

The flag dates from 1946. It is based on the city's arms but is identical to the flags of Salzburg and Vorarlberg.

Vorarlberg

Like the flags of Salzburg and Vienna, Vorarlberg's bicolor flag is based on the provincial arms.

Hungary

Adopted October 1, 1957 | **Ratio** 1:2 | **Usage** National and Civil

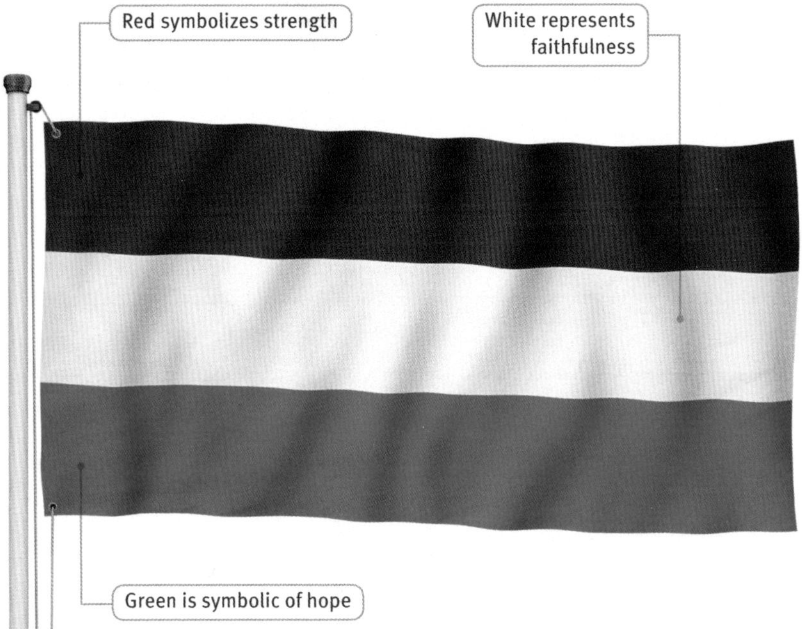
Red symbolizes strength
White represents faithfulness
Green is symbolic of hope

The current flag was first used in the 1848–1849 uprising. Its pattern was derived from the French *Tricolore* used during the French Revolution. The colors—red, white, and green—date back to the 9th century. They were first used in 1608 during the reign of King Matthias II. Until 1945, the royal crown was featured in the center of the national flag. During Hungary's brief period as a republic from 1945–1949 the royal crown was replaced by the "*Kossuth*" coat of arms. When the Communists took power, they added a Soviet-style emblem to the flag. In 1990, the arms of the kingdom were readopted, but they were not replaced on the flag.

ARMS OF HUNGARY

The red and white stripes probably originated from Spain in the late 12th or early 13th century
The crown of St. Stephen, the first king of Hungary
The patriarchal cross was added to the Hungarian arms about 800 years ago

Czechia (Czech Republic)

Adopted March 30, 1920 | **Ratio** 2:3 | **Usage** National and Civil

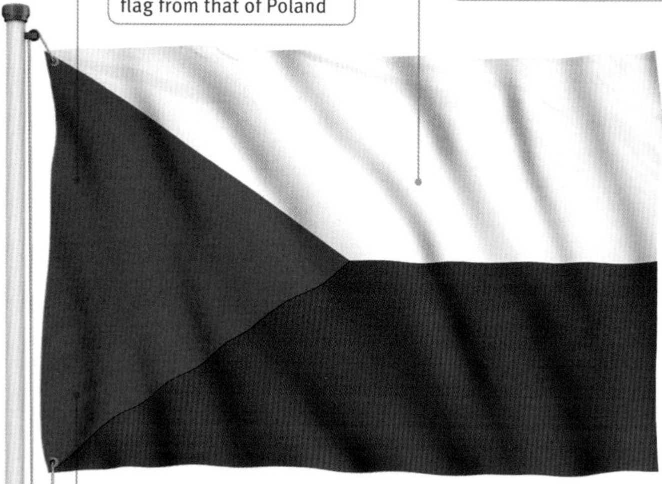
The blue triangle was added to distinguish the flag from that of Poland
White and red are the heraldic colors of Bohemia
Blue represents the state of Moravia

The first flag of Czechoslovakia was based on the arms and was white over red. This was identical to the flag of Poland, so a blue triangle was added at the hoist. The flag was banned by the Nazis in 1938, and a horizontal tricolor of white, red, and blue was enforced. The original flag was restored in 1949.

THE NEW CZECH REPUBLIC
When Czechoslovakia separated into the Czech Republic and Slovakia in 1993, the Czechs decided to keep their existing flag, recalling the two principal parts of the country.

The greater coat of arms depicts a quartered shield reflecting the regions of Czechia.

GREATER ARMS OF CZECHIA

The white lion on a red field is the traditional emblem of Bohemia
The red-and-white eagle on a blue field is from the arms of Moravia
The black eagle on a yellow field is taken from the arms of Silesia
The Bohemian arms are repeated to fill the shield

Slovakia

Adopted September 3, 1992 | **Ratio** 2:3 | **Usage** National and Civil

A version of this flag was first used in the 19th century
White, blue, and red are Pan-Slavic colors
The arms of Slovakia

The first Slovak flags, used during the 19th century, were like the contemporary Russian flag, to whom they looked for aid in gaining independence. As Czechoslovakia, a red and white flag with a blue triangle was used. During the Second World War, Slovakia readopted the white, blue, and red tricolor, with the arms in the center.

ARMS OF SLOVAKIA

The arms uses colors of the early flags, a white patriarchal cross rising from blue mountains on a red shield.

On gaining independence in 1993, the red, white, and blue tricolor was retained as the national flag, but the arms was placed toward the hoist.

The President's flag has the arms, bordered by the national colors.

THE PRESIDENT'S FLAG

The flag is bordered by stripes in the national colors—white, blue, and red
A patriarchal cross
A stylized image of Slovakia's mountains

Slovenia

Adopted June 25, 1991 | **Ratio** 1:2 | **Usage** National and Civil

The order of the tricolor is the same as the flag for Slovenia, when it was part of Yugoslavia
The coat of arms was added in 1991 when Slovenia became independent

Slovenia has been at the crossroads of many cultures and empires for centuries but finally emerged as an independent state in 1991 following the breakup of the former Yugoslavia.

The colors are derived from the arms of the Duchy of Caniola, and the tricolor of white, blue, and red was first used in 1848 as a revolutionary banner. After gaining independence, Slovenia placed its arms in the upper hoist of this tricolor, to create a distinct national flag.

The arms depicts mountain peaks, above wavy blue lines symbolizing the sea coast. The stars are from the arms of the Duchy of Selje.

ARMS OF SLOVENIA

The wavy lines symbolize Slovenia's sea coast
The three stars are from the arms of the former Duchy of Selje
The three mountain peaks represent the Triglav, part of the Alps

Croatia

Adopted December 21, 1991 | **Ratio** 1:2 | **Usage** National and Civil

Red, white, and blue are traditional Croatian colors
Arms of Croatia
The tricolor charged with the coat of arms was first used during the Second World War

While part of Yugoslavia, Croatia's flag was designed in the Pan-Slavic colors, red, white, and blue. These are also traditional Croatian colors used in the 19th century.

During the Second World War, Croatia became a semi-independent state and added the arms of Croatia to the center of its flag. Following the war, Croatia retained its tricolor, but the arms was replaced by a gold-edged red star on the orders of Tito, the leader of Yugoslavia at that time. Before gaining independence, the present flag was adopted, based on the one used during the war.

The shield of Croatia is in the red and white checks. Above is a row of shields of its various territories.

ARMS OF CROATIA

The red and white checks are traditional emblems of Croatia
The small shields at the top are taken from the arms of Croatia's regions: the ancient arms of Croatia, Dubrovnik, Dalmatia, Istria, and Slavonia (from left to right)

Bosnia & Herzegovina

Adopted February 4, 1998 | **Ratio** 1:2 | **Usage** National and Civil

The dark blue and yellow, and the stars, refer to the flag of Europe
The flag was imposed by the international High Representative
The geographical shape of Bosnia is a triangle

After Bosnia-Herzegovina broke away from Yugoslavia in 1992, a neutral plain white flag was adopted by Parliament. The country's independence triggered a civil war between the country's three ethnic groups—Muslims, Croats, and Serbs. After the Dayton, OH, peace agreement was signed in 1995, the "neutral" Bosnian flag became unacceptable to the Croats and Serbs. In February 1998, the international High Representative, who safeguards the peace in Bosnia-Herzegovina, imposed a new flag. However, it was designed by a committee with members from all three ethnic groups.

The country's coat of arms was adopted in 1998, replacing the design that had been in use since 1992.

BOSNIA-CROAT FEDERATION FLAG

The shield's shape alludes to the shape of the country
Three-pointed shield recalls the country's three main ethnic groups

Montenegro

Adopted July 13, 2004 | **Ratio** 1:2 | **Usage** National and Civil

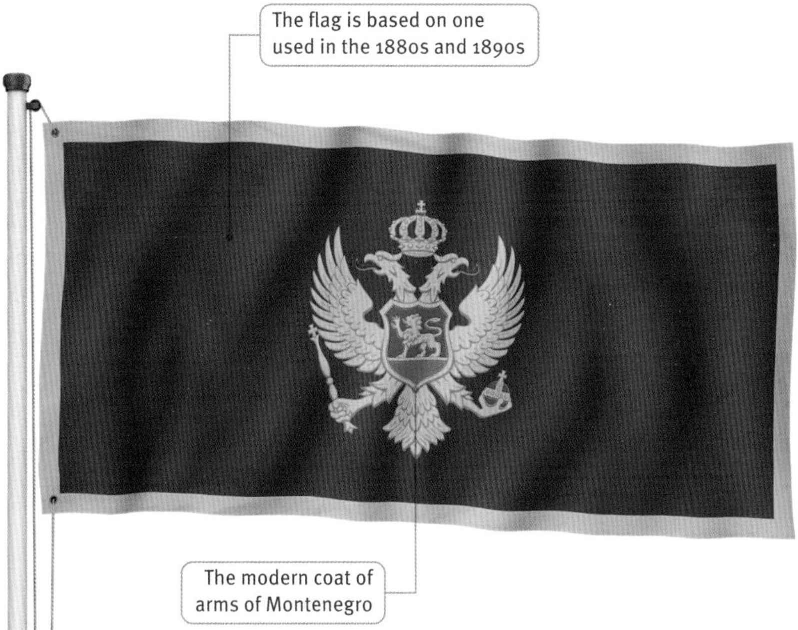
The flag is based on one used in the 1880s and 1890s
The modern coat of arms of Montenegro

Long an independent kingdom, Montenegro, like the other Yugoslav states, had used the Pan-Slav colors. Montenegro, like Serbia, inverted the Russian flag into a horizontal tricolor of red, blue, and white. In 1914, it was accepted that the royal monogram of King Nikola should be added to the flag. In the communist state (1946–1991), the monogram was replaced by a gold-edged red star. With the end of communist rule, the star was removed. To distinguish the flag from that of Serbia, the blue was made lighter. In 2004, the present—and completely different—flag was adopted.

NATIONAL FLAG IN 1914

POST-COMMUNIST FLAG

Serbia

Adopted November 11, 2010 | **Ratio** 2:3 | **Usage** National and Civil

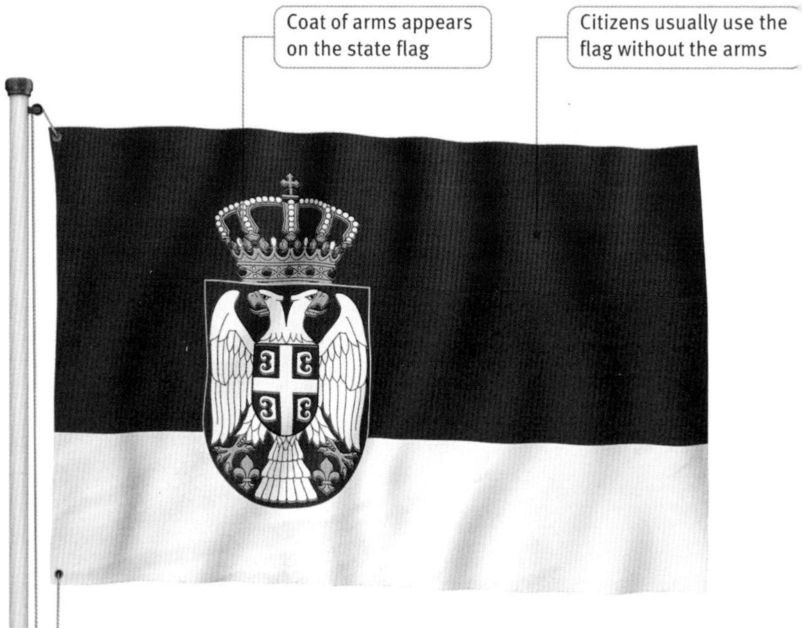
Coat of arms appears on the state flag
Citizens usually use the flag without the arms

Like other countries in the region, Serbia used the Pan-Slav colors by inverting the Russian flag.

When Serbia became part of newly formed Yugoslavia in 1946, it kept its own flag, but a gold-edged red star was added to the center. After the break up of Yugoslavia in 1991, and following an inconclusive referendum, the star was removed and by 2004 the Serbian coat of arms had been added.

This form became official after the final separation of Serbia and Montenegro in 2006.

The arms features a white double-headed eagle, representing strength and power, on a red shield. The current version was redesigned in 2010.

FLAG OF YUGOSLAVIA (1919–2006)

FLAG OF SERBIA IN COMMUNIST YUGOSLAVIA (1946–1992)

Kosovo

Adopted February 17, 2008 | **Ratio** 5:7 | **Usage** National and Civil

Blue and yellow are from the European Union Flag, while white is for peace
Six stars are for the six communities in Kosovo
Golden map of county outline on a blue field

In September, 2008, Kosovo controversially declared its independence from Serbia.

The flag is a result of an international competition, which produced a short list of three designs for consideration. Of these, one by Muhamer Ibrahimi was adapted to create the new flag.

The modified version has six white stars that represent Kosovo's six main ethnic groups, arranged in an arc above a golden map of Kosovo.

The flag is unusual for using a map of the nation it represents, with the flag of Cyprus being the only other national flag to use the same device.

The arms of Kosovo mirror the flag design with the white stars and golden map set on a blue, gold-edged shield.

ARMS OF KOSOVO

The arms is a shield in the same design as the flag

Albania

Adopted April 7, 1992 | **Ratio** 5:7 | **Usage** National

The traditional heraldic Albanian flag first used in 1912 when independence was restored

Albanians call their country, *Shqipëria*, meaning "land of the eagle"

The black eagle first appeared on the Albanian flag in the 15th century when Albania became part of the Byzantine Empire. According to legend, the Albanians are the descendants of the eagle. The red flag, with the eagle in the center, was adopted in 1912, when independence was restored. Parts of the Italian arms were included on the flag after the invasion of 1939, but the original flag was restored in 1942.

In 1946, the flag changed again, to incorporate a gold-edged red star above the eagle, representing the Communist regime. The star was removed in 1991, by order of the new multiparty government.

ARMS OF ALBANIA

The black eagle has been an emblem of Albania since the 15th century

The two-headed eagle first appeared on flags used during the struggle against Turkish occupation

North Macedonia

Adopted October 5, 1995 | **Ratio** 1:2 | **Usage** National and Civil

Red was the traditional color of the Macedonian flag
The radiant sun was added in 1995 to replace the controversial "Star of Vergina"

As part of Yugoslavia, Macedonia was the only region not to use the Pan-Slavic colors. Its flag was red, with a gold-edged red star in the canton.

A CONTROVERSIAL NEW FLAG

At independence in 1992, the country retained its red flag but added a gold star in a gold sun. This was soon changed to the Star of Vergina, an ancient Macedonian emblem from the tomb of Philip of Macedon, father of Alexander the Great. Greece objected to this, claiming the star as a Greek emblem. In 1995, the star was replaced by a radiant sun.

North Macedonia's arms is similar in design to former Soviet emblems.

ARMS OF NORTH MACEDONIA

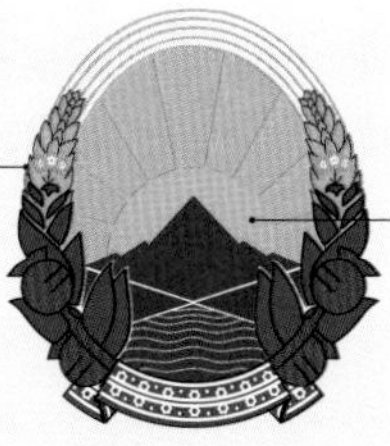
Symmetrical wreaths of wheat
A radiant sun, also used on the national flag

Bulgaria

Adopted November 22, 1990 | **Ratio** 3:5 | **Usage** National and Civil

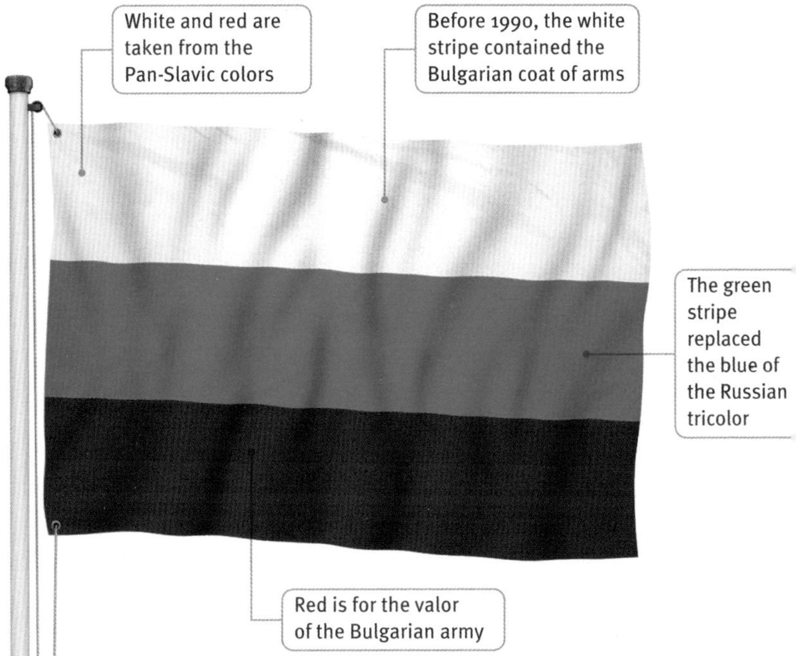
White and red are taken from the Pan-Slavic colors
Before 1990, the white stripe contained the Bulgarian coat of arms
The green stripe replaced the blue of the Russian tricolor
Red is for the valor of the Bulgarian army

While under Turkish rule, Bulgaria had no national flag. When it became a principality in 1878, a slight variation of the Pan-Slavic colors, widely used during the independence movements of the late 19th century, was adopted. The horizontal arrangement of the tricolor was based on the Russian flag at the time, but for Bulgaria's national flag, the central blue stripe was substituted by green.

THE PEOPLE'S REPUBLIC

No change was made to the flag during Bulgaria's period as an independent kingdom 1908–1946, but with the formation of the People's Republic in 1947, a coat of arms was added in the white stripe near the hoist. This depicted a rampant lion, a red star representing Communism, and later a cogwheel symbolizing industrialization. The coat of arms was removed from the flag in 1990 because of its Communist connotations. No arms now appear on the flag.

THE SYMBOLISM OF THE COLORS

Although based on the Pan-Slavic colors, the white band is said to represent a love of peace, and red, the valor of the people. The green stripe, substituted for the traditional Pan-Slavic blue in 1878, was intended to represent the youthfulness of the emerging nation.

Greece

Adopted January 13, 1822 | **Ratio** 2:3 | **Usage** National and Civil

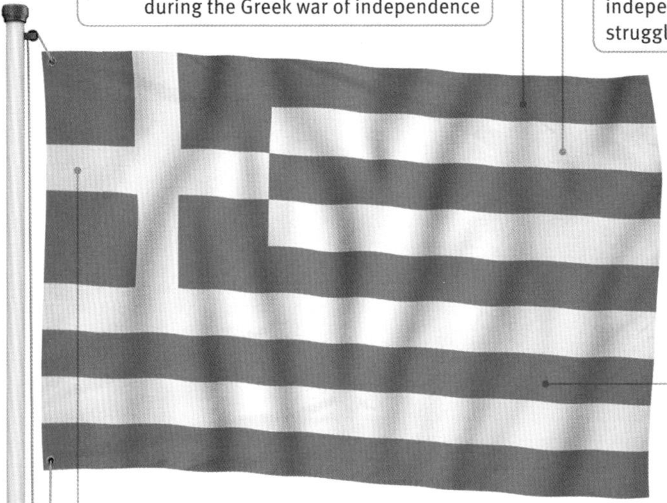
The nine stripes represent the nine syllables in the cry "Freedom or Death," uttered during the Greek war of independence
White reflects the purity of the Greek independence struggle
Blue represents the sea and sky
The cross in the canton represents Greek religious faith

The flag flown by Greece is in the same colors as the one that was raised following independence from the Ottoman Empire in the early 19th century. At times, Greece has used a plain white cross on blue as its land flag and the striped flag at sea. Today the plain Cross Flag is preserved in the president's flag and in the canton of the blue-and-white striped national flag.

The shade of blue of the flag has also varied. Today, it is the original light blue color of 1822. It was altered in the 1970s and the blue was changed to a much darker, navy shade.

THE PRESIDENT'S FLAG

The original white cross on a blue field is retained in the president's flag and the national arms
A wreath of laurels surrounds the Cross flag

Romania

Adopted December 27, 1989 | **Ratio** 2:3 | **Usage** National and Civil

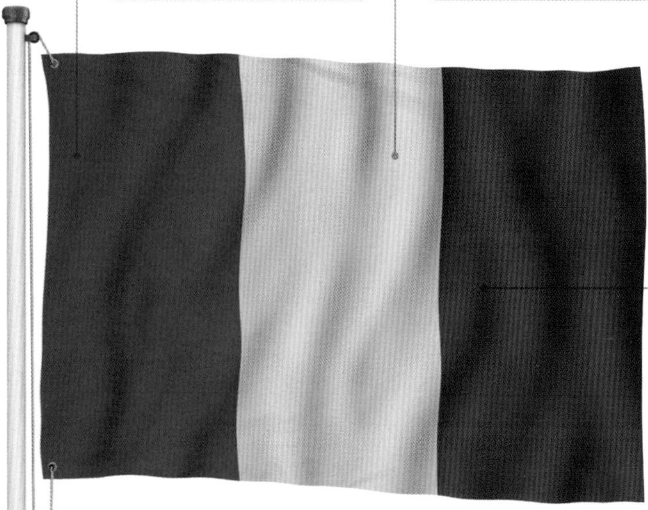
Blue formed part of the province of Moldavia's flag
Yellow formed part of the province of Wallachia's flag
Red was featured in the flags of both Moldavia and Wallachia and is the color of Romanian unity

The current flag was created in 1848 by combining the colors of Wallachia and Moldavia–the Ottoman provinces that made up Romania. In 1867, the Royal Arms was set in the yellow stripe. The coat of arms was modified many times, and in 1948, it was replaced with a Communist emblem. This was jettisoned following the fall of the Ceausescu regime in 1989.

NEW NATIONAL ARMS

In 1992, the old coat of arms was restored by the new parliament. It features a combination of motifs that look back to Romania's past as a powerful medieval state.

ARMS OF ROMANIA

The eagle grips an Eastern Orthodox cross in its beak
Sword recalls St. Stephen the Great of Moldavia
The scepter of St. Michael the Brave of Wallachia
The smaller shield displays the arms of some of Romania's provinces

Moldova

Adopted April 27, 1990 | **Ratio** 1:2 | **Usage** National and Civil

The blue, yellow, and red colors reflect strong links with Romania
The arms of Moldova

The blue, red, and yellow tricolor of Moldova is almost identical to the Romanian flag, reflecting the two countries' cultural affinity.

ARMS OF MOLDOVA

On Moldova's flag, the yellow stripe is charged with the national arms. Like the Romanian coat of arms, the Moldovan arms, adopted in 1990, features a golden eagle holding an Eastern Orthodox cross in its beak. However, instead of a sword, the eagle is holding an olive branch. The blue and red shield on the eagle's breast is also different–on it are an ox's head, a star, a rose, and a crescent–all traditional symbols of Moldova.

THE ARMS OF MOLDOVA

A star
A rose
An olive branch symbolizing peace
An eagle holds an Eastern Orthodox cross, similar to that in the arms of Romania
A crescent
An ox's head

Belarus

Adopted June 7, 1995 | **Ratio** 1:2 | **Usage** National and Civil

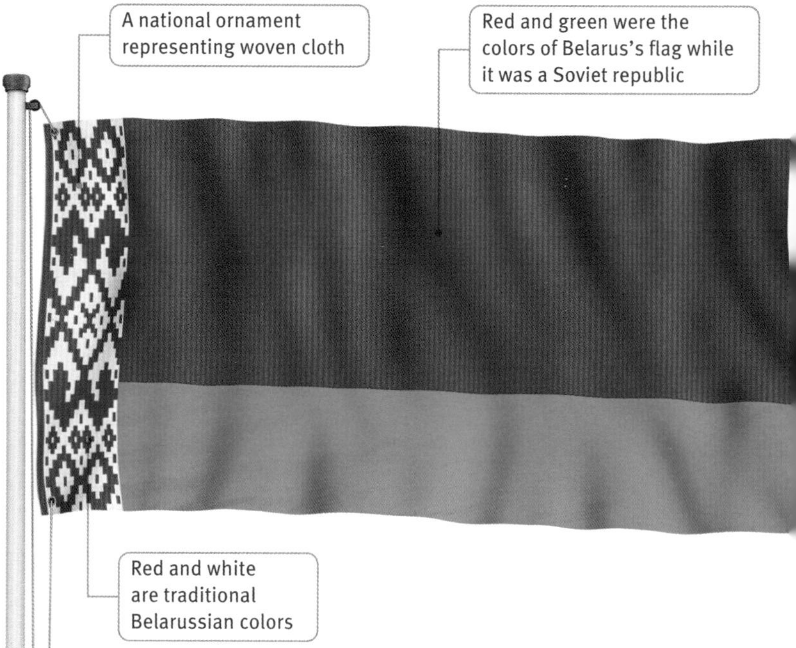
A national ornament representing woven cloth
Red and green were the colors of Belarus's flag while it was a Soviet republic
Red and white are traditional Belarussian colors

The original flag of Belarus while under Soviet administration in 1922 was similar to that of the USSR. It was changed in 1951, and the flag used today is similar to this second flag, except that the Communist hammer, sickle, and star have been removed, and the red and white portions of the hoist ornamentation have been reversed.

A REVISED DESIGN

Following independence from the USSR in 1991, Belarus adopted a flag of three equal horizontal stripes of white-red-white. This was the same flag that had been associated with a brief period of Belarussian independence in 1918, and its colors were derived from the arms of the republic. The design was rejected in a referendum in 1995.

The flag of Belarus, adopted following the referendum, reflects its growing ties with Russia. The unusual ornamentation in the hoist is described as a national ornament and represents woven cloth.

ARMS OF BELARUS

The Soviet-style coat of arms, retained on gaining independence, also reflects the dominant Russian influence. This depicts an outline of the state against a sun rising from behind a globe. This is entirely surrounded by wreaths of wheat and flowers.

Ukraine

Adopted January 28, 1992 | **Ratio** 2:3 | **Usage** National and Civil

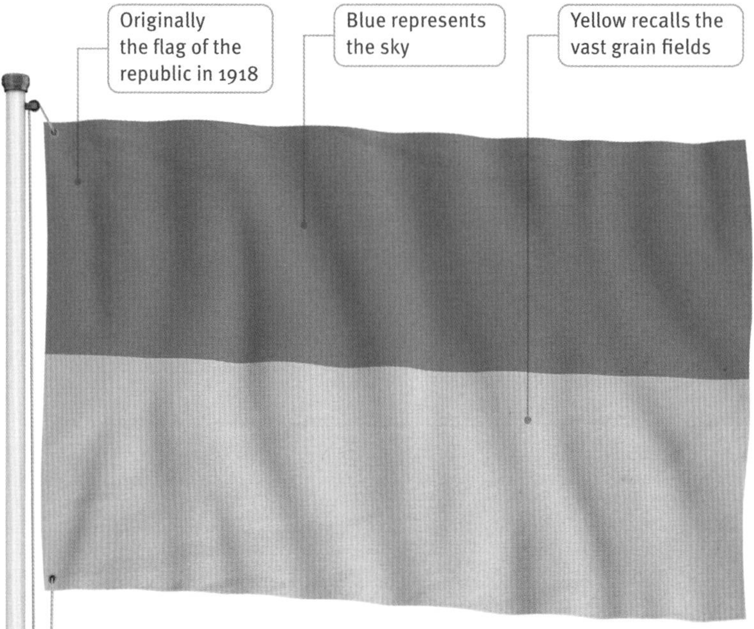
Originally the flag of the republic in 1918
Blue represents the sky
Yellow recalls the vast grain fields

The bicolored flag flown in Ukraine today was the official flag of the country in 1918 when Ukraine enjoyed a brief period of independence. With the invasion of the Red Army, the flag was suppressed until the German occupation of 1941–1944. After the war, it was banned again by the Soviet Union. When Ukraine gained its independence in 1991, the country readopted its original flag. Blue represents the sky and yellow the vast fields of grain of the country's agriculture.

The Ukrainian coat of arms is in the national colors and features an ancient trident symbol.

ARMS OF UKRAINE

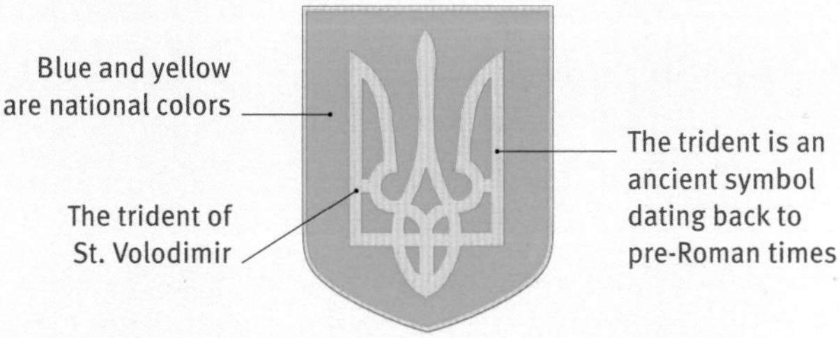
Blue and yellow are national colors
The trident of St. Volodimir
The trident is an ancient symbol dating back to pre-Roman times

Russia

Adopted December 11, 1993 | **Ratio** 2:3 | **Usage** National and Civil

The colors of the flag were orginally the colors of Moscow; white, blue, and red are Pan-Slavic colors

Since its official adoption in 1799, the Russian tricolor has had a major influence on other east European flags

At the end of the 17th century, Czar Peter the Great of Russia visited western Europe. Following this visit, he decided to adopt a variation of the Dutch flag as a civil ensign for Russian ships. This was a horizontal tricolor of white, blue, and red. It was only officially recognized in 1799. Peter the Great also adopted a flag for the Russian navy, which was white with the blue diagonal Cross of St. Andrew.

THE PAN-SLAVIC COLORS

Both the color and tricolor design of this first flag had a major influence on many of the flags of eastern European nations during the 19th century, who looked to Russia for help in liberating them from foreign domination. They have since become known as the Pan-Slavic colors.

THE HAMMER, SICKLE, AND STAR

After the Russian Revolution of 1917, the Communists abolished all former flags and instead adopted the Red Flag as the flag of the Soviet Union. This contained a gold hammer and sickle—symbols of the proletariat and the peasants—under a gold-edged red star, to represent unity. As a Soviet republic, Russia used this flag with a vertical blue bar at the hoist. When the Soviet Union collapsed in 1991, the former flags of Russia, including the white, blue, and red tricolor were restored.

Republic flags

Unlike many other countries, the flags of the Russian republics are all new, adopted since 1991.

Adygeya

Designed by British politician David Urquhart who helped resist annexation of the republic by Russia, the arrows are for resistance. Green is for agriculture and gold is for freedom.

Altay

Blue represents the clear sky, mountains, rivers, and lakes of Altay. White is for eternity, and to encourage the revival of love and harmony between the Altay people.

Bashkortostan

Blue is for charity and virtue, white for openness and willingness, and green for freedom and eternal life. The *kurai* flower represents the seven races of the Bashkir people.

Buryatia

Blue is for the sky and water, white for purity, and yellow for freedom and prosperity. The *Soembo*—the moon, sun, and hearth—recall reconciliation, family life, and hospitality.

Chechnya

Green is for Islam. Red is for the blood shed for freedom. White is the road leading to the future, and the gold is the national ornament.

Republic flags (continued)

Chuvashia

The red base is the Chuvash land, from which grows the "Tree of Life." The three suns are an ancient Chuvash emblem. Gold is for future and prosperity.

Daghestan

The upper green stripe is for agriculture and hope. The blue stripe is for the Caspian Sea that borders the republic. Red represents fidelity and courage.

Ingushetia

The white stripe is for the pure intentions and actions of the people and green is for nature, fertility, and Islam. The central emblem represents a sun symbolizing peace and creativity, and its color recalls the people's struggles.

Kabardino-Balkaria

The flag's colors evoke the blue sky, the white snowcapped mountains, and the green prairies of Kabardino-Balkaria. In the center is a stylized representation of the Elbrus Mountains.

Kalmykia

The vibrant yellow is symbolic of the faith of the people of Kalmykia and also represents the sun warming their land. The blue circle signifies the eternal road to the sacred lotus in the center.

Karachay-Cherkessia

Blue symbolizes peace, kind motives, and tranquility. Green represents nature, fertility, and wealth. Red is for the warmth and unity of the people. The mountains in the center recall the scenery of the republic.

Karelia

The many lakes of Karelia are recalled by the central blue stripe and its vast pine forests by green. The red stripe symbolizes warmth, unity, and continuing cooperation between the people of Karelia.

Khakassia

The horizontal white, blue, and red stripes are taken from the Russian national flag. The vertical green stripe is for eternal life and is charged with an ancient Khakassian solar symbol.

Republic flags (continued)

Komi

The three colors of the flag recall the republic's northerly location in blue, its forests in green, and its snows in white. They are also symbolic of virtues such as cleanliness, unity, and purity.

Mari El

Mari El's flag was changed in 2011. The new emblem of the flag of Mari El is a bear. The animal, popularly known as "forest man," symbolizes the Mari people. The sword is facing down, which represents their peaceful nature.

Mordovia

The flag of Mordovia was adopted in 1995 and has the same colors as the Russian flag. In the center is the sun emblem also found on the flags of Mari El and Udmurtia.

North Ossetia-Alania

White symbolizes spirituality and cleanliness of intentions. Yellow represents the region's farming. The red stripe recalls a willingness to fight for freedom.

Sakha (Yakutia)

The flag recalls the blue sky and shining sun. Beneath is a white stripe recalling the snow. Red is for courage and constancy; green is for the forests of Sakha.

Tatarstan

The upper green stripe of the flag represents the majority of Muslim Tatar population of Tatarstan. The lower red stripe is for the Russian minority. The white fimbriation represents the peace that unites them.

Tuva

The original Tuvan flag adopted in 1918 was also blue, yellow, and white. Today, the colors are said to represent courage and strength in blue, prosperity in yellow, and purity in white.

Udmurtia

The eight-pointed solar sign in the center of the flag is said to guard the people from misfortune. The earth and stability are symbolized in black, morality and the cosmos in white, and life and the sun in red.

Asia

35
12
20
10
44
2
3
24
40
46
22
17
16
45
19
42
36
15
21
1
4
34
32
13
29
6
47
31
49
5
39
26

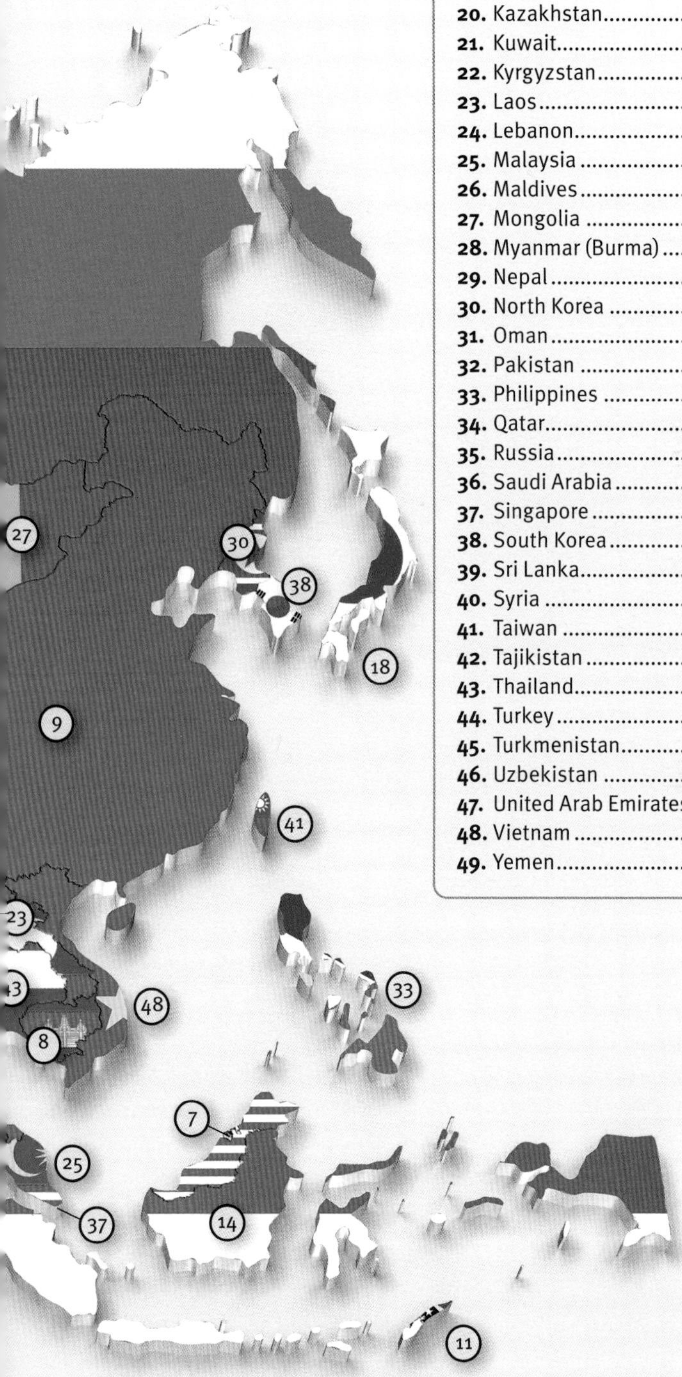
27
30
38
18
9
41
23
48
8
33
7
25
37
14
11

Azerbaijan

Adopted February 5, 1991 | **Ratio** 1:2 | **Usage** National and Civil

The colors represent the Azerbaijani motto to "Turkify, Islamisize, and Europeanize"
Blue is often associated with the Turkic people
Green is the traditional color of Islam
Each point of the star represents a Turkic peoples
Red recalls European influence

The flag dates back to the brief period of Azerbaijani independence during 1918–1920 and replaced the one used in the Soviet era. The white crescent and eight-pointed star were intentionally similar to the emblem on the Turkish flag, since Turkey has traditionally been an ally of the country. The eight points on the flag's star stand for the eight groups of Turkic-speaking peoples—the Azeris, Ottomans, Jagatais, Tatars, Kipchaks, Seljuks, and Turkomans.

THE NATIONAL ARMS

The coat of arms, adopted in 1993, is set on a round shield in the colors of the flag.

ARMS OF AZERBAIJAN

The flame at the star's center symbolizes a new era
The shield is in the color of the national flag—blue, red, and green
The star has eight points, each representing one of the eight Turkic peoples
The golden ear of corn reflects Azerbaijan's agriculture

Armenia

Adopted August 24, 1990 | **Ratio** 1:2 | **Usage** National and Civil

Red recalls Armenian blood spilled during the struggle for independence
Blue is for hope and the Armenian skies
Orange represents the blessings of hard work

Armenia achieved independence following the collapse of the Russian Empire in 1918, and the flag used today dates from this time. Its origin is in a design from the Armenian Institute in Venice of 1885, although this flag used the colors red-green-blue. After independence from a further period of Russian control in 1991, the Soviet flag was replaced by the 1920 tricolor of red, blue, and orange.

ARMS OF ARMENIA

In 1991, the arms of 1920 replaced the Soviet coat of arms. The four emblems within the shield each represent an Armenian royal dynasty. In the center is a stylized image of Mount Ararat.

ARMS OF ARMENIA

Mount Ararat, the supposed resting place of Noah's Ark
The shield is supported by an eagle and a lion.
Four quarters of the shield represent former Armenian royal dynasties
Below the shield lie a broken leaf, a sheaf of wheat, a pen, and a sword

Turkey

Adopted June 5, 1936 | **Ratio** 2:3 | **Usage** National and Civil

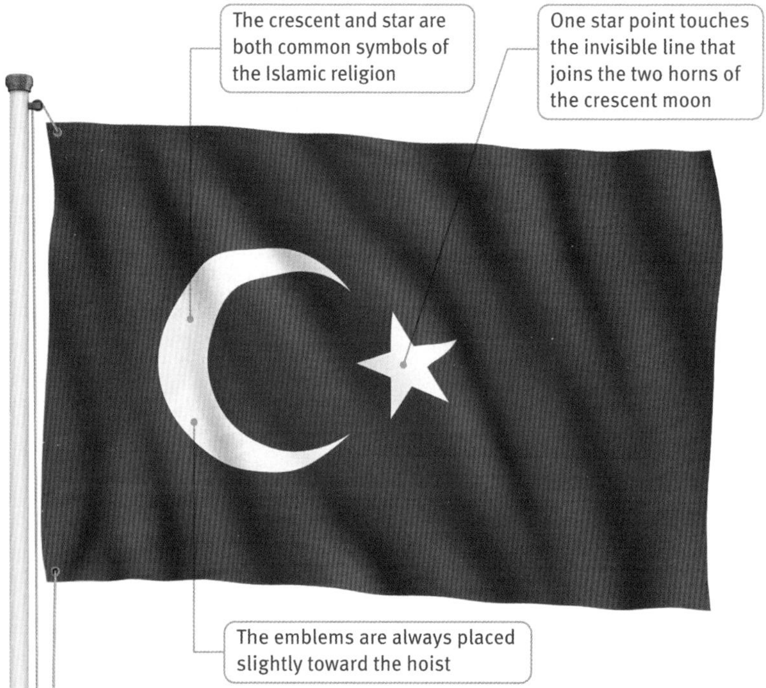
The crescent and star are both common symbols of the Islamic religion
One star point touches the invisible line that joins the two horns of the crescent moon
The emblems are always placed slightly toward the hoist

Turkey's flag dates from 1844, although similar red flags were used as early as the 17th century within the Ottoman Empire. Between 1920–1923, when Turkey became a republic, all the emblems of the Sultan were abolished and the flag became the main emblem.

THE CRESCENT AND STAR

Pairing both the crescent and star emblems together is a more recent custom; use of a single crescent dates back to the Middle Ages. It is a symbol associated with Islam and also with Osman, the founder of the Ottoman Empire. The star first appeared on the flag in 1793. Initially it had eight points, but by the early 19th century, it usually had the five seen today. In 1936, the national flag and all the other flags used in Turkey today were fully defined and specified.

A PAN-ISLAMIC SYMBOL

The crescent-and-star has become an emblem of the Pan-Islamic movement supported by Turkey in the late 19th century; these symbols are now widely used on the flags and national arms of many Muslim countries.

Turkey does not have a coat of arms, but there are individual flags for the president and senior members of the Turkish navy. These also contain the traditional crescent and star.

Georgia

Adopted January 25, 2004 | **Ratio** 3:5 | **Usage** National and Civil

Red cross, typical of St. George, Georgia's patron saint
Smaller crosses, possibly based on the "Jerusalem" cross

During the "Rose Revolution" of 2003, the Georgian flag achieved prominence as the symbol of the opposition National Movement. On taking power in 2004, the party adopted it as the new national flag.

UNCERTAIN ORIGINS

The exact historical background of the flag is unknown. References are made in a 14th-century text to a similar flag from Sivas, in modern Turkey. Georgians may have adopted it after invading the territory.

Another theory suggests Georgian links with the Holy Land saw the addition of the four small crosses. These were based on the "Jerusalem cross." However, it is true that St. George is the patron saint of Georgia, perhaps explaining the basic red crosses on a white field.

THE SOVIET ERA

While part of the USSR, Georgia flew a variant of the Red Flag, adopted in 1951. It had a red field, with a thin blue stripe close to the top. The canton contained the traditional hammer, sickle, and star emblems—unusually in red and on a blue disk from which emanated 24 rays.

Following independence from the USSR in 1991, Georgia officially readopted a flag used during its brief independence between 1918 and 1921. The field was deep red, with black and white stripes in the canton.

Lebanon

Adopted December 7, 1943 | **Ratio** 2:3 | **Usage** National

The two red stripes are a symbol of self-sacrifice
The cedar tree represents holiness, eternity, and strength
The white band symbolizes peace

The present Lebanese flag was adopted in 1943 just prior to independence from France. It was designed to be a neutral flag, not allied to any one of Lebanon's religious groups. Red is thought to be for the color of the uniforms worn by the Lebanese Legion during the First World War. Officially, the red is said to represent the people of Lebanon's sacrifice during the struggle for independence, while white represents purity.

THE CEDAR OF LEBANON

Although the flag has existed for only a little over half a century, the tree at the center of the flag—the Cedar of Lebanon—has been an emblem of the country since the time of King Solomon, almost 3,000 years ago. Specifically, the cedar is the symbol of the country's Maronite Christian community. It first appeared on a flag in 1861 when the Lebanon was part of the Ottoman Empire. Soon after its collapse, the country became mandated to France and its flag was a French *Tricolore*, with the Cedar of Lebanon in the white band of the *Tricolore*. The cedar symbolizes happiness and prosperity for the country.

The present flag, with the cedar's foliage and trunk in green, has a variant in which the tree trunk is brown—although this is not officially recognized.

Syria

Adopted March 29, 1980 | **Ratio** 2:3 | **Usage** National and Civil

An earlier version of the flag had three stars, in anticipation of a union incorporating Syria, Egypt, and Iraq

White, black, red, and green are Pan-Arab colors

The two green stars originally represented Syria and Egypt, although they are now said to represent Syria and Iraq

In 1920, while still a French colony, Syria flew a green-white-green tribar with a French *Tricolore* in the canton. At independence this was changed to a green, white, and black tricolor, with three red stars for its provinces across its center. Its current red-white-black Pan-Arabic flag was adopted when Syria became part of the United Arab Republic, but with three stars. On leaving the union in 1961, Syria briefly reverted to its original flag, before readopting the Arab Liberation colors in 1963.

The arms of Syria depicts the Hawk of Quraish, bearing a shield charged with the national flag.

ARMS OF SYRIA

The shield is in the form of a national flag

The banner's Arabic inscription reads "Arab Republic of Syria"

The hawk was the emblem of the Quraish tribe to which the Prophet Muhammad belonged

Cyprus

Adopted August 16, 1960 | **Ratio** 2:3 | **Usage** National and Civil

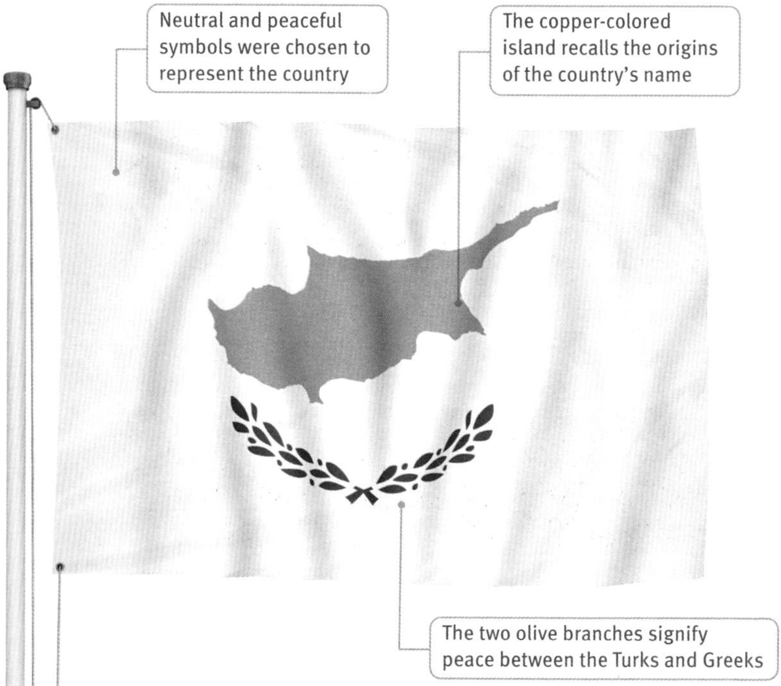
Neutral and peaceful symbols were chosen to represent the country
The copper-colored island recalls the origins of the country's name
The two olive branches signify peace between the Turks and Greeks

Adopted at independence in 1960, the Cypriot flag was designed around peaceful and neutral symbols in an attempt to promote harmony after centuries of conflict. Despite this effort, communities still struggle to resolve the deeply entrenched difficulties that exist between the Greek and Turkish Cypriots.

As a consequence of this, the north and south of the island have been divided by a UN buffer zone since 1964, and in 1974, Turkish forces occupied the northern part of the island, forming the "Turkish Republic of Northern Cyprus." The two parts of the island also fly the national flags of Greece and Turkey.

THE ISLE OF COPPER

The map of the island on the flag is copper-colored, to express the meaning of the island's name—the Isle of Copper. The two olive branches on the white field represent peace between the two ethnic groups.

THE NATIONAL EMBLEM

Cyprus's national emblem is a dove holding an olive branch in its beak. This is a symbol of peace and reconciliation arising from the biblical story of Noah and the Ark. The dove is also symbolic of Aphrodite, the Greek goddess whose legend originated from the island.

Israel

Adopted October 28, 1948 | **Ratio** 8:11 | **Usage** National

The blue and white colors of the flag are derived from the Jewish prayer shawl
The central emblem is the Shield of David, which has a long association with the Jewish people

The flag was designed for the Zionist movement by David Wolfsohn in 1891, over 50 years before the state of Israel was officially declared.

STAR OF DAVID

The central emblem in the form of a hexagram is known as the "*Magen David*" (Shield of David), an emblem that had been used on Jewish flags for centuries before being adopted as the national flag of Israel. The blue and white colors recall the colors of the *tallith* (Jewish prayer shawl). The blue is officially described as "Yale Blue." It is a lighter shade than is used in other Israeli flags.

The merchant flag was adopted in 1948. There is also a naval ensign of similar design.

THE CIVIL AND THE NAVAL ENSIGNS

Like other variant Israeli flags, civil (below, left) and naval (below, right) ensigns are a darker shade of blue than the national flag.

The Shield of David is slightly elongated

Jordan

Adopted April 18, 1928 | **Ratio** 1:2 | **Usage** National and Civil

Red, black, green, and white are Pan-Arab colors
The seven-pointed star represents the seven verses of Islamic belief that open the Qur'an

The colors of the Jordanian flag are those of the Pan-Arab flag. They were first used in 1917 to represent "Pan-Arabianism," which sought independence from the Ottoman Empire. The star at the hoist was added in 1928, when Jordan gained nominal independence. It represents seven verses of Islamic belief.

JORDAN'S COAT OF ARMS
The coat of arms is similar to that designed in 1949 for the King. The crest is a crown in his honor. The current inscription on the scroll reads "The King of the Hashemite Kingdom of Jordan, Abdullah bin al-Hussein bin A'oun, Beseeches the Almighty for Aid and Success."

ARMS OF JORDAN

The current coat of arms is very similar to that designed for King Abdullah I in 1949
An Arabic inscription asking for the Almighty's aid
The crown of His Majesty the King
The black eagle symbolizes the banner of the Messenger of God

Saudi Arabia

Adopted March 15, 1973 | **Ratio** 2:3 | **Usage** National and Civil

A number of versions of the green flag have been used by the Wahabi sect since the 19th century
Green was thought to be a favorite color of the Prophet Muhammad
The *shahada*, is the Muslim Statement of Faith

The flag of Saudi Arabia symbolizes the Arab people of the desert. Used in various forms since the late 19th century, the green is favored by the Wahabi sect and is believed to be the favorite color of the prophet Muhammad.

FLAG INSCRIPTION

In 1901, the *shahada*, the Muslim Statement of Faith, was added to the flag in white letters, making it one of the few national flags to contain an inscription.

By law, it must be able to be read correctly—from right to left—on both sides of the flag. The sword is the symbolic sword of Abd-al-Aziz, who conquered part of Arabia in the early 20th century. It has appeared in different forms in the past, sometimes as two crossed swords.

THE SHAHADA

The inscription reads "There is no god but Allah and Muhammad is the Prophet of Allah"
This version of the sword was added in 1981
The sword represents that given to Abd-al-Aziz by his father

Yemen

Adopted May 22, 1990 | **Ratio** 2:3 | **Usage** National and Civil

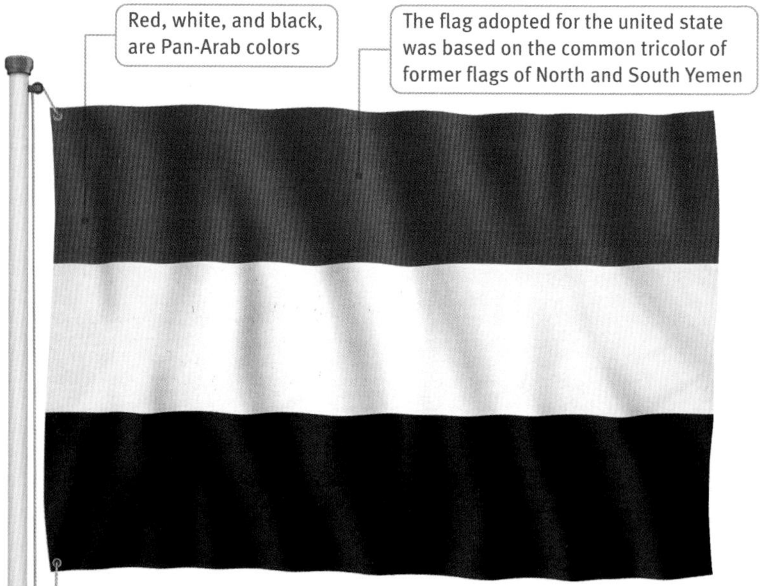
Red, white, and black, are Pan-Arab colors
The flag adopted for the united state was based on the common tricolor of former flags of North and South Yemen

The first flag of Yemen, used while the Imams were in power, was red, with a white sword placed horizontally in the center, and five white stars representing the five duties of a devout Muslim. Yemen was originally two countries, each having its own flag.

SOUTH YEMEN

Formally the British Aden Protectorate, the flag of the People's Democratic Republic of Yemen was modeled on the Egyptian Pan-Arab flag. It was a red, white, and black tricolor, and it bore a blue triangle, representing the Yemeni people in the hoist, while a red star represented the Socialist ruling party.

NORTH YEMEN

The flag of the Yemen Arab Republic formally the Kingdom of Yemen, was also modeled on the Egyptian flag. It was a red, white, and black tricolor, but it was simply charged with a single, five-pointed green star in a central white band, representing Arab unity.

A UNIFIED FLAG

When Yemen unified in 1962, the stars and the triangle were dropped, but the common elements of their flags—the Pan-Arab red, white, and black stripes—were preserved for the united flag. The new flag's pattern suggests a compromise between the officially secular south and the Islamic north.

Oman

Adopted April 25, 1995 | **Ratio** 1:2 | **Usage** National and Civil

The emblem of the ruling dynasty
White is for the Imam of Oman and for peace
The red field is common in the flags of the Gulf states
Green represents the mountains and fertility

Until 1970, Oman used the plain red banner of the indigenous people, the Kharijite Muslims. In 1970, the Sultan introduced a complete new set of national flags. Bands of green and white were added to the fly, and the national emblem, the badge of the Abusaidi Dynasty, was placed in the canton. This depicts crossed swords surmounted by a *gambia*, a traditional curved dagger.

THE SYMBOLISM OF THE COLORS
White has been associated historically with the Imam, the religious leader of Oman and at times, the political rival to the ruling Sultan. It also symbolizes peace. Green is traditionally associated with the *Jebel al Akhdar* or "Green Mountains," which lie toward the north of the country. Red is a common color in Gulf state flags.

THE NATIONAL EMBLEM

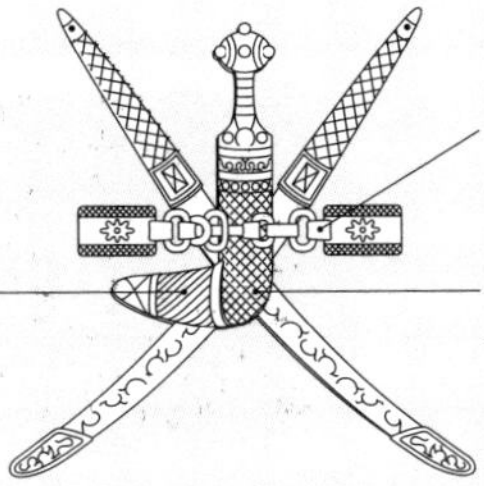
The national emblem is said to date back to the middle of the 18th century
An ornate horse's bit links the weapons
A curved dagger is fastened over a pair of crossed swords

United Arab Emirates

Adopted December 2, 1971 | **Ratio** 1:2 | **Usage** National and Civil

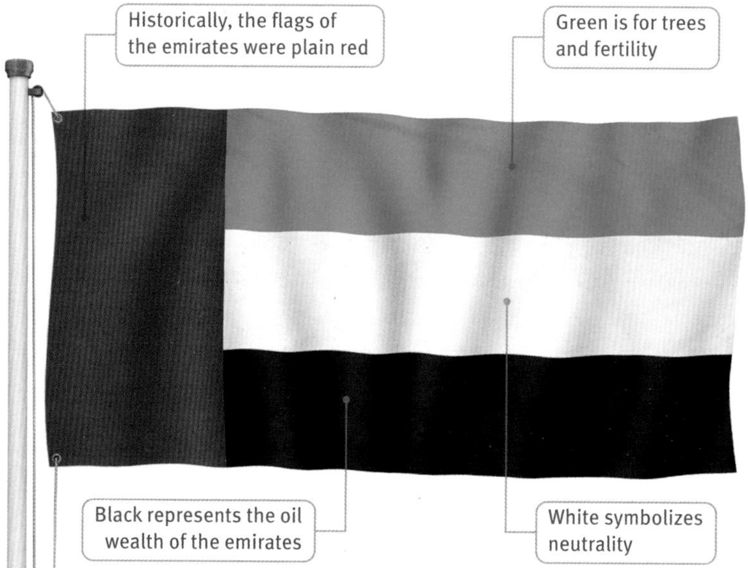
Historically, the flags of the emirates were plain red
Green is for trees and fertility
Black represents the oil wealth of the emirates
White symbolizes neutrality

Following a General Treaty in 1820, the seven emirates that now form the United Arab Emirates came under British protection. Red and white flags were taken up by all except the Emirate of Fujairah, a non-signatory to the treaty, which adopted a plain red flag. With minor alterations, the flags are still retained for local use. The first flag of the federation, adopted in 1968, was also red and white, but with a green star.

THE PAN-ARAB COLORS

On independence in 1971, a flag in the Pan-Arab colors—red, green, white, and black—was adopted to express Arab unity and nationalism. The red also recalls the color of the flags of the member states.

FLAG OF DUBAI

Like the other six emirates, Dubai retains its individual red and white flag
The flag colors remain constant, but the proportions have changed in recent decades

Qatar

Adopted July 9, 1971 | **Ratio** 11:28 | **Usage** National and Civil

The maroon coloring and proportions distinguish the flag from Bahrain's flag
The nine-pointed serrated line indicates that Qatar is the ninth member of the "reconciled Emirates" following a 1916 treaty
"Qatar maroon" derives from the action of sun on natural red dye

Qatar's flag was originally plain red, like the flag of Bahrain, to which it was once linked. The peoples of both countries are Kharijite Muslims, whose traditional banner was red. The flag evolved into its present form around the middle of the 19th century and was officially adopted when Qatar became independent from Britain in 1971.

"QATAR MAROON"

The flag's maroon color is said to have come about from the action of the desert sun's heat on the red vegetable dyes formerly used for its flags. This color, now known as "Qatar maroon," was officially adopted in 1948. The white area derives from a British request in the 1820s that all friendly states around the Gulf add a white band to their flags to distinguish them from pirate flags. The serrated edge indicates that Qatar is one of the nine "reconciled Emirates" that signed a treaty with Great Britain in 1916. During its earlier usage, before Qatar's independence, the flag also bore the name of the state in white lettering and red diamonds were placed on the white band.

THE EMBLEM OF QATAR

The circular badge of Qatar uses both the colors and serrated pattern of the flag around its edge. In the center is a local sailing boat, passing an island. This is set between two crossed swords. It is inscribed with the name of the state in Arabic.

Bahrain

Adopted February 14, 2002 | **Ratio** 3:5 | **Usage** National and Civil

The serrated edge was originally a straight line
Red and white are the traditional colors of the Gulf states

After centuries of complex history, Bahrain became a British protectorate in 1820. At this time, the flag was a plain red design, but as part of a maritime treaty with the British a white bar was added at the hoist. This became serrated in 1932 to help distinguish it from other flags in the region. Soon after independence in 1971, the large number of serrations was reduced to just eight.

The current version of the flag arose in 2002 when Bahrain became a Kingdom and the number of serrations was set at five, said to represent the five pillars of Islam.

The national arms was adopted in 1932. It is based on the colors and design of the national flag.

ARMS OF BAHRAIN

The coat of arms dates from 1932; it was designed by Sir Charles Belgrave, the Sheik's political adviser
The shield contains the characteristic serrated division line, as on the national flag

Kuwait

Adopted September 7, 1961 | **Ratio** 1:2 | **Usage** National and Civil

Black represents the defeat of the enemy
Green stands for fertility
Red symbolizes the blood of the enemy
White symbolizes purity

Before 1961, the flag of Kuwait, like those of other Gulf states, was red and white. The present flag is in the Pan-Arab colors, but each color is also significant in its own right. Black symbolizes the defeat of the enemy, while red is the color of blood on the Kuwaiti swords. White symbolizes purity, and green is for the fertile land. The idea for the flag's distinctive design—a horizontal tricolor with a black trapezium in the hoist—may have come from the flag used by Iraq until the late 1950s.

KUWAIT'S COAT OF ARMS

The arms depicts a hawk above which sails an Arab *dhow* on stylized waves.

ARMS OF KUWAIT

The inscription is the name of the state
A hawk with outstretched wings
An Arab *dhow*—a traditional sailing boat
A shield in the national colors

Iraq

Adopted January 22, 2008 | **Ratio** 2:3 | **Usage** National and Civil

Red represents courage
"God is great" (*Takbir*) written in Arabic
White symbolizes generosity
Black recalls the triumphs of Islam

The flags of Iraq have always included the Pan-Arab colors of red, white, black, and green. The colors represent the qualities of those who follow Islam. Red represents courage; white stands for generosity; black is for the triumphs of Islam; and green is for Islam itself.

Three green stars were added to the flag in 1963, based on the then flag of Egypt (see p.104). In 1991, the inscription was added. It was modified and the stars removed in 2008.

THE NATIONAL ARMS

Also in 1963 the golden Eagle of Saladin became the national arms. It always shows the national flag on its chest.

ISLAMIC VERSE

The Islamic verse was added to the flag in 1991 and modified in 2004 and 2008

The *takbir* reads "*Allahu Akbar*" ("God is Great")

Iran

Adopted July 29, 1980 | **Ratio** 4:7 | **Usage** National and Civil

The four crescents symbolize the growth of the Muslim faith
The sword represents strength and fortitude
Kufic script from the Qur'an
The globe shape stands for the power of the world's downtrodden people

The traditional green, white, and red of the Iranian flag date back to the 18th century, although there is no agreed explanation of the colors. The colors were arranged in horizontal stripes in 1906. In 1980, a new flag was introduced with the addition of emblems expressive of the Islamic Revolution.

A REVOLUTIONARY EMBLEM

The emblem in the center of the flag is a highly stylized composite of various elements representing different facets of Islamic life: Allah, the Book, the Sword, the five principles of Islam, balance, unity, neutrality, and the universal government of the downtrodden.

THE KUFIC SCRIPT (STYLIZED VERSION)

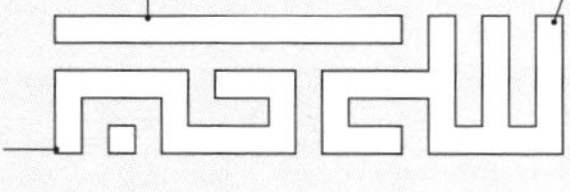
Along the edges of the green and red stripes appears the phrase *"Allahu Akbar"* ("God is Great")
A stylized version of Kufic script, used for the Qur'an
The script, repeated 22 times, is the date in the Islamic calendar on which Ayatollah Khomeini returned from exile in 1979

Turkmenistan

Adopted January 24, 2001 | **Ratio** 2:3 | **Usage** National and Civil

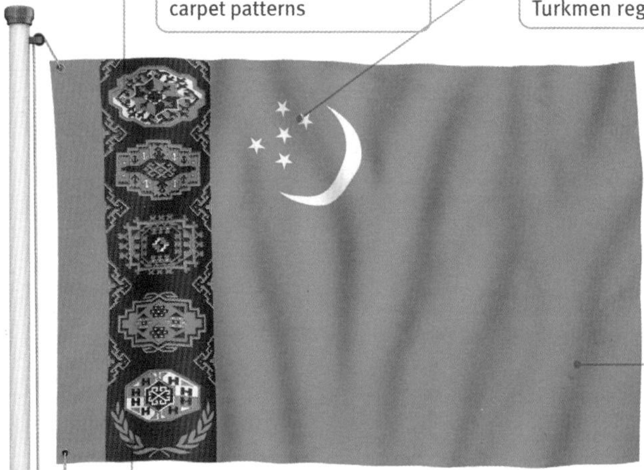
The five designs are representative of traditional carpet patterns
Each star represents one of the five Turkmen regions
Green is a color revered in Turkmenistan
The wreath of olive leaves is identical to that on the United Nations flag and was added in 1997

The original design of the flag was adopted on February 19, 1992, following a competition, and is based on national traditions. In the official interpretation, the five stars stand for the new regions established by the constitution of 1992. The carpet design contains five medallions or *guls*, which represent the traditional designs used by the tribes who produced the country's famous carpets. The wreath of olive leaves was added in 1997 to "immortalize the policy of neutrality" declared by Turkmenistan in 1995.

The state emblem recalls the region's important agricultural products and famous horses.

STATE EMBLEM OF TURKMENISTAN

The five *guls* from the national flag
Cotton and wheat both featured on the emblem of the former Soviet Republic of Turkmenistan
An *akheltikin* horse, famed in Turkmenistan
Cotton represents the country's most important agricultural product

Uzbekistan

Adopted November 18, 1991 | **Ratio** 1:2 | **Usage** National and Civil

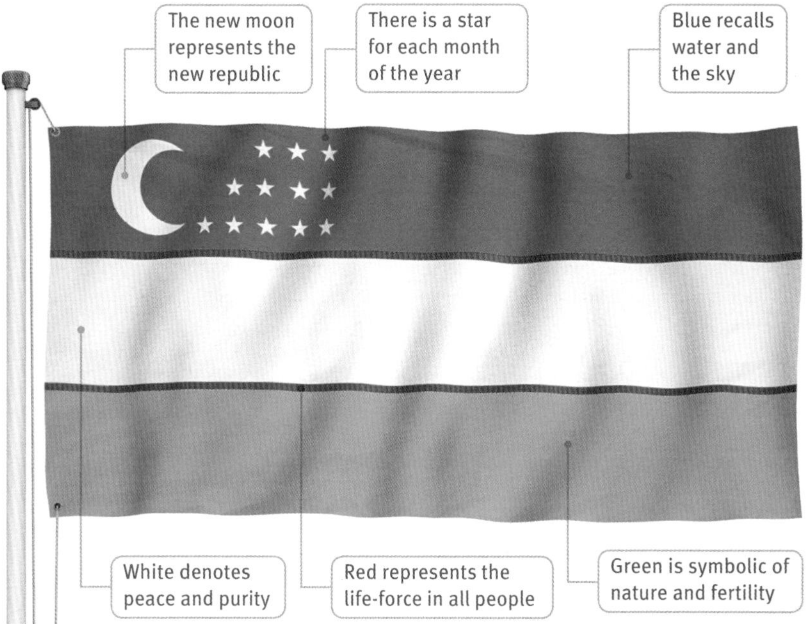
The new moon represents the new republic
There is a star for each month of the year
Blue recalls water and the sky
White denotes peace and purity
Red represents the life-force in all people
Green is symbolic of nature and fertility

Uzbekistan was the first of the Central Asian republics to adopt its own non-Communist national flag, although the new design is partially derived from that of the former Soviet Uzbekistan.

The blue stripe symbolizes water and the sky. It is also the color of the flag of Timur, who ruled an Uzbek Empire in the 14th century. The white stripe is a sign of peace and purity. Green is a Muslim symbol of nature and fertility. Red is for the life-force found in all people. The new moon suggests the birth of the new republic, while the 12 stars represent the months of the Islamic calendar.

STATE EMBLEM OF UZBEKISTAN

The emblem features a bird whose outstretched wings form a crescent, framing a rising sun over a landscape of mountains and rivers
Cotton is Uzbekistan's chief natural resource
Islamic crescent and star
Wheat represents the country's staple food crop
The ribbon bears the name of the state

Kazakhstan

Adopted June 4, 1992 | **Ratio** 1:2 | **Usage** National and Civil

The sky blue field symbolizes the skies stretching over the many Kazakh people
A *berkut*, or steppe eagle, beneath a shining sun
The traditional "*koshkar-muiz*" pattern is placed close to the hoist

Kazakhstan's post-Communist flag was adopted in 1992. Its sky blue background recalls the endless skies over the Kazakh people. It also symbolizes well-being, tranquility, peace, and unity. In the center of the flag, below a golden sun with 32 rays, soars a bird of the species known locally as the *berkut*, or steppe eagle. Together they represent love, freedom, and the aspirations of the Kazakh people. A traditional pattern called "*koshkar-muiz*" (the horns of the ram) forms a vertical stripe near the hoist.

The new state emblem is also based around a radiant sun. It depicts traditional features of Kazakhstan.

STATE EMBLEM OF KAZAKHSTAN

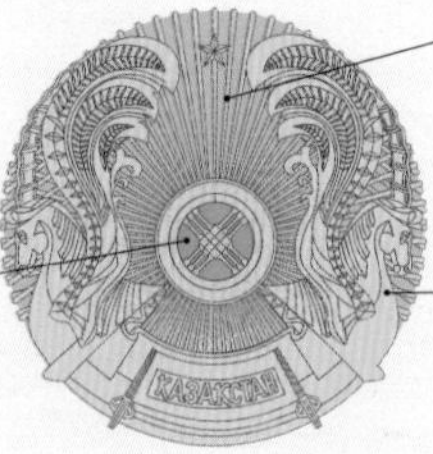
The center of the emblem is like the upper part of a *yurt*, the ancient felt tent of the Kazakh nomads
The sun's rays spread out like a *yurt*'s supporting structure
Winged and horned horses represent historical traditions and beliefs

Mongolia

Adopted January 12, 1992 | **Ratio** 1:2 | **Usage** Civil and State

The *soyonbo* device combines a number of Buddhist emblems
Sky blue is the national color of Mongolia
Originally the color of Communism, red today represents progress

The current national flag replaced the Red Flag of revolution in 1940. The red field is retained at the fly and hoist, although the color's original Socialist connotations have given way to more general themes of progress and prosperity. The sky blue panel represents the people of Mongolia and invokes the imperial days of Genghis Khan. The flag bears a 17th-century Buddhist emblem at hoist called the *soyonbo*. The *soyonbo* comprises various ideograms representing different elements from the Buddhist view of the world. The Communist star that appeared above the *soyonbo* was removed in 1992.

THE *SOYONBO*

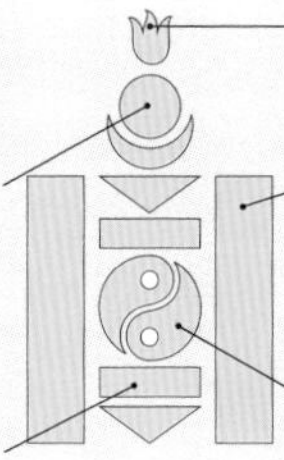
The sun and moon represent the eternal existence of the Mongolian nation
Horizontal bars indicate that vigilance is required from the highest and lowest in society
The tongues of the flame stand for past, present, and future
The vertical columns illustrate the Mongolian proverb "Two friends are stronger than stone"
The fish stand for vigilance because fish never sleep

Kyrgyzstan

Adopted March 3, 1992 | **Ratio** 3:5 | **Usage** National and Civil

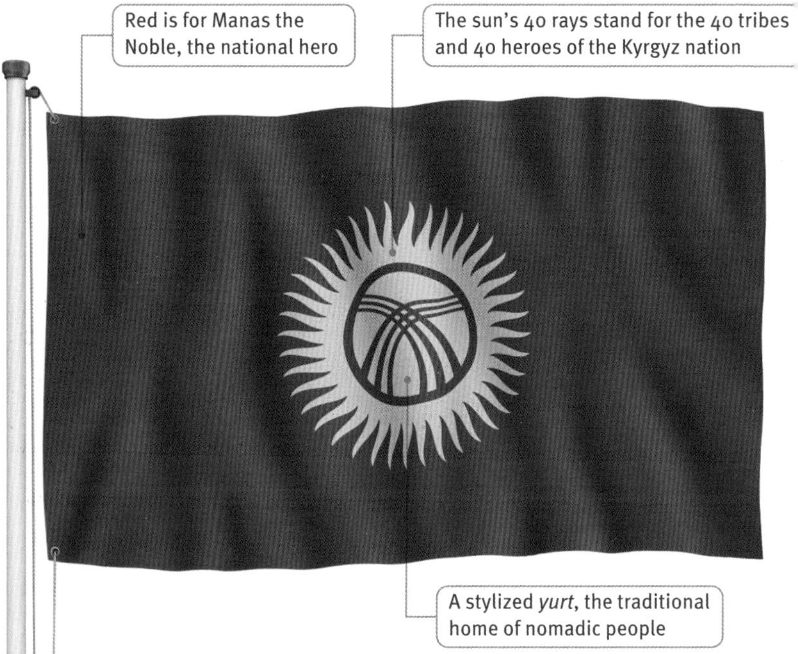
Red is for Manas the Noble, the national hero
The sun's 40 rays stand for the 40 tribes and 40 heroes of the Kyrgyz nation
A stylized *yurt*, the traditional home of nomadic people

Independent since 1991, a post-Communist flag was not adopted until 1992. The flag's red background is associated with the national hero, Manas the Noble, who welded 40 tribes together to form the Kyrgyz nation. The red also represents the bravery and valor of the Kyrgyz people.

In the center of the flag is a yellow sun with 40 rays, representing the tribes and the legendary 40 heroes of Manas. The sun's rays run clockwise on the obverse of the flag and counterclockwise on the reverse.

A TRADITIONAL *YURT*

At the sun's center is a stylized bird's-eye view of the roof, or *tunduk*, of a Kyrgyz *yurt*, the traditional tent used by the nomadic people of the steppe. It symbolizes the unity of time and space, the origin of life, hearth and home, and the history of the nomads.

ARMS OF KYRGYZSTAN

The coat of arms of Kyrgyzstan is round and does not contain a traditional shield. In the center is a white eagle with spread wings. Behind this are snowcapped mountains, representing the mighty Tien Shan, and a radiant, rising sun. This scene is bordered by wreaths of cotton and wheat, both major agricultural products in Kyrgyzstan. The name of the state is inscribed in Cyrillic script at the top.

Tajikistan

Adopted November 24, 1992 | **Ratio** 1:2 | **Usage** National and Civil

The crown and stars stand for Tajikistan's state sovereignty
White is the color of cotton, Tajikistan's main industry
Green represents farm produce

In 1992, Tajikistan became independent from the USSR and adopted a new flag. The red, white, and green stripes are the same as those chosen in 1953 for the flag of the Tadzhik Soviet Socialist Republic. Red is the color of the flag of the USSR; white is for cotton, Tajikistan's main export; and green recalls other farm produce.

SYMBOLS OF THE NEW STATE
The center of the flag features a gold crown and an arc of seven stars. These symbols refer to the state sovereignty of Tajikistan, friendship between all nations, and the "unbreakable union of workers, peasants, and the intellectual classes" of the republic.

STATE EMBLEM OF TAJIKISTAN

The flag colors of red, white, and green
The mountains recall the country's many peaks
Crown and stars from the national flag
Wheat and cotton, both major crops, surround the arms

Afghanistan

Adopted January 4, 2004 | **Ratio** 2:3 | **Usage** National

Black recalls previous flags used in Afghanistan
The new arms of Afghanistan
Green represents Islam

With the election of a democratic government in 2004, the present flag was adopted. Black, red, and green have been traditional in most Afghan flags. Black is from the first recognized Afghan flag, red is for bravery, and green for Islam. The white emblem in the center is the state coat of arms. This too is a traditional design.

The arms show the Muslim Mehrab (the niche that shows the direction to the Muslim Holy City of Mecca) and Minbar (the pulpit from which sermons are preached). These are shown within a traditional image of a mosque, flanked by two national flags and surrounded by sheaves of wheat. Four inscriptions also appear at the top and bottom of arms.

ARMS OF AFGHANISTAN

The Arabic inscription "God is Great"
The date 1298 in the Muslim calendar (AD 1919), is the date Afghanistan was internationally recognized as an independent state
The Arabic inscription reads: "There is no god but Allah, and Muhammad is the Prophet of Allah"
The name of Afghanistan in Arabic script

Pakistan

Adopted August 11, 1947 | **Ratio** 2:3 | **Usage** National

The white strip represents non-Muslim and other minority groups in Pakistan
Star symbolizes light and knowledge
Dark green represents Islam
The crescent represents progress

The flag was designed by Muhammad Ali Jinnah, founder of the nation. It is associated with the flag used by the All-India Muslim League as an emblem of its aim of achieving an independent Muslim state. Their flag was green, with a central white star and crescent. At independence in 1947, a white stripe was added at the hoist to represent the state's minorities.

THE SYMBOLISM OF THE COLORS

The green and white together stand for peace and prosperity. The crescent symbolizes progress and the star represents light and knowledge.

The flag of the president is similar to the national flag. The emblems are in gold and are enclosed within a wreath of laurel. Beneath is the name of the state in Urdu.

THE PRESIDENT'S FLAG

The field of the president's flag is green and white, like the national flag
The crescent and star are symbols of Islam
The name of the state is written in Urdu

Nepal

Adopted December 16, 1962 | **Ratio** 11:9 | **Usage** National and Civil

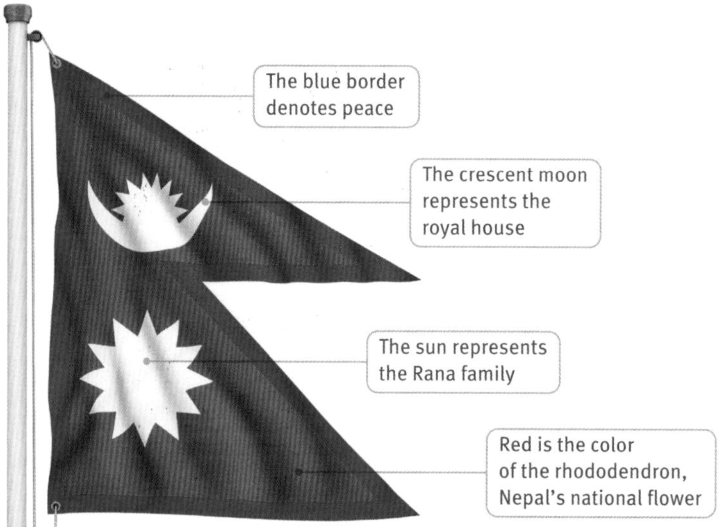
The blue border denotes peace
The crescent moon represents the royal house
The sun represents the Rana family
Red is the color of the rhododendron, Nepal's national flower

The flag of Nepal is the only national flag that is not rectangular or square. Originally, two separate triangular pennants were flown one above the other; these were then joined to form a single flag. Its crimson red is the color of the rhododendron—the country's national flower. Red is also the sign of victory in war. The blue border is the color of peace.

THE SUN AND THE MOON

Until 1962, the flag's emblems, the sun and the crescent moon, had human faces. They were removed to modernize the flag. The sun retains the face on the Royal Standard. The crescent represents the royal house, and the sun denotes the Rana family, the hereditary prime ministers until 1961.

THE ROYAL STANDARD (1960–2008)

The Royal Standard shows a rampant lion holding a lance with a flag
The sun has a face, as did the national flag until 1962

Bhutan

Adopted Circa 1965 | **Ratio** 2:3 | **Usage** National and Civil

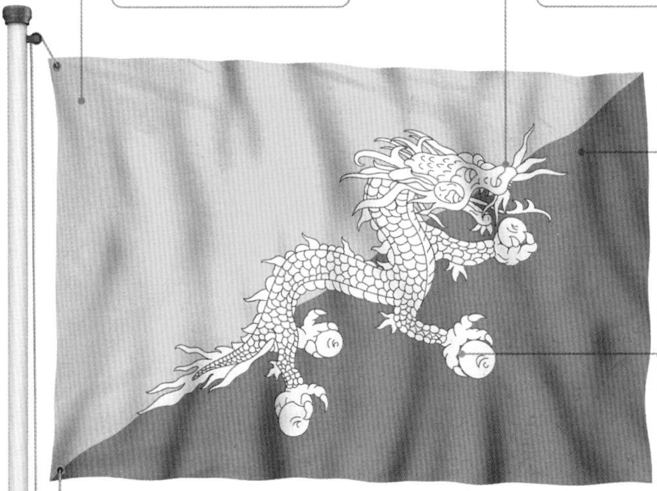
Saffron yellow denotes the authority of the King
The "Thunder Dragon"
Orange represents the Drukpa monasteries and religious practices
White represents purity and loyalty

In Bhutan, thunder is believed to be the sound of dragons roaring. In about 1200, a monastery called the *Druk* (the "Thunder Dragon"), was set up, with a sect called the Drukpas named after it. The name and the emblem of the dragon have been associated with Bhutan ever since. The dragon on the flag is white to symbolize purity.

TEMPORAL AND SPIRITUAL POWER
The two colors of the flag, divided diagonally, represent spiritual and temporal power within Bhutan. The orange part of the flag represents the Drukpa monasteries and Buddhist religious practice, while the saffron yellow field denotes the secular authority of the royal dynasty of the Wangchuks.

EMBLEM OF BHUTAN

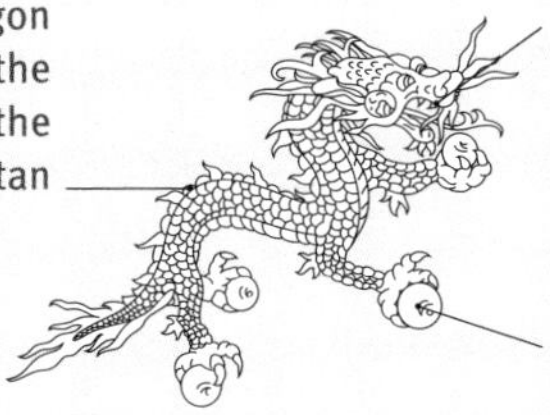
The dragon symbolizes *Druk*, the Tibetan name for the Kingdom of Bhutan
The snarling mouth expresses the strength of the male and female deities protecting the country
Jewels clasped in the dragon's claws symbolize wealth

India

Adopted July 22, 1947 | **Ratio** 2:3 | **Usage** National

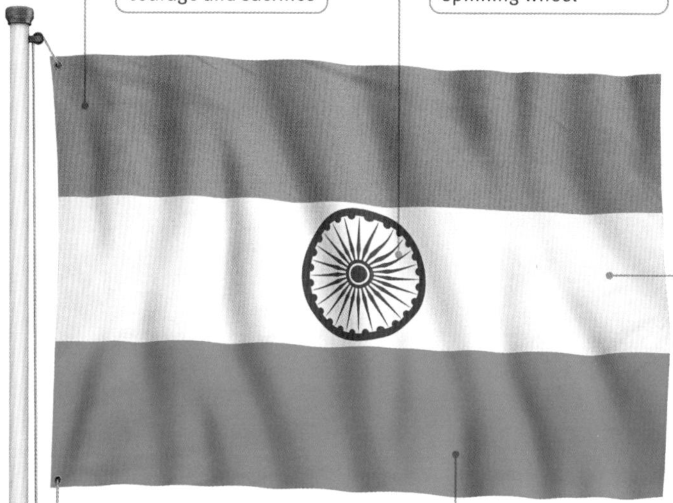
Orange represents courage and sacrifice
The *Chakra*, or Buddhist spinning wheel
White symbolizes peace and truth
Green symbolizes faith and chivalry

The national flag, adopted in 1947, is based on the flag of the Indian National Congress, which was established in 1885 to press for independence. The flag's orange color symbolizes courage and sacrifice, white stands for peace and truth, green is for faith and chivalry, and blue represents the color of the sky and the ocean.

THE CHAKRA

The central motif is a *Chakra*, or Buddhist spinning wheel. The 24 spokes of the wheel correspond with the 24 hours of the day, symbolizing that there is life in movement and death in stagnation. The naval ensign is adapted from British practice. The gold National Emblem was added in 2004.

INDIAN NAVAL ENSIGN

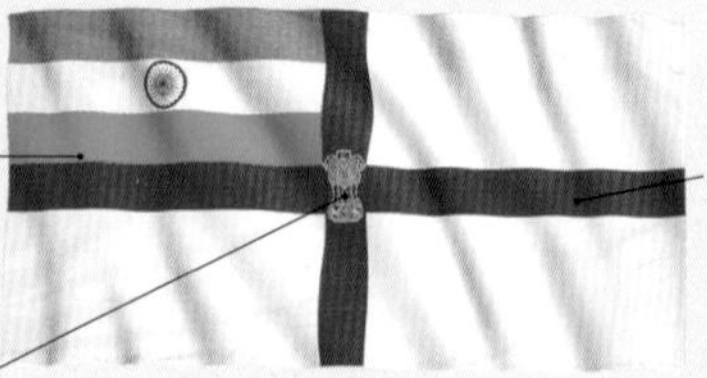
The national flag is placed in the canton
The gold National Emblem of India appears in the center
The design derives from British naval practice

Maldives

Adopted July 25, 1965 | **Ratio** 2:3 | **Usage** National and Civil

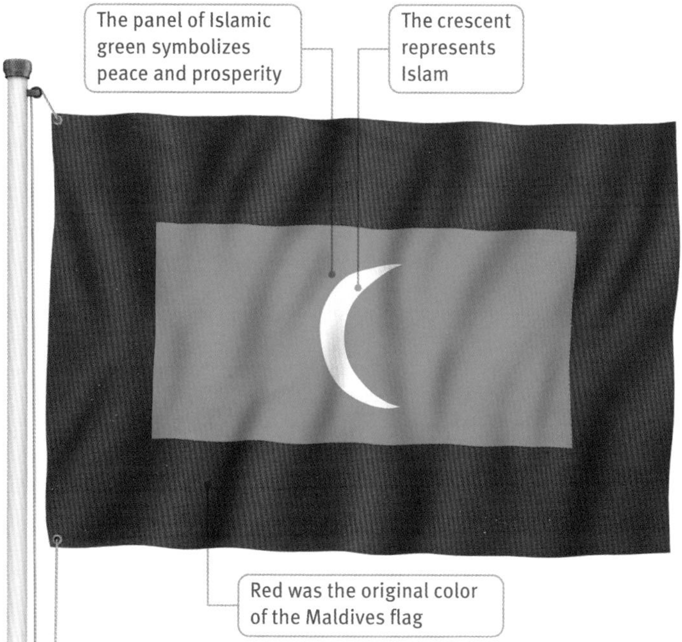
The panel of Islamic green symbolizes peace and prosperity
The crescent represents Islam
Red was the original color of the Maldives flag

Until the beginning of the 20th century, the flag of the Maldives was plain red, reflecting the culture of the Arab traders from the Persian Gulf who operated among the islands. This flag remained in use after the British Protectorate was set up in 1887. The flag later acquired a white crescent facing the hoist—another sign of Islamic influence.

A NEW DESIGN

The flag was redesigned in 1948 after the independence of Ceylon (now Sri Lanka), of which the islands had been a dependency. The crescent was turned around and placed on an Islamic green panel. A pattern of black and white diagonal stripes was added along the hoist. This was dropped after independence from Britain in 1965. A modern interpretation of the colors suggests that red symbolizes the blood shed in the struggle for independence, while green stands for peace and progress.

THE NATIONAL EMBLEM

The national emblem of the Maldives contains the Islamic crescent and star emblem beneath a date palm. Below the crescent is a scroll with the inscription, in Dihevi, "State of a Thousand Islands," which recalls the many islands—over 2,000—that make up the Maldives. The crescent is flanked by two national flags.

Sri Lanka

Adopted December 17, 1978 | **Ratio** 1:2 | **Usage** National and Civil

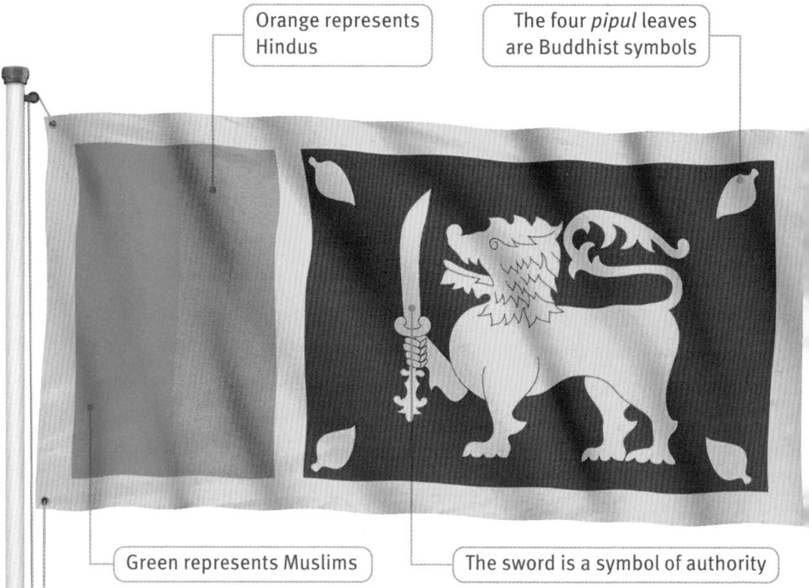
Orange represents Hindus
The four *pipul* leaves are Buddhist symbols
Green represents Muslims
The sword is a symbol of authority

The original flag of Sri Lanka featured just the lion and sword on a red field, recalling that the Sinhalese word for lion—"Sinhala"—is the basis of the island's name. The flag's yellow border symbolized the protection of the nation by Buddhism.

The flag was derived from the flag of the Sinhalese kingdom of Kandy. It proved unpopular with minority groups, so vertical bands of green, for Muslims, and orange, for the Hindu Tamils, were added in 1951.

When the country's name changed from Ceylon to Sri Lanka in 1972, four leaves were added. They denote the tree under which Siddhartha sat when he received enlightenment and became the Buddha. This version of the flag was in official use from 1978.

FLAG OF KANDY

The "Lion Flag" was the national flag of Ceylon prior to 1815 when it became a British colony
The finials are derived from the spire on top of a Buddhist temple

Bangladesh

Adopted January 17, 1972 | **Ratio** 3:5 | **Usage** National

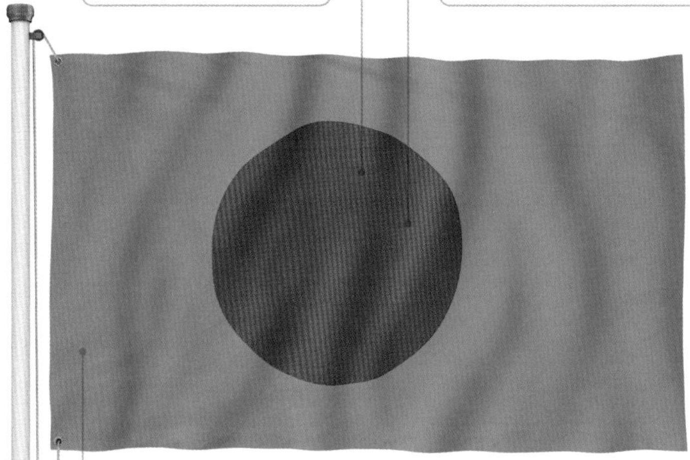
The red circle is set slightly toward the hoist
The red disk symbolizes the struggle for independence
Green represents the land

The flag was originally adopted in March 1971, when the country gained independence, at which time it had a yellow silhouette map of the country in the red disk. This flag was used throughout the struggle for independence, but when the state was formally established in 1971, the outline map was omitted from the new national flag.

NATIONAL EMBLEM OF BANGLADESH
The coat of arms was adopted in 1972. It consists of the national flower, a water lily, known locally as the *shapla*, growing from stylized waves. Around it are ears of rice, and above is a sprig of jute, with four golden stars. The emblem appears in the center of the president's flag, set on a deep purple field.

THE PRESIDENT'S FLAG

Wreath of rice
A *shapla* (water lily) on stylized waves
The name of the state in Bangla
A sprig of jute, with four golden stars representing nationalism, socialism, democracy, and secularism

Myanmar (Burma)

Adopted October 21, 2010 | **Ratio** 4:7 | **Usage** National and Civil

Yellow symbolizes solidarity
Green represents peace and tranquility
Red is for courage and decisiveness
The white star is from the flag of the Burman Resistance in the Second World War

Myanmar's flag came into use in 2010, having been introduced in the 2008 constitution. It is completely different from the two flags that Myanmar had had since independence. The old flags were red with a blue canton featuring six stars and later a socialist emblem. The new flag features three stripes and a single large star, similar to that on one of Myanmar's pre-independence flags, that of the Burman Resistance.

The emblem was also changed by the 2008 constitution. A map of Myanmar within a laurel wreath is surrounded by an ornate structure that incorporates two Burmese lions, a star, and a scroll with the name of the country in Burmese script.

EMBLEM OF MYANMAR

The central emblem is guarded by two ornate Burmese lions
The central emblem is a map of Myanmar

Thailand

Adopted September 28, 1917 | **Ratio** 2:3 | **Usage** National and Civil

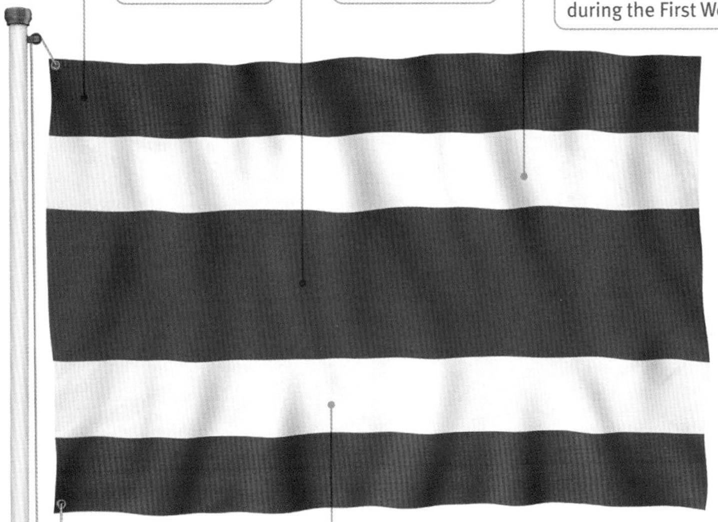
Red symbolizes lifeblood
Blue represents the monarchy
The blue and white stripes were added during the First World War
White stands for the purity of the Buddhist faith

Thailand is also known as the "Land of the White Elephant," and this emblem appeared on its plain red flag in the 19th century. During the First World War, horizontal white stripes were added above and below the elephant.

In 1917, the elephant was abandoned, and a blue stripe was added to the middle of the flag in order to express solidarity with the Allies, whose flags were mostly red, white, and blue. This flag is known as the *Trairanga* (tricolor).

The Royal Arms of Thailand was introduced in 1910. The arms features the *garuda*, a bird-man in Hindu mythology.

ARMS OF THAILAND

The *garuda* of Hindu mythology is the enemy of all things poisonous
The red *garuda* is placed on a field of royal yellow for the Royal Standard

Laos

Adopted December 2, 1975 | **Ratio** 2:3 | **Usage** National and Civil

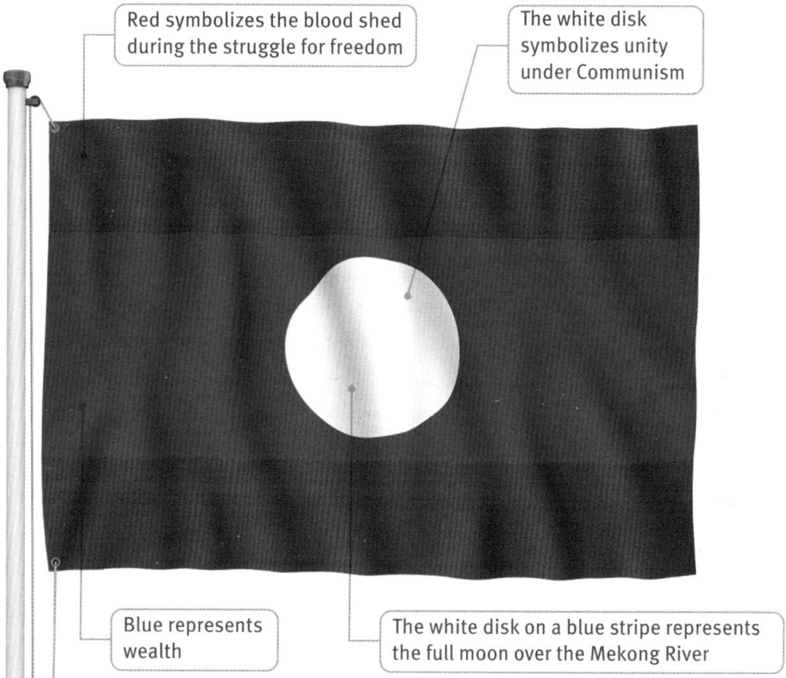
Red symbolizes the blood shed during the struggle for freedom
The white disk symbolizes unity under Communism
Blue represents wealth
The white disk on a blue stripe represents the full moon over the Mekong River

The national flag of Laos was adopted in 1975, when the country became a people's republic. It is one of the few Communist flags that does not use the five-pointed star as an emblem. This flag replaced the original flag of Laos, which was red, with a triple-headed white elephant on a pedestal beneath a parasol. This expressed the ancient name of the country, "Land of a Million Elephants," and dated from the 19th century.

A FLAG FOR THE REPUBLIC

From 1953 onward, the royal government waged war with the Pathet Lao, whose flag was blue with a white disk and red borders at the top and bottom. From 1973–1975, the Pathet Lao formed part of the government coalition, before assuming power directly and prompting the abdication of the king. Their flag was then adopted as the national flag.

In the center is a white disk, symbolizing the unity of the people under the leadership of the Lao People's Revolutionary Party and the country's bright future. The red stripes stand for the blood shed by the people in their struggle for freedom, and the blue symbolizes their prosperity.

The white disk on a blue background is also said to represent a full moon against the Mekong River.

Cambodia

Adopted June 29, 1993 | **Ratio** 2:3 | **Usage** National and Civil

Red and blue are traditional colors
The famous temple of Angkor Wat has appeared in various forms on Cambodia's flag

The flag used today is the same as that established in 1948, although since then five other designs have been employed. These have almost all made use of the image of the temple of Angkor Wat in one form or another. This famous temple site, dating from the 12th century, was built by the Mahidharapura monarchs. It has five towers, but these were not always all depicted in the stylized version used on flags. The temple also appears on the arms. The monarchy was restored in September 1993, the 1948 flag having been readopted in June of that year.

STATE EMBLEM OF CAMBODIA

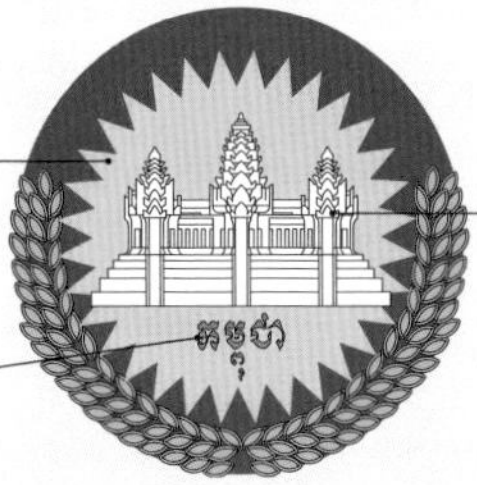
The glowing sun represents national rebirth
The inscription is the name of the country
Angkor Wat is a symbol of the nation and its greatness

Vietnam

Adopted November 30, 1955 | **Ratio** 2:3 | **Usage** National and Civil

Red symbolizes revolution and bloodshed
The gold five-pointed star is for the unity of five groups of workers in building socialism

Vietnam's national flag was adopted in 1976, at the end of the Vietnam War, when North and South Vietnam were reunited under the new name of the Socialist Republic of Vietnam. This flag had been used by Communist North Vietnam since 1955, a year after partition.

It is essentially the same as the flag used by the national resistance movement, led by Ho Chi Minh, in its struggle against the occupying Japanese forces during the Second World War.

SYMBOLISM OF THE COLORS

The red color of the field stands for the revolution and for the blood shed by the Vietnamese people.

The five-pointed yellow star represents the unity of workers, peasants, intellectuals, youths, and soldiers in the building of socialism.

NATIONAL EMBLEM OF VIETNAM

The national emblem, which was also readopted in 1976, had been used by North Vietnam since 1956. It depicts a cogwheel, symbolic of industry, and the yellow five-pointed star of socialism, enclosed by a garland of rice—the country's main agricultural product. The name of the country is inscribed on a scroll at the base of the emblem. The symbols on both the arms and the flag were inspired by the Chinese flag.

Malaysia

Adopted September 16, 1963 | **Ratio** 1:2 | **Usage** National and Civil

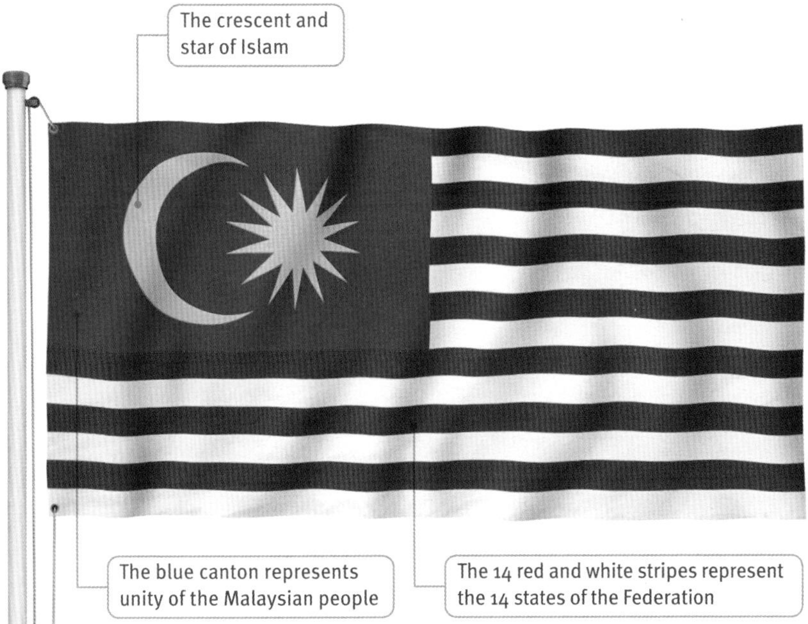

The first flag of independent Malaya was based on the Stars and Stripes of the United States of America, combined with Islamic symbolism. It had 11 red and white stripes and a blue canton, like the US flag, with a gold crescent and an 11-pointed star, traditionally associated with Islam. Both the number of stripes and points on the star denoted the 11 states of the Federation.

THREE NEW STATES

In 1963, three new states—Singapore, Sabah, and Sarawak—joined the Federation to form Malaysia. To reflect this, the flag was amended to 14 red and white stripes representing the 14 states. When Singapore seceded in 1965, the flag remained unaltered. The 14th stripe is now said to stand for the federal district of Kuala Lumpur.

THE SYMBOLISM OF THE COLORS

The blue canton represents the unity of the Malaysian people. The crescent is for Islam, the dominant religion. The 14 points of the star are for unity among the states of the country. Yellow is the traditional color of the rulers of the Malay states. Red and white are also traditional colors in Southeast Asia.

The national motto appears on a scroll in the coat of arms. It is repeated in both Jawi and Roman script and means "Unity is Strength."

Malaysia: State flags

The flags of the Malaysian states were mostly derived from those of the 19th century and were originally flags of the princes or sultans.

Johore

The blue field represents the government. The red canton is for the "*Hulubalang*" warrior caste, who defend the state. The crescent and star represent the ruler.

Kedah

Red is the traditional color of Kedah. The sheaves of yellow paddy or rice are for prosperity. The green crescent signifies Islam, and the yellow shield is for sovereignty.

Kelentan

The red field is symbolic of the loyalty and sincerity of the people, while the white emblem represents the ruler. Kelentan has 36 royal and official flags.

Kuala Lumpur

Blue is for the unity of the population of Kuala Lumpur; red is for courage and vigor; white is for purity, cleanliness, and beauty; and yellow is for sovereignty and prosperity.

Labuan

The colors are those of the national flag and they have the same symbolism—white recalls the purity of Buddhism and red represents the lifeblood of the people.

Melaka

The colors and pattern are taken from the national flag. Unlike the Malaysian flag, the flag of Melaka has only two stripes—one in red and one in white—and a five-pointed star.

Negeri Sembilan

This flag reflects the hierarchy of power in Malaysia. The yellow field symbolizes the ruler; the black triangle, the district rulers; and the red triangle, the people.

Pahang

White is for the ruler, because it can change to any other color, reflecting how a ruler can be influenced by popular opinion. Black represents the people standing firm.

State flags (continued)

Perak

The three stripes represent different levels of the royal family. The Sultan is evoked by white, the Raja Muda by yellow, and the Raja di-Hilir by black. The latter two are junior members of the ruling family.

Perlis

Yellow represents the ruler, and blue represents the people. The colors are arranged as two equal horizontal stripes to signify the close cooperation that should exist between the ruler and his subjects.

Pinang

Light blue represents the blue seas around the island of Pinang. White is for the peace and serenity of the state, and yellow for its prosperity. The tree is the Pinang palm, after which the state is named.

Sabah

The zircon blue (top stripe) is for tranquility, white for purity and justice, red for courage, ice blue (canton) for unity and prosperity, and royal blue for strength. The mountain is Kinabalu.

Sarawak

Yellow is the traditional color of Borneo, where the state lies. Red and black are from the flag of the former Raja of Sarawak. The star has nine points for the nine districts of the state.

Selangor

The yellow and red quarters are symbolic of flesh and blood, the combination necessary for life. The crescent and star in the canton represent Islam, the dominant religion of the state.

Terengganu

The white background stands for the Sultan. It envelopes the black field, symbolizing the people. This reflects how the Sultan provides protection to his subjects.

Indonesia

Adopted August 17, 1945 | **Ratio** 2:3 | **Usage** National and Civil

The flag is based on the banner of the 13th-century Indonesian Empire
Red represents the body
White symbolizes the soul

The flag is based on the banner of the 13th-century Empire of Majahapit, red and white being the holy colors of Indonesia at that time. These colors were revived in the 20th century as an expression of nationalism against the Dutch. The first red and white flag flew in Java in 1928 and was adopted as the national flag of the republic in 1945 when the country declared its independence. The red stripe is symbolic of physical life, while white represents spiritual life. Together they stand for the complete human being, body and soul. Red and white are also traditional colors of many Southeast Asian nations.

NATIONAL EMBLEM OF INDONESIA

The emblem shows a shield supported by a mythical bird, the *garuda*. The 17 wing feathers and 8 tail feathers refer to the day and month (August 17) on which independence was declared in 1945
The shield depicts a buffalo head, a banyan tree, and sheaves of rice and cotton
The yellow star represents religious belief
The national motto means "Unity in Diversity"
BHINNEKA TUNGGAL IKA

East Timor

Adopted May 20, 2002 | **Ratio** 1:2 | **Usage** National and Civil

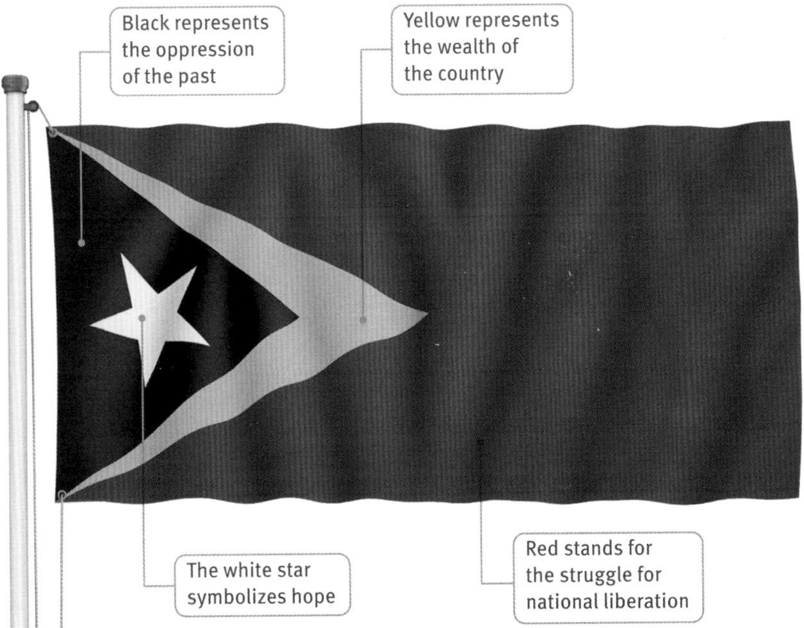
Black represents the oppression of the past
Yellow represents the wealth of the country
The white star symbolizes hope
Red stands for the struggle for national liberation

At midnight on 19 May 2002, the UN flag was replaced with the flag of newly independent East Timor outside the government offices in Dili, the capital. The new country, now a member of the United Nations, is slowly resolving the legacy of decades of occupation.

NEW STATE, OLD FLAG

The flag was actually designed by the Fretilin party for the "Democratic Republic of Timor" in 1975, following the transition from Portuguese colony to independence. However, the infant nation's subsequent invasion and occupation by Indonesia led to the adoption of that country's flag for the last quarter of the 20th century.

SYMBOLISM OF THE FLAG

The black triangle represents the darkness of four centuries of colonial oppression under the Portuguese. The golden-yellow arrowhead recalls the long struggle for independence, as well as the hope of the country's future prosperity. The red field reflects the blood shed by the Timorese people on their journey toward autonomy—a symbol that has taken on greater poignancy since the referendum for independence and the massacre of thousands of East Timorese by pro-Indonesian militias in 1999. The white of the star symbolizes peace, while the star itself represents the guiding light, which gives hope for the future.

Singapore

Adopted December 3, 1959 | **Ratio** 2:3 | **Usage** National and Civil

The crescent is for the new nation
The five stars symbolize ideals of democracy, peace, progress, justice, and equality
Red stands for universal brotherhood and equality
White represents the purity and virtue of the Singaporean people

The flag dates from when Singapore became a self-governing British colony in 1959. It was preserved when Singapore joined the Malaysian Federation and adopted as the national flag when Singapore became fully independent in 1965.

The colors of red and white are those of the Malay people. Red is supposed to represent universal brotherhood and equality, while white symbolizes purity and virtue. The white crescent signifies the new nation of Singapore, while the five stars next to it represent the ideals of democracy, peace, progress, justice, and equality.

The President's flag is a plain red field with the crescent and star emblem in the center.

THE PRESIDENT'S FLAG

The President's flag simply enlarges and centers the crescent and stars motif from the national flag
Red and white represent the Malay people

Brunei

Adopted September 29, 1959 | **Ratio** 1:2 | **Usage** National and Civil

Black and white stripes represent Brunei's chief ministers
The national emblem was placed in the center in 1959
Yellow represents the Sultan of Brunei

A similar version of this flag, without the coat of arms, was first used in 1906. The flag's main color, yellow, is associated with the Sultan, while the black and white stripes that cut across it are the colors of the Brunei's two chief ministers. The coat of arms in the center of the flag was added in 1959.

THE NATIONAL ARMS

The coat of arms bears testament to Brunei's Muslim traditions with the crescent, a traditional symbol of Islam, at its center. The Arabic motto on the crescent translates as, "Always render service by God's guidance," below it, a scroll bears the inscription "*Brunei Darussalam*" (City of Peace).

STATE EMBLEM OF BRUNEI

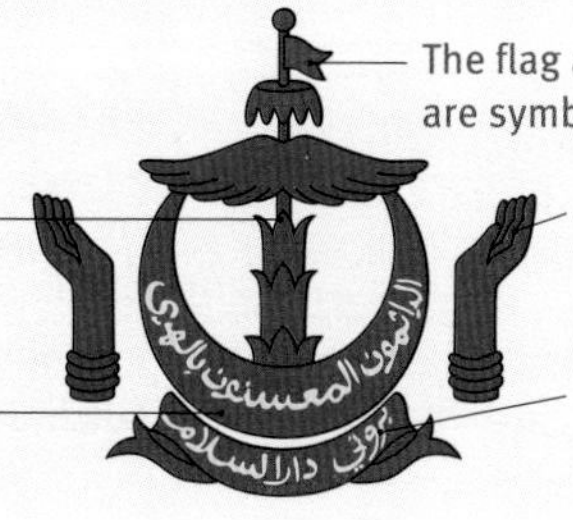
The central mast is a symbol of the state
The crescent is symbolic of the Islamic faith
The flag and umbrella are symbols of royalty
The upturned hands signify the benevolence of the government
The inscription is the country's official title "*Brunei Darussalam*"

Philippines

Adopted May 19, 1898 | **Ratio** 1:2 | **Usage** National and Civil

The white triangle symbolizes purity and peace
Blue represents patriotism
Red symbolizes bravery
The sun and stars represent the three main areas of the country—Luzon, the Visayas, and Mindanao

The flag was first used by Filipino nationalists in exile while the Spanish still controlled the islands. When they were ceded to the US, the Philippines became far more autonomous, and the flag was flown freely from 1898. It was banned by the Americans from 1907–1919, and the Stars and Stripes was flown exclusively on the islands.

The sun and stars are Masonic in origin. The eight rays of the sun are for the eight provinces that revolted against the Spanish. The three stars represent the country's three main geographical areas. White stands for purity and peace, red for bravery, and blue for patriotism. When used at war, the red stripe is flown at the top of the flag, representing courage.

THE PRESIDENT'S FLAG

The sun is taken from the national flag
The three stars and a golden sea lion were adapted from the arms of Manila
A ring of 52 white stars of Manila

Taiwan

Adopted October 28, 1928 | **Ratio** 2:3 | **Usage** National

A blue flag with a white sun was the party flag of the Kuomingtang; each ray represents two hours of a day
The flag is said to represent "a white sun in a blue sky over red land"
Red recalls the Han Chinese, the dominant race in China

The flag adopted for Taiwan, or Formosa, as it was known, had been the national flag of China. It was used from 1928–1949 when the Kuomingtang, the Chinese Nationalist Party, was in power.

The red field represents China, the blue canton, and white sun was the party flag of the Kuomingtang. The 12 rays of sunshine symbolize unending progress, each ray represents two hours of the day.

THE TAIPEI OLYMPIC FLAG

This flag was adopted by Taiwan in 1980 specifically for use at the Olympic Games, where its national flag was not accepted. It combines red, white, and blue—the national colors of Taiwan and the Olympic emblem.

THE TAIPEI OLYMPIC FLAG

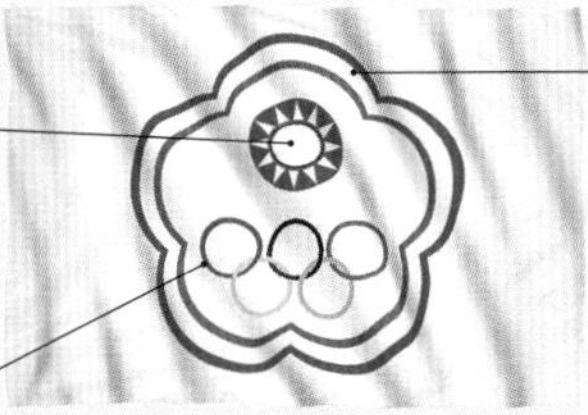
The sun symbol is taken from the national flag
The emblem of connected rings shows that it is an Olympic flag
Blue, red, and white are the national colors

China

Adopted October 1, 1949 | **Ratio** 2:3 | **Usage** National and Civil

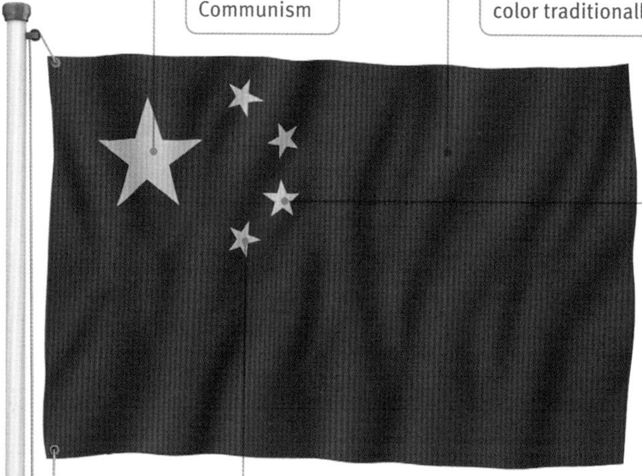
The large star represents Communism
The red field symbolizes the Communist revolution and is also a color traditionally used in China
The use of five stars reflects the importance of the number five in Chinese philosophy
The four smaller stars represent the social classes of the Chinese people

China's first national flag originated in 1872. It was yellow with a blue dragon, representing the Manchu (Qing) Dynasty, which ruled China from 1644 to 1912. The revolt of 1911 saw the changing of the flag to five different colored stripes. Soviet republics were established in the 1920s, each of which was represented by a red flag referring to the Soviet fatherland. The present flag dates from 1949, when the People's Republic was formed.

A NEW CHINESE FLAG

The design was created by Zeng Liansong who responded to a government notice published in a newspaper. Around 3,000 designs were received, which were reduced to a short list of 38. Further discussions were held until Mao, the leader of China at the time, eventually decided on Liansong's design. The flag was officially raised for the first time on October 1, 1949 in Tiananmen Square, Beijing.

SYMBOLISM

The red field signifies the Chinese Communist Revolution and echoes the ancient Han Dynasty of 206 BCE. The five stars symbolize the unity of the Chinese people under the leadership of the government. The large yellow star represents the Communist Party of China and the four smaller stars represent the four social classes of China as defined in Mao's writings: peasants, workers, petty bourgeoisie, and patriotic capitalists.

North Korea

Adopted September 8, 1948 | **Ratio** 1:2 | **Usage** National and Civil

The two blue stripes stand for sovereignty, peace, and friendship
The white stripes symbolize purity
The star is a symbol of Communism
Red represents the Communist revolution

The flag was adopted in 1948, when North Korea became an independent Communist state. The regime retained the traditional Korean colors of red, white, and blue and added a red star on a white disk.

Although often used as a motif for Communism, in this case the star specifically represents revolutionary traditions. The red stripe expresses patriotism and determination, the white stripes symbolize unity, while the blue indicates the desire to strive for independence, peace, and friendship.

The prominent theme of the Soviet-style coat of arms is industrialization, depicted with an electricity tower and a large dam.

ARMS OF NORTH KOREA

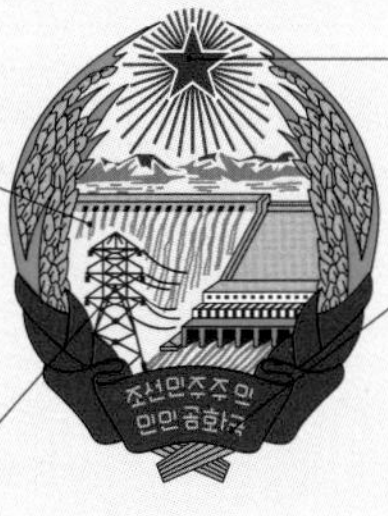
A hydroelectric power station within a wreath of rice-ears
Industrial elements feature heavily on the arms of Korea and include a large dam and electricity tower
The star represents revolutionary traditions
The inscription on the scroll is the country's official name—The Democratic People's Republic of Korea

South Korea

Adopted July 12, 1948 | **Ratio** 2:3 | **Usage** National and Civil

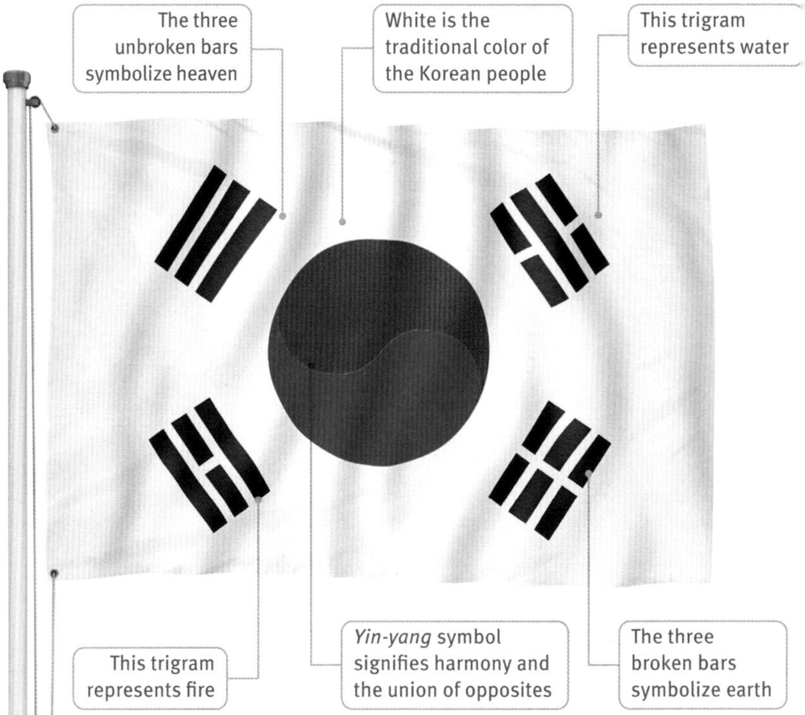
The three unbroken bars symbolize heaven
White is the traditional color of the Korean people
This trigram represents water
This trigram represents fire
Yin-yang symbol signifies harmony and the union of opposites
The three broken bars symbolize earth

The flag used by the Kingdom of Korea before 1910 featured the traditional colors: red, white, and blue. When South Korea separated from the north in 1948, the original flag was retained, but a few alterations were made.

A NEW SOUTH KOREAN FLAG

At the flag's center is a disk containing an S-shaped line, the upper half being red and the lower half blue. This is derived from the Eastern *yin-yang* symbol, which represents the harmony of opposites in nature, for example, good and evil; male and female. When North and South Korea separated, the shape of the *yin-yang* was stylized in the form of a Japanese *mon*. These are simplified versions of everyday objects, shown in symmetrical and regular forms. *Yang* is represented by red and *yin* by blue.

The other alteration to the original flag in 1948 was to the trigrams (*kwae*) surrounding the *yin-yang*, which were reduced from eight to four. They are the basic trigrams from the *I-Ching*, a divination system widespread in the East. On the South Korean flag they symbolize the four polarities: heaven (upper hoist), water (upper fly), fire (lower hoist), and earth (lower fly). The white field of the flag represents peace and the white clothing traditionally worn by the Korean people.

Japan

Adopted February 27, 1870 | **Ratio** 2:3 | **Usage** National and Civil

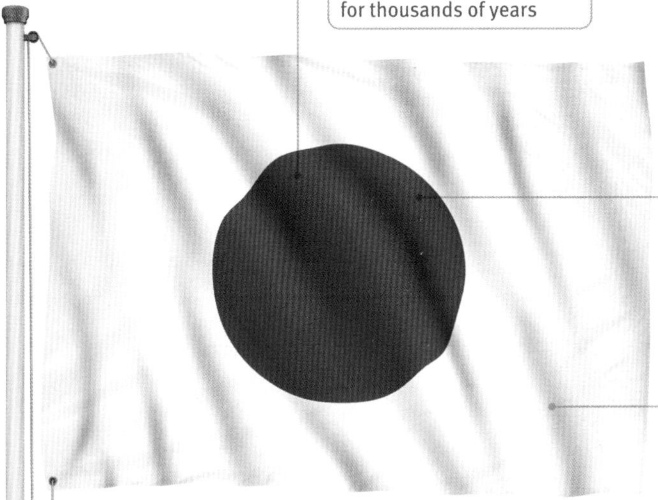
The sun symbol has been an element in Japan's flags for thousands of years
The red disk is named *Hinomaru* or Lucky Sun
The white field expresses honesty and purity

Japan is known as "The Land of the Rising Sun." The Emperor of Japan and his predecessors descend from the House of Yamato, which united the country in AD 200, and they claim to be direct descendants of the sun goddess, Amaterasu Omikami.

The current flag was officially established as the national flag of Japan in 1870.

THE *HINOMARU*

The Lucky Sun, or *Hinomaru*, in the center of the flag, has been an imperial badge since the 14th century. The white field stands for purity and integrity, and some suggest the red disk represents brightness, sincerity, and warmth. The Japanese Maritime SDF ensign is an unusual adaptation of the national flag.

JAPANESE MARITIME SDF ENSIGN

Adopted in 1889, the naval ensign consists of the sun-disk with red rays extending to the border of the flag
Rays extend to the edge of the flag to recall the rising sun

Australasia & Oceania

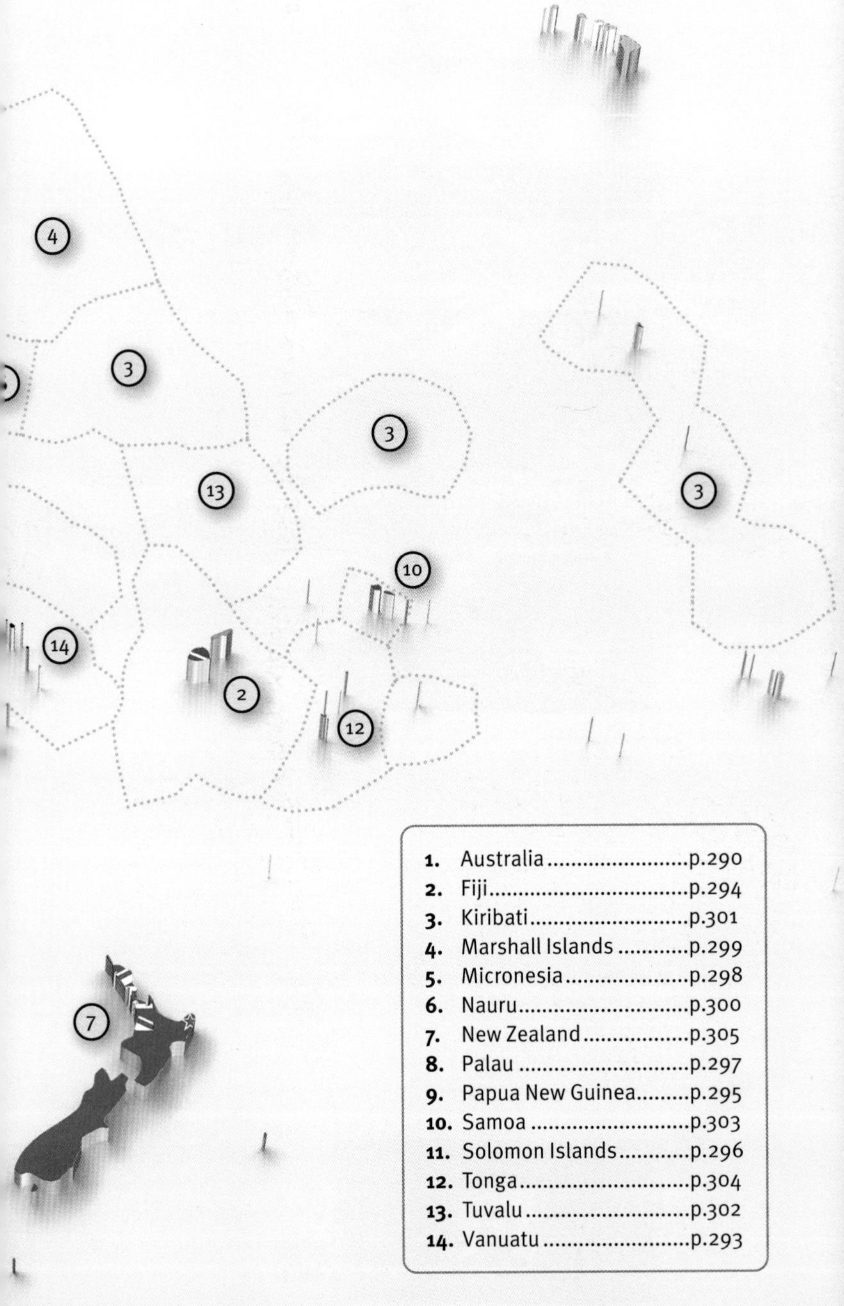
4
3
3
3
13
10
14
2
12
7

Australia

Adopted September 1, 1901 | **Ratio** 1:2 | **Usage** National and Civil

The Union Jack is retained in the canton
The stars of the Southern Cross
The points of the "Commonwealth Star" represent the members of the Federation

The first national flag was adopted in 1901 following various design competitions, but its use was restricted. It includes a blue ensign and three motifs, celebrating key aspects of Australian statehood.

THE SOUTHERN CROSS

This constellation is visible throughout the year in southern night skies and has been used as a navigational aid for centuries. It helped guide early European ships to the continent and became a popular emblem for the new settlers. The five stars of the cross appear on the fly, with seven points for the brightest stars, and five for the lesser Epsilon Crucis.

THE UNION JACK

First flown on Australian soil by the explorer Captain Cook in 1770, it was the national flag from 1788 and remained the official citizens' land flag until 1954. It occupies the canton, denoting Australia's historical links with the UK.

THE "COMMONWEALTH STAR"

This large star affirms the federal nature of government in Australia. Originally there were six points for the six federal states. The seventh point was added in 1909, to represent the Northern Territory together with the six other external territories administered by the Australian Federal Government.

Australia: State flags

The state flags use the British Blue Ensign, with the state badge in the canton. The two territories do not follow this pattern.

Australian Capital Territory

The capital territory became self-governing in 1989. The flag, adopted in 1993, depicts Canberra's city coat of arms and the Southern Cross in the city colors of blue and gold.

New South Wales

A gold star adorns each arm of the St. George's Cross, with a golden lion *passant guardant* at the center. This more distinctive badge replaced a previous design in 1876.

Northern Territory

Adopted by the territory in 1978, the flag depicts the Southern Cross and a stylized Sturt's desert rose against black and ocher, which are the territorial colors.

Queensland

The state badge depicts the Royal Crown at the center of a Maltese cross. The design of the crown was altered at the coronation of HM Queen Elizabeth II in 1953.

South Australia

The state emblem of the piping shrike (a magpie) is shown with outstretched wings on a yellow background. The piping shrike was adopted as the flag badge in 1904.

State flags (continued)

Tasmania

The Red Lion *passant* on a white background recalls historical ties with England and has remained essentially unchanged since its adoption in 1875.

Victoria

The Royal Crown was added in 1877. The present arrangement, with the crown surmounting the Southern Cross, became the state arms in 1910.

Western Australia

The Black Swan has been Western Australia's emblem since the first British colony was founded at Swan River. The flag was adopted in 1953.

Australia has two official flags for its First Nations:

Australian Aboriginal flag

Artist Harold Thomas designed this flag in 1971 and it is one of the few in the world adopted as an official emblem where the artist retains intellectual property rights (we were unable to obtain permission to show it in this edition, unfortunately). The flag consists of a black upper half representing the Aboriginal people, and a red lower half echoing the red ochre earth of Australia. A central yellow disc represents the sun, giver of life and protection. It became an official Australian flag in 1995.

Torres Strait Islander flag

Green represents the land; blue, the Torres Strait; the white star, the five main island groups; and the white *dhari* headress, the Torres Strait Islander peoples. The flag was designed by Bernard Namok and became official in 1995.

Vanuatu

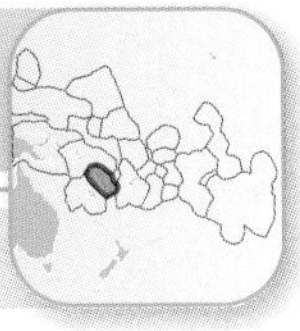

Adopted February 13, 1980 | **Ratio** 3:5 | **Usage** National and Civil

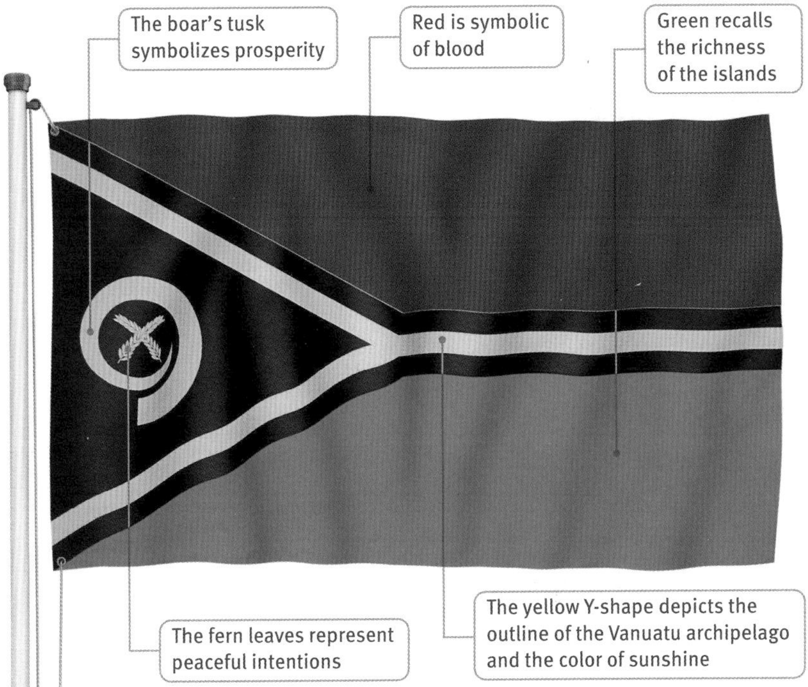
The boar's tusk symbolizes prosperity
Red is symbolic of blood
Green recalls the richness of the islands
The fern leaves represent peaceful intentions
The yellow Y-shape depicts the outline of the Vanuatu archipelago and the color of sunshine

After the anglophone Vanuaaku Party led Vanuatu to independence from Britain and France in 1980, the colors of the party flag—red, black, green, and yellow—were adopted as the basis for the design of a new national flag. The final design was chosen a few months before independence by a parliamentary committee from designs submitted by a local artist.

THE SYMBOLISM OF THE COLORS

The yellow symbolizes sunshine; the green reflects the richness of the islands. The red is symbolic of blood, and the black is for the Melanesian people. The Prime Minister requested the inclusion of the yellow and black fimbriations to give more prominence to the color representing the people.

The yellow Y-shape denotes the general pattern of the islands in the Pacific Ocean.

THE BOAR'S TUSK

Between the arms of the "Y" lies the traditional emblem of a boar's tusk—the symbol of prosperity, worn as a pendant on the islands—crossed by two leaves of the local *namele* fern. The leaves are a token of peace, and their 39 fronds represent the 39 members of Vanuatu's legislative assembly.

Fiji

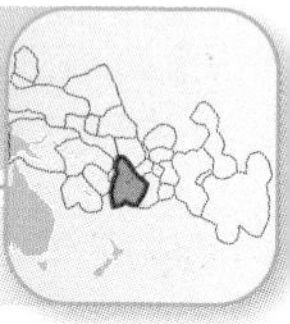

Adopted October 10, 1970 | **Ratio** 1:2 | **Usage** National and Civil

The Union Jack denotes the historical links with Great Britain
The design is based on the British Blue Ensign
The blue field represents the Pacific Ocean

The flag was adopted in 1970, when Fiji achieved independence. Its bright blue background symbolizes the Pacific Ocean, which plays an important part in the lives of the islanders, both in terms of the fishing industry and the burgeoning tourist trade. The Union Jack reflects the country's links with Great Britain.

ARMS OF FIJI
The shield is derived from the country's official coat of arms, which was originally granted by Royal Warrant in 1908. The images depicted on the shield represent agricultural activities on the islands and the historical associations with Great Britain.

ARMS OF FIJI

On the chief, a British lion holds a coconut between its paws
The first quarter shows sugarcane; the second, a coconut palm; the third, a dove of peace; and the fourth, a bunch of bananas
The coat of arms was granted in 1908; it is a white shield, with a red cross and a red chief (the upper third of a shield)

Papua New Guinea

Adopted July 1, 1971 | **Ratio** 3:4 | **Usage** National and Civil

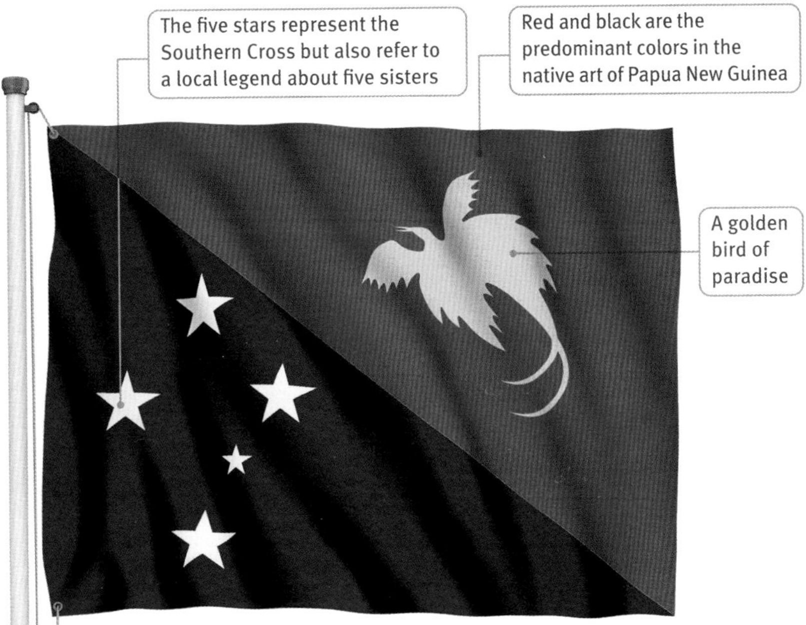
The five stars represent the Southern Cross but also refer to a local legend about five sisters
Red and black are the predominant colors in the native art of Papua New Guinea
A golden bird of paradise

The current flag of yellow and white symbols on black and red was designed by a 15-year-old art student, Susan Karike, and officially accepted in 1971. When Papua New Guinea became independent from Australian administration in 1975, it was retained as the national flag.

Prior to the adoption of the current flag, the Australian administration had attempted to introduce a flag in 1970. Its choice was never popular with local people, which led to the nationwide design competition from which the current flag emerged.

FLAG COLORS AND SYMBOLOGY

The colors of the field—red and black—were chosen because of their widespread use in the native art of the country.

The flag is halved diagonally. The lower half features the Southern Cross constellation in white on black, as it would appear in the night sky over Papua New Guinea. This signifies the link with Australia and also recalls a local legend about five sisters.

The upper half contains a golden Raggiana bird of paradise on a red background, seemingly soaring above the Southern Cross. As the national bird of Papua New Guinea, the bird of paradise also features on the national emblem. Its feathers are widely used for traditional dress and in festivals and ceremonies.

Solomon Islands

Adopted November 18, 1977 | **Ratio** 1:2 | **Usage** National and Civil

The five stars represent the five main groups of islands
The yellow stripe symbolizes sunshine
Green represents the land

Before the current flag was adopted in 1977, three different coats of arms had represented the islands.

The national flag, adopted in 1977, is divided diagonally by a stripe of yellow representing the sunshine of the islands. The two triangles formed by the diagonal stripe are blue and green, signifying water and the land. The five stars were initially incorporated to represent the country's five districts. The islands were later divided into seven districts, and the symbolism of the stars was modified to refer to the five main groups of islands.

The coat of arms is also in the colors of the national flag.

ARMS OF THE SOLOMON ISLANDS

The crest is a traditional canoe (in section) and a shining sun
A freshwater crocodile
The national motto—"To lead is to serve"
TO·LEAD·IS·TO·SERVE
A shark
The shield depicts frigate birds, an eagle, two turtles, a shield, and bow and arrow, all representing districts of the Solomon Islands
The compartment is a stylized frigate bird

Palau

Adopted January 1, 1981 | **Ratio** 5:8 | **Usage** National and Civil

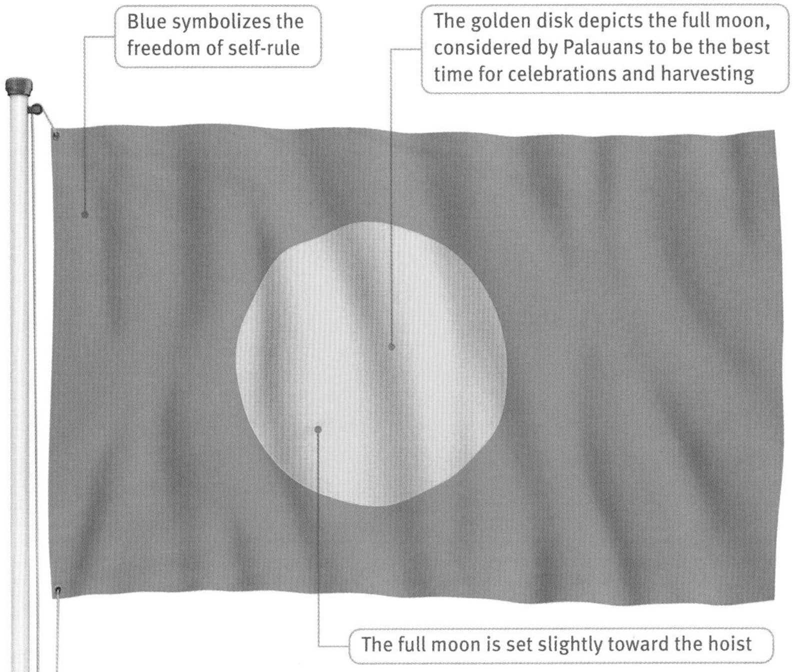
Blue symbolizes the freedom of self-rule
The golden disk depicts the full moon, considered by Palauans to be the best time for celebrations and harvesting
The full moon is set slightly toward the hoist

The current flag was introduced in 1981 when Palau became a republic. Previously, the flag of the Trust Territory of the Pacific Islands was flown jointly with the United Nations and United States flags.

THE SYMBOLISM OF THE FLAG

The flag's very simple design belies the depth of meaning attributed to it. The explanation for the choice of colors is rooted in the history and customs of the Palauan people. The bright blue of the field, which might be assumed to be symbolic of the Pacific Ocean, is in fact a representation of the transition from foreign domination to self-government. The golden disk, which sits slightly off center toward the hoist, represents the full moon. The Palauans consider the full moon to be the optimum time for celebration, as well as for other communal tasks such as harvesting, planting, fishing, tree-felling, and carving traditional canoes. The moon is a symbol of peace, love, and tranquility.

THE SEAL OF PALAU

Palau does not have a coat of arms but has a seal, adopted in 1981, when the country became a republic. The seal is not colored. It depicts a traditional Palauan triangular hut, above the date of adoption. This is surrounded by the title of the state.

Micronesia

Adopted November 10, 1979 | **Ratio** 10:19 | **Usage** National and Civil

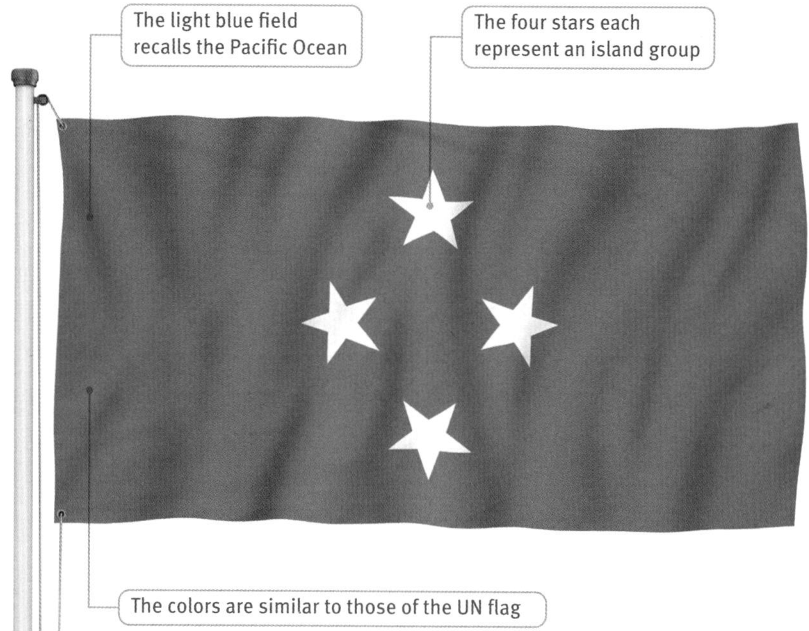
The light blue field recalls the Pacific Ocean
The four stars each represent an island group
The colors are similar to those of the UN flag

The flag, adopted in 1978, is in the colors of the UN flag. The light blue also represents the Pacific Ocean. In an echo of US practice, the stars are for the four islands, arranged like the points of the compass.

MICRONESIAN STATES

Chuuk

The white coconut palm shows that the people depend on coconut resources. The white stars represent the 38 municipal units in the territory.

Kosrae

The olive branches symbolize peace. The four stars are for the islands' four units. The *fafa* stone is traditionally used for grinding food.

Pohnpei

The 11 stars are for the district's 11 municipalities. The half coconut shell represents the *sakau* cup used in traditional ceremonies.

Yap

The outer and inner rings show a *rai*, a traditional symbol of unity. The white outrigger canoe symbolizes the desire to reach state goals.

Marshall Islands

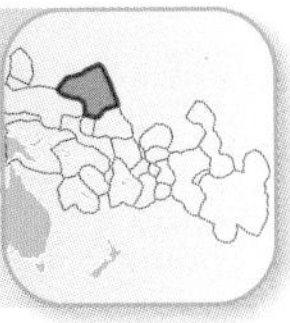

Adopted May 1, 1979 | **Ratio** 10:19 | **Usage** National and Civil

A 24-pointed star, one for each of the districts on the islands
Blue field for the Pacific Ocean
The two stripes, orange over white, represent the two parallel chains of the Marshall Islands

The Marshall Islands became a self-governing territory on May 1, 1979, and on that day a new national flag was adopted. Designed by Emlain Kabua, wife of the president of the new government, it was the winning entry in a competition that had attracted 50 designs.

A FLAG FOR A PACIFIC ISLAND

The flag's dark blue field represents the vast area of the Pacific Ocean over which the islands are scattered. The star symbolizes the geographical position of the islands, which lie a few degrees above the Equator. The star has 24 points, representing the 24 municipalities of the Marshall Islands. Four of its rays extend farther than the others and stand for the capital, Majuro, and the administrative districts of Wotji, Yaluit, and Kwajalein. They also form a cross, signifying the Christian faith of the Marshallese.

SYMBOLS OF PROSPERITY

The two parallel stripes extending across the flag symbolize the two parallel chains of the Marshall Islands: the Ratak (Sunrise) Chain is white, while the Ralik (Sunset) Chain is orange. The stripes extend and widen upward. This is said to signify the increase in growth and vitality of life on the islands. Orange also symbolizes courage and prosperity, while white represents peace.

Nauru

Adopted January 31, 1968 | **Ratio** 1:2 | **Usage** National and Civil

The blue field represents the island's blue skies and the Pacific Ocean
The gold stripe represents the Equator
The 12-pointed star recalls the 12 original tribes of Nauru

The flag, chosen in a local design competition, was adopted on the day of independence, January 31, 1968. It depicts Nauru's geographical position, one degree below the Equator. A gold horizontal stripe representing the Equator runs across a blue field for the Pacific Ocean. Nauru itself is symbolized by a white 12-pointed star. Each point represents one of the 12 indigenous tribes on the island.

ARMS OF NAURU

This is also a local design and includes the chemical symbol for phosphorus; phosphates are Nauru's main export. Beneath it are a frigate bird and a sprig of *tomano*.

ARMS OF NAURU

NAOERO
GOD'S WILL FIRST
The shield is surrounded by coconut leaves
The chemical symbol for phosphorus
A frigate bird
The 12-pointed star, as featured on the flag, representing the 12 tribes of Nauru
The feathers of a frigate bird
A sprig of *tomano*

Kiribati

Adopted July 12, 1979 | **Ratio** 1:2 | **Usage** National and Civil

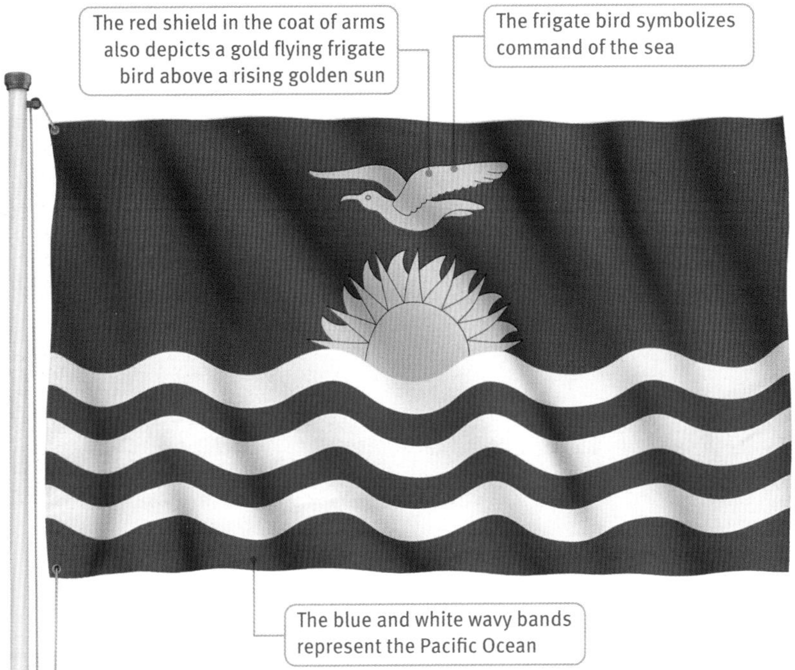
The red shield in the coat of arms also depicts a gold flying frigate bird above a rising golden sun
The frigate bird symbolizes command of the sea
The blue and white wavy bands represent the Pacific Ocean

Kiribati's flag is one of only three national flags that are armorial banners—flags having a design that corresponds exactly to that of the shield in the coat of arms.

ARMS OF KIRIBATI

The coat of arms dates back to May 1937 when it was granted to the Gilbert and Ellice Islands, as Kiribati and Tuvalu were then known. The shield was then incorporated into the center of the fly half of a British Blue Ensign as the state ensign of the colony.

Shortly before independence was granted in 1979, a local competition was held to choose a new national flag and a design based on the colonial coat of arms was submitted to the College of Arms. The College of Arms decided to modify the design. Both the golden frigate bird and the sun were enlarged to occupy more of the top of the flag and the width of the blue and white wavy bands was reduced.

THE ORIGINAL DESIGN

However, the local people insisted on the original design, in which the top and bottom halves of the flag were equal, the sun and local frigate bird small, and the various design elements outlined in black.

The new flag was hoisted during the independence day celebrations in the capital, Tarawa on July 12, 1979.

Tuvalu

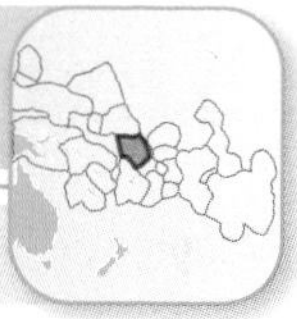

Adopted April 11, 1997 | **Ratio** 1:2 | **Usage** National and Civil

The Union Jack signifies continuing links with Britain
The nine stars are for the nine islands

Tuvalu means "eight islands," although there are in fact nine, each of which is represented by a star on the flag. The stars' arrangement reflects the islands' general geographic distribution.

This flag was chosen after independence in 1978 because it symbolizes the continuing links with Britain and the Commonwealth. However, anti-Commonwealth feeling rose and in 1995, the government decided on a new flag without the Union Jack. The new flag, introduced later that year, retained the stars but included the arms in a triangle at the hoist. In April 1997 the original design was readopted, following a change of government.

ARMS OF TUVALU

The coat of arms depicts a local meeting house, or *maneapa*
Eight sets of objects reflect the country's title, "Eight Together"
The border contains eight sea shells and eight banana leaves
The motto means "Tuvalu for God"
TUVALU·MO·TE·ATUA

Samoa

Adopted January 1, 1962 | **Ratio** 1:2 | **Usage** National and Civil

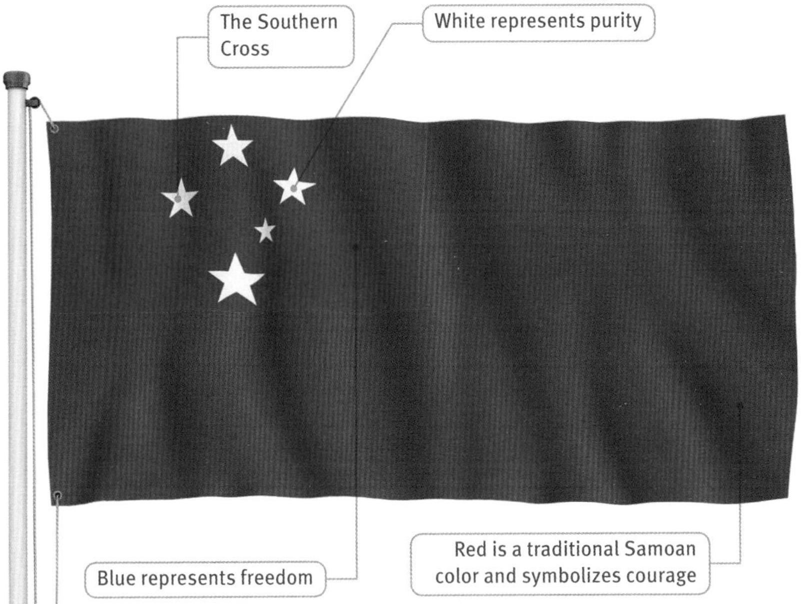
The Southern Cross
White represents purity
Blue represents freedom
Red is a traditional Samoan color and symbolizes courage

Prior to 1899, when Samoa was partitioned by Germany and the US, it was ruled by the rival kingdoms of Malietoa and Tamasese.

The flag of Malietoa was probably inspired by missionaries. It was a plain red field, with a white cross and a white star in the canton. The rival King of Tamasese favored the German cause and used flags with black crosses.

A UNITED FLAG

In 1948, by then a territory of New Zealand, Samoa was granted its current flag. This was created jointly by the kings of Malietoa and Tamasese. It comprised a red field taken from the former flag of Malietoa and the Southern Cross from the flag of New Zealand, on a blue field in the canton.

In 1949, the smaller fifth star was added, making the Southern Cross more like that on the Australian flag. The flag was retained when independence was granted in 1962.

ARMS OF SAMOA

The coat of arms was adopted in 1951 and contains symbols reflecting the Christian faith of the Samoan people. It depicts a shield of the Southern Cross, below a coconut palm from the previous colonial badge. Above the shield is a cross recalling the national motto—"May God be the foundation of Samoa."

Tonga

Adopted November 4, 1875 | **Ratio** 1:2 | **Usage** National and Civil

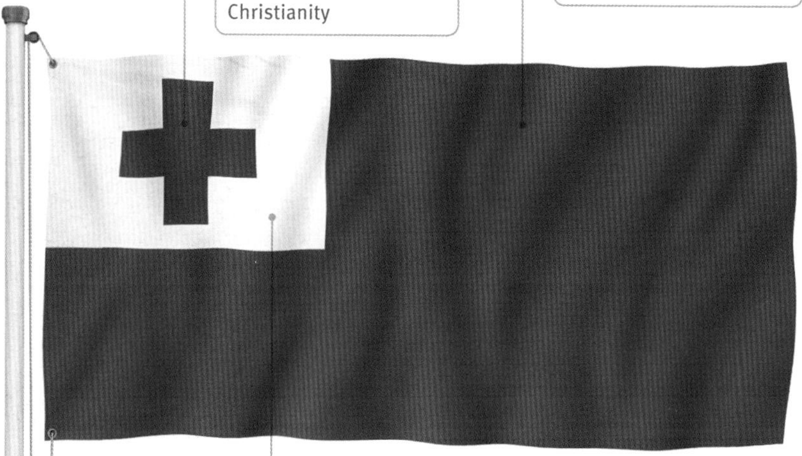
The red cross represents the king's devotion to Christianity
Red represents the blood Jesus shed on the cross
White symbolizes purity

The flag dates from 1862 when the king at the time, who had converted to Christianity in 1831, called for a national flag that would symbolize the Christian faith.

A NEW "CHRISTIAN" FLAG

The first design was a plain white flag with a red couped cross, but this was later found to be too similar to the International Red Cross flag, adopted in 1863, and so the white flag was placed in the canton of a red one. The cross and the red color signify the sacrifice of Christ's blood. The 1875 constitution states that the flag shall never be altered.

The naval ensign, introduced in 1985, also has a red couped cross on white in the canton.

TONGAN NAVAL ENSIGN

Red couped cross in the canton
The naval ensign, introduced in 1985, recalls the flag of Imperial Germany
A red cotised, or bordered, Scandinavian cross

New Zealand

Adopted March 24, 1902 | **Ratio** 1:2 | **Usage** National

The Union Jack in the canton recalls New Zealand's colonial ties to Britain
The stars all vary slightly in size
Four white-bordered red stars represent the Southern Cross

The current flag was designed and adopted for restricted use in 1869 and became the national flag in 1902. It is the British Blue Ensign, with a highly stylized representation of the Southern Cross constellation. It depicts only four of the five stars in the constellation.

In 2016, the current flag won a referendum on whether to adopt a new flag design or keep the original Blue Ensign.

MAORI FLAG

The *Tino Rangatiratanga* was designed in 1990 by Hiraina Marsden, Jan Smith, and Linda Munn using the traditional Maori colors of black, white, and red. The white bar forms a stylized *koru*, or fern frond. It was officially recognized in 2009 for use on Waitangi Day.

OVERSEAS TERRITORIES

Cook Islands

The 15 stars on the fly represent the 15 main islands of the group; they are arranged in a ring to indicate that each island is of equal importance.

Niue

The link with the UK is shown by the use of the Union Jack; that with New Zealand by the four stars. The large central star represents Niue itself.

Other Flags & Signal Flags

International flags

Many international organizations have adopted flags to help raise their profile worldwide. Here is a selection of flags belonging to well-known global organizations.

United Nations (UN)

The UN is an international organization responsible for peacekeeping missions. Its flag shows olive branches, which are a symbol of peace, and the map represents the people of the world.

Commonwealth of Nations

The Commonwealth of Nations is an intergovernmental organization of 53 member states. The gold "C" symbol centers on a globe, emphasizing the global nature of the organization.

European Union (EU)

An economic and political union of 27 member states, the EU's flag consists of 12 gold stars on an azure field. The stars represent the European people in a circle—a symbol of unity.

African Union (AU)

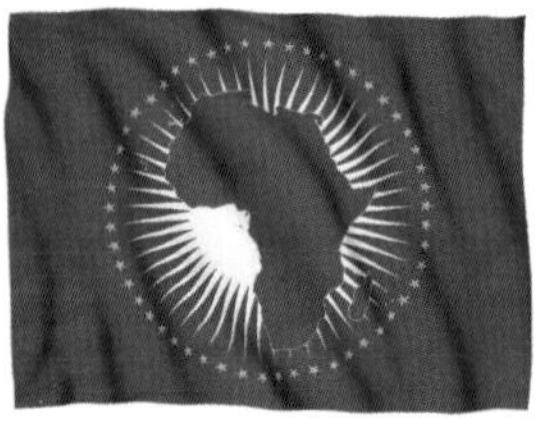

The current flag of the African Union was adopted in 2010. It shows rays of light coming out of the continent, symbolizing hope; and the 53 gold stars represent the member states.

Arab League

The flag is a green field bearing the seal of the League of Arab States. The script gives the name of the organization, while the 22 links in the chain represent the original 22 members when it was formed.

Commonwealth of Independent States (CIS)

The CIS is a regional organization whose participating countries are former Soviet Republics. The poles around the sun represent the eight members who signed the treaty in 1991.

Association of Southeast Asian Nations (ASEAN)

The ASEAN is a geopolitical and economic organization made up of 10 countries in the region. The flag depicts 10 rice stalks in the middle of a red circle. The image represents prosperity.

Secretariat of the Pacific Community

An intergovernmental agency focusing on development in the Pacific region, SPC's flag bears 27 stars representing all its members. The sail and ocean recalls linkage and the sharing of ideas.

International flags (continued)

Union of South American Nations (UNASUR)

UNASUR is committed to South American integration. Its flag is navy blue and bears the organization's logo, which depicts a whirlwind symbolizing dynamism and the spirit of change.

Caribbean Community and Common Market (CARICOM)

CARICOM's main purpose is to promote economic integration among its 15 Caribbean nations. The interlocking Cs symbolize the unity of its members and a break from its colonial past.

North Atlantic Treaty Organization (NATO)

The North Atlantic Treaty Organization's flag depicts a compass, symbolizing its endeavor to remain on a path of peace. The circle represents the unity that binds together the 14 member states.

International Maritime Organization (IMO)

The IMO's flag is based on the UN flag. It shows the world map on two crossed anchors, surrounded by laurel leaves, which symbolize the organization's knowledge of the world's oceans.

Organization of Petroleum Exporting Countries (OPEC)

The Organization of Petroleum Exporting Countries consists of 11 nations whose economy is reliant on oil revenues. The flag bears the logo, with the letters stylized to resemble oil barrels.

Red Cross, Red Crescent, Red Crystal

These are the variant flags of the global humanitarian aid organization (adopted to show religious sensitivity). The symbols serve as protective markings in armed conflicts.

Greenpeace

The largest international environmental organization in the world, Greenpeace's flag bears a rainbow over a world map, which symbolizes its determination to protect the environment by peaceful means.

International Federation of Vexillological Assoc. (FIAV)

The flag of the International Federation of Vexillological Associations depicts two halyards (ropes) forming two interlaced loops. The image symbolizes the link between all the countries of the world.

Disputed territories

There are a number of disputed or occupied territories around the world, each with varying degrees of international recognition and political autonomy. This is a selection of some of these territories and does not represent a definitive list.*

Artsakh

Located in the Caucasus between Armenia, Azerbaijan, and Iran, the flag of Artsakh is based on that of Armenia (red for the struggles of the Armenian people, blue for their wish for peace, and orange for their creativity), combined with a distinctive step pattern at the fly, based on local carpet designs.

Kurdistan

The Kurdish people live in an area that overlaps the borders of Turkey, Syria, Iraq, and Iran. The flag design dates back to the Paris Peace Convention of 1920. Red is for martyrdom, white is for peace, green is for the beauty of Kurdistan, and the golden 21-rayed sun is for life. Twenty-one is a special number to the Kurds.

Northern Cyprus

Cyprus is split into two parts, separated by a UN-controlled buffer zone. The flag of the northern part was designed by Emin Çizenel and introduced in 1984. It is based on the flag of Turkey with the colors reversed and two additional red horizontal lines.

Palestine

Palestine lies at the eastern end of the Mediterranean Sea. The flag was adopted in 1964 and is based on the flag of the 1916 Arab Revolt. This used the colors of the caliphates: horizontal stripes of black (Abbasid), green (Fatimid/Rashidun), and white (Umayyad) with a red (Hashemite) triangle at the hoist.

Somaliland

Somaliland is on the northern side of the Horn of Africa. Since 1996, its flag has been three horizontal stripes of green (for prosperity), white (for peace), and red (for the fallen heroes of liberation), with the Islamic *Shahada* on the green stripe and the Black Star of Africa on the white.

South Ossetia

This small enclave lies between northern Georgia and Russia. The flag is the same as that of North Ossetia in Russia and was adopted in 1990. It has three horizontal stripes, white for purity, red for martial courage, and gold for prosperity.

Transnistria

Transnistria is located in the thin strip of Moldova between the Dniester River and Ukraine. The flag was officially adopted in 2000 and is actually that of the old Moldavian Soviet Socialist Republic. The obverse also features the old Soviet emblem at the hoist, while the reverse is plain.

Western Sahara

Western Sahara lies on the western coast of Africa, south of Morocco. The flag, designed by El Ouali and adopted in 1976, is based on that of Palestine but with an added crescent and star for Islam.

*Inclusion of territories on this list is for information purposes only and does not imply any specific status.

Signaling flags

Signaling at sea is one of the oldest uses of flags. Signals were sent with flaglike objects called vexilloids during the wars between the Greeks and the Persians (478–47 BCE). By the Middle Ages, the Genoese and Venetian fleets of Italy had more elaborate signals. The first specially made signal flag was the "Banner of Council" introduced for the English fleet in 1369 (used to call the captain to the admiral's ship). Signals were also sent by hoisting ordinary flags in special positions.

CODE OF SIGNALS

The first regular code of signals dates from the 17th century in England, and numeral flags were invented in the 1800s. These numbers could also represent letters of the alphabet, and they were used to send messages and commands in the heat of battle. Each ship also used pennants to represent its name. In 1812, Sir Home Popham introduced special flags for letters of the alphabet, and by 1889 there was a specific flag for each letter and numeral. The first International Code of Signals (ICS) was introduced on January 1, 1901.

INTERNATIONAL CODE OF SIGNALS (ICS) FLAGS

The purpose of this set of signals is to offer a means of communication to help mariners navigate their vessels safely. Below is a listing of the numeral or letter of the alphabet that each flag denotes.

NUMBERS

0

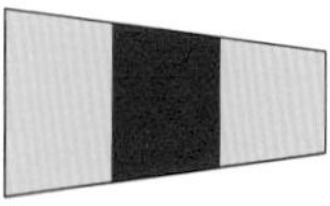

1

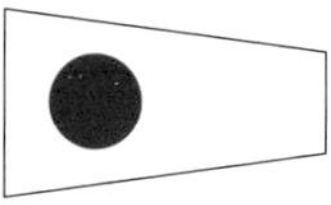

2

3

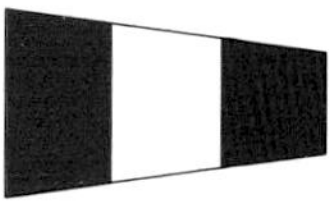

4

5

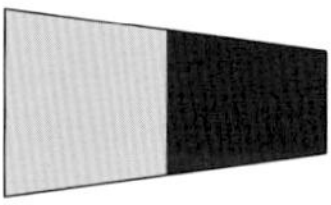

6

7

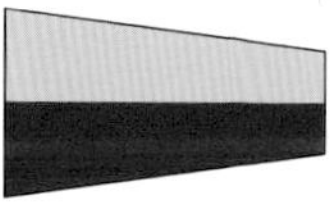

8

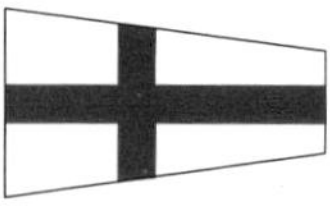

9

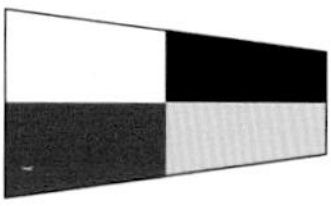

First repeat

Second repeat

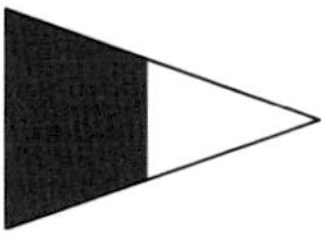

Third repeat

These flags indicate a repeat of the first, second, and third flag in that hoist, thus avoiding the need for multiple sets of flags.

LETTERS

A

B

C

D

E
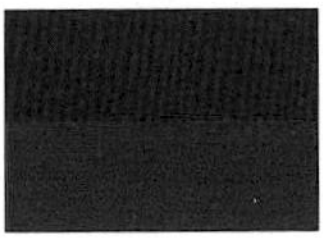
F

G

H
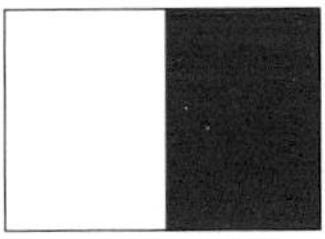
I

J

K

L

M

N

O

P

Q

R

S
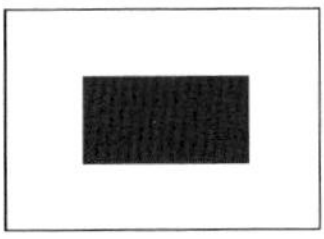
T

U

V

W

X

Y

Z

Signaling flags (continued)

SIGNAL COMBINATIONS

While each flag carries its own message — for example, hoisting flag H means "I have a pilot on board"—flags hoisted in combination convey a wide variety of different messages. These signals are internationally recognized and can be looked up in a code book held by both parties. Below is a selection of signals.

A
C
I am abandoning my vessel

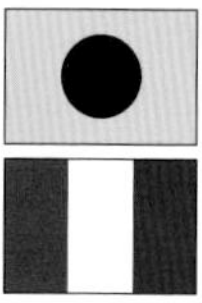
I
T
I am on fire

M
A
C
I request you arrange hospital admission

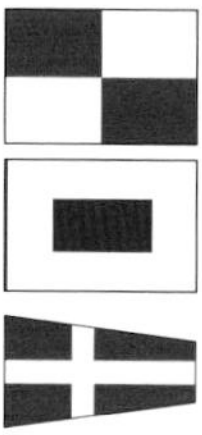
U
S
4
Nothing can be done until weather moderates

N
T
Distress signal

A
N
I need a doctor

NAVAL MANEUVERING SIGNALS

The ICS has also created a set of flags that vessels can use to indicate the maneuvers they are making and issue commands to other vessels. Some of the signs provide information of a vessel's course or an action it is about to take, while others are distress signals that prompt those nearby to keep their distance. Below are some of the most commonly used maneuvering signals.

Code/answer

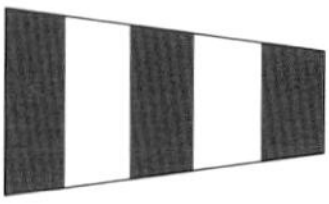

Preparative

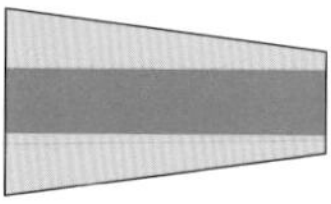

Question

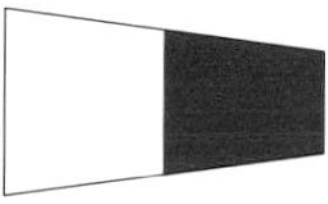

Negation

Designation

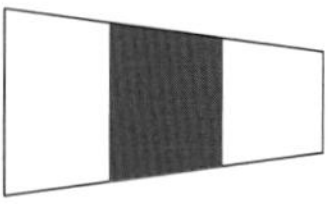

Course Pennant

Turn

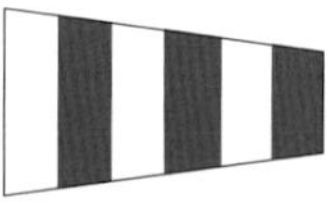

Smoke

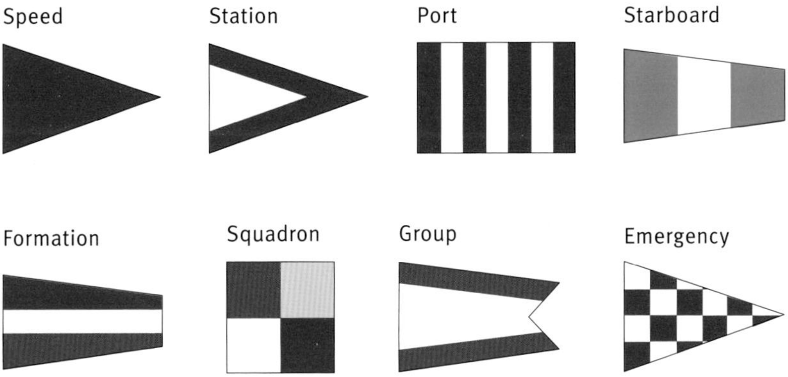
Speed
Station
Port
Starboard
Formation
Squadron
Group
Emergency

"ENGLAND EXPECTS..."

Nelson's famous signal at Trafalgar in 1805 was composed of hoists taken from Popham's *Dictionary of Signals,* except for the last word "Duty." This had to be spelled out using the numerals from an earlier official signal book. Nelson also wanted to use the word "confides," but this was also absent from the dictionary.

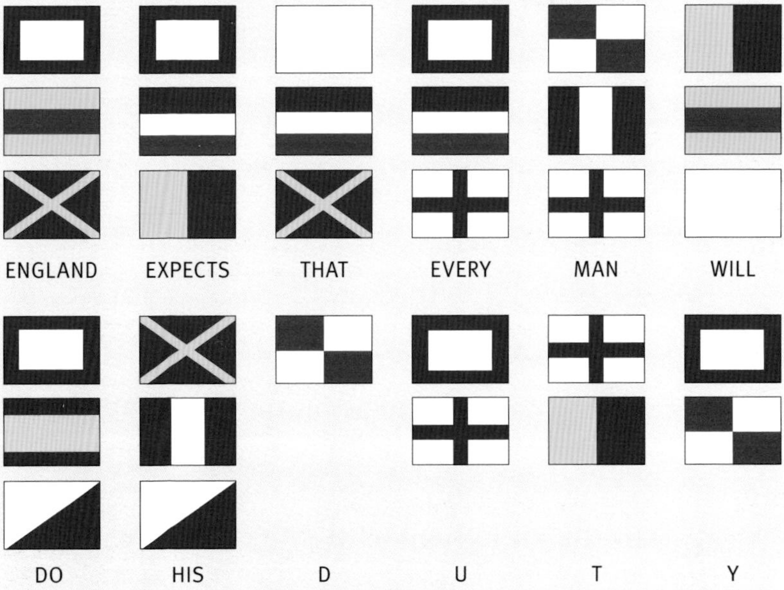
ENGLAND
EXPECTS
THAT
EVERY
MAN
WILL
DO
HIS
D
U
T
Y

Index

KEY
❍ Country
❑ Overseas territory
☆ Disputed or occupied territory

Index (continued)

Acknowledgements

Dorling Kindersley would like to thank:
Senior DTP Designer: Vishal Bhatia
Desk Editor: Saumya Agarwal

The publisher would like to thank the following for their kind permission to reproduce their photographs:
(Key: a-above; b-below/bottom; c-center; f-far; l-left; r-right; t-top)

1 Dreamstime.com: niroworld. **10 Dorling Kindersley:** National Maritime Museum, London (br). 12 Corbis: Pascal Le Segretain / Sygma (b). **Dorling Kindersley:** National Maritime Museum, London (tr). **13 NASA:** Charles M. Duke Jr. / JSC (t)

All other images © Dorling Kindersley. For further information see: www.dkimages.com